LEO THE GREAT

Pope Leo I's theological and political influence in his own time (440–61) and beyond far outweighs the amount of attention he has received in recent scholarship. That influence extended well beyond Rome to the Christian East through his contribution to preparations for the Council of Chalcedon and its outcome. For this he was alternately praised and vilified by the opposing parties at the Council. Leo made his views known through letters, and a vast number of homilies. While so many of these survive (123 letters and 97 homilies of certain attribution), Leo and his works have not been made the subject of a major English-language socio-historical study in over fifty years.

In this brief introduction to the life and works of this important leader of the early church, we gain a more accurate picture of the circumstances and pressures which were brought to bear on his pontificate. A brief introduction surveys the scanty sources which document Leo's early life, and sets his pontificate in its historical context, as the Western Roman Empire went into serious decline, and Rome lost its former status as the western capital. Annotated translations of various excerpts of Leo's letters and homilies are organised around four themes dealing with specific aspects of Leo's activity as bishop of Rome:

- Leo as spiritual adviser on the life of the faithful
- Leo as opponent of heresy
- the bishop of Rome as civic and ecclesiastical administrator
- Leo and the primacy of Rome.

Taking each of these key elements of Leo's pontifical activities into account, we will gain a more balanced picture of the context and contribution of his best-known writings on Christology. This volume offers an affordable introduction to the subject for both teachers and students of ancient and medieval Christianity.

Bronwen Neil is Burke Lecturer in Ecclesiastical Latin at Australian Catholic University, Brisbane. Her previous publications include *Seventh-Century Popes and Martyrs: The Political Hagiography of Anastasius Bibliothecarius* (2006), and, co-authored with Pauline Allen, *Maximus the Confessor and his Companions: Documents from Exile* (2002).

THE EARLY CHURCH FATHERS
Edited by Carol Harrison
University of Durham

The Greek and Latin fathers of the Church are central to the creation of Christian doctrine, yet often unapproachable because of the sheer volume of their writings and the relative paucity of accessible translations. This series makes available translations of key selected texts by the major Fathers to all students of the Early Church.

CYRIL OF JERUSALEM
Edward Yarnold, S.J.

EARLY CHRISTIAN LATIN POETS
Caroline White

CYRIL OF ALEXANDRIA
Norman Russell

MAXIMUS THE CONFESSOR
Andrew Louth

IRENAEUS OF LYONS
Robert M. Grant

AMBROSE
Boniface Ramsey, O.P.

ORIGEN
Joseph W. Trigg

GREGORY OF NYSSA
Anthony Meredith, S.J.

JOHN CHRYSOSTOM
Wendy Mayer and Pauline Allen

JEROME
Stefan Rebenich

TERTULLIAN
Geoffrey Dunn

ATHANASIUS
Khaled Anatolios

SEVERUS OF ANTIOCH
Pauline Allen and C.T.R. Hayward

GREGORY THE GREAT
John Moorhead

GREGORY OF NAZIANZEN
Brian E. Daley

EVAGRIUS PONTICUS
A.M. Casiday

THEODORET OF CYRUS
István Pásztori Kupán

THEOPHILUS OF ALEXANDRIA
Norman Russell

THEODORE OF MOPSUESTIA
Frederick McLeod

LEO THE GREAT

Bronwen Neil

Routledge
Taylor & Francis Group

LONDON AND NEW YORK

BR
65
.L42
I54
2009

First published 2009
by Routledge
2 Park Square, Milton Park, Abingdon, Oxon OX14 4RN

Simultaneously published in the USA and Canada
by Routledge
270 Madison Ave., New York, NY 100016

*Routledge is an imprint of the Taylor & Francis Group,
an informa business*

© 2009 Bronwen Neil

Typeset in Times New Roman by Taylor & Francis Books
Printed and bound in Great Britain by
TJ International Ltd, Padstow, Cornwall

British Library Cataloguing in Publication Data
A catalogue record for this book is available from the British Library

Library of Congress Catalog in Publication Data
Leo I, Pope, d. 461.
[Selections. English. 2009]
Leo the Great / [selection, translation, and introductions by]
Bronwen Neil.
p. cm. – (Early church fathers)
Includes bibliographical references and index.
1. Theology. 2. Leo I, Pope, d. 461–Correspondence. 3. Popes–
Correspondence. 4. Sermons, Latin–Translations into English.
5. Sermons, Early Christian. I. Neil, Bronwen. II. Title.
BR65.L42E54 2009
270.2–dc22
2009000544

ISBN13: 978-0-415-39480-2 (hbk)
ISBN13: 978-0-415-39481-9 (pbk)
ISBN13: 978-0-203-87490-5 (ebk)

TO MY GRANDFATHER
ROBERT WILLIAM WADDELL
† 8.XI.2008

CONTENTS

Acknowledgements   xii
Abbreviations   xiv

PART I
Introduction   **1**

1 Leo's life and times   3

Bishops of Rome as civic leaders   4
Barbarian invasions   8
Building the church   11
The Leonine corpus   13
Leo's literary style   15

2 Pastoral caregiver   18

Fasting and almsgiving   18
Condemnation of astrology, and other 'pagan' religious
   practices   21
Importance of the Christian calendar   22

3 Theologian and opponent of heresy   27

Leo's soteriology and christology   27
The struggle against heresy   29
Inquiry against the Manichees   31
Pelagianism   33
Nestorianism   35
Eutychianism   37

CONTENTS

4 Heir of St Peter   39

Primacy of the bishop of Rome 40
Old Rome versus New Rome: conflict with the church
of Constantinople 42

5 Administrator of the wider church   45

The dispute with Hilary of Arles 45
The reception of Leo's letters into canon law 46
Conclusion 49

PART II
Texts   **51**

6 General introduction to the translations   53

7 Pastoral caregiver   55

Homily 87 on the September Fast 55
Homily 85 on the Feast of St Lawrence 58
Homily 27 on the Feast of the Nativity 61
Homily 69 on Holy Saturday 67

8 Theologian and opponent of heresy   73

Homily 16 on the December Fast 73
Homily 73 on the Ascension 78
Letter 15 to Turibius, Bishop of Astorga 82
Letter 28 to Flavian, Bishop of Constantinople 94
Letter 124 to the monks of Palestine 104

9 Heir of St Peter   113

Homily 82B on the Feast of the Apostles 113
Homily 84 on the anniversary of Alaric's sack of Rome 118
Letter 6 to Anastasius, Metropolitan of Thessalonica 120
Homily 4 on the anniversary of Leo's ordination 125

10 Administrator of the wider church   131

Letter 2 to Septimus, Bishop of Altinum 131
Letter 108 to Theodore, Bishop of Fréjus 133
Letter 137 to Emperor Marcian 136

CONTENTS

Letter 167 to Rusticus, Bishop of Narbonne   138
Letter 170 to Gennadius, Bishop of Constantinople   146

Notes   149
Bibliography   170
Index   179

ACKNOWLEDGEMENTS

Many people and institutions have contributed to the completion of this book. The research undertaken for this volume was partially funded by The Australian Research Council in the form of a Discovery Project on 'Poverty and Welfare in Late Antiquity'. My collaborators on that project in the Centre for Early Christian Studies, Australian Catholic University, were Prof. Pauline Allen, Dr Wendy Mayer, Dr Silke Sitzler and Dr Edward Morgan. I am most grateful to them for their generous exchange of ideas and resources. Dr Geoffrey Dunn served as both proofreader and interlocutor on all things papal.

An Alexander von Humboldt-Stiftung Fellowship at the Friedrich-Wilhelms-Universität Bonn for six months in 2008 enabled me to complete the manuscript. I am particularly indebted to my colleagues in the Evangelisch-Theologische Fakultät, Abteilung für Kirchengeschichte, especially Prof. Wolfram Kinzig, Dr Jochen Schmidt, and visiting research fellow Prof. Wessam Farag, as well as to Prof. Ulrich Volp, now at Johannes Gutenberg-Universität, Mainz. The grant of a Return-to-Work award by Australian Catholic University offered teaching relief and research leave for this period. My research assistant, Dorthe Schmücker, proved a resourceful and persuasive emissary to various libraries in Bonn. I also thank the library staff at McAuley campus, Australian Catholic University, for their patience and ingenuity in tracking down inter-library loans.

Carol Harrison, general editor of this series, and the editorial team at Routledge have provided excellent advice. The initial shaping of the volume was aided by the reviews of three anonymous readers. All responsibility for those defects which remain is of course my own.

Finally I need to thank my family for their indefatigable support. Damien Casey has withstood the buffets of every wave of doctrine and cheerfully fulfilled the sensitive role of critic during the course of this project. Our daughter Ursula helped me keep a sense of perspective. My late grandfather, Robert Waddell, embodied respect for religious traditions other than his own (evangelical Protestantism), and first introduced me to the concept of universal salvation. May he know the fullness of life.

Bonn, December 2008

ABBREVIATIONS

ACO	Acta conciliorum oecumenicorum, ed. E. Schwartz
CCSL	Corpus Christianorum series Latina
CCSL a	*Sancti Leonis magni Romani pontificis tractatus septem et nonaginta*, ed. A. Chavasse
CFML	Corpus fontium Manichaeorum series Latina, ed. H.G. Schipper and J. van Oort
CIL	Corpus inscriptionum latinarum
CSEL	Corpus scriptorum ecclesiasticorum Latinorum
FOTC	Fathers of the Church
FOTC 34	*St Leo the Great, Letters*, trans. E. Hunt.
ILCV	*Inscriptiones latinae christianae veteres*, ed. E. Diehl
JK	*Regesta pontificum Romanorum*, ed. P. Jaffé et al.
LP	*Liber Pontificalis*, eds L. Duchesse and C. Vogel
Mansi	*Sacrorum conciliorum noua et amplissima collectio*, ed. J.D. Mansi
MGH	Monumenta Germaniae Historica
NPNF	Nicene and post-Nicene Fathers
ODB	*Oxford Dictionary of Byzantium*, ed. A.P. Kazhdan et al.
PG	Patrologia Graeca, ed. J.-P. Migne
PL	Patrologia Latina, ed. J.-P. Migne
PLRE II	*The prosopography of the later Roman Empire II: AD 395–527*, ed. A.H.M. Jones et al.
SC	Sources chrétiennes
ST	Textus et documenta, series theologica, ed. C. Silva-Tarouca

Part I

INTRODUCTION

Leo the Great (440–61) had the misfortune to live in interesting times. Fortunately he seems to have thrived on adversity throughout his twenty-one years as bishop of Rome, during a period of tremendous social and religious turmoil. Inheriting a see that had recently been riven by domestic strife and sectarian divisions and was inundated with refugees from Africa, both orthodox and heretical, Leo was able to maintain social order. In the tinderbox conditions surrounding the theological disputes of the late 440s and 450s, he managed to keep his head. He undertook the leadership of a church that under his predecessors had been operating well over budget. Imperial coffers had dried up and the western emperor himself, resident in Ravenna and Rome in the 440s, then solely in Rome from about 450, was ineffectual. The city, battered by barbarian attack, had lost many of its wealthy citizens and much of its self-respect. By taking over the reins of leadership, and stressing the privilege and responsibilities of Petrine succession, Leo managed to restore some sense of civic pride in Rome and its church. Leo sought to make Christianity a truly civic religion by implementing a new liturgical calendar of feasts that would eclipse the worn-out pagan traditions and bringing the papacy to the fore in negotiations with rivals for power over Rome.

Leo's influence extended well beyond his own see of Rome, to the Christian East, through his contribution, *in absentia*, to the Council of Chalcedon (451). His achievements in the areas of Roman primacy and christology were not uncontroversial, however, and certainly not universally embraced. To further his causes in the areas of doctrine, Roman authority and church discipline, Leo made numerous doctrinal and canonical communications in the form of letters and homilies.

1

Easily the most famous is his *Tome to Flavian*, a work that was pivotal in the christological disputes of the mid-fifth century but whose impact extended well into the Middle Ages. Leo's contribution to Chalcedonian theology has long dominated scholarship on this pope, and continues to do so.[1]

The present volume attempts to redress the balance by offering a new English version of eighteen homilies and letters attributed to Leo. The selected texts are grouped under four themes, which had a major bearing on Leo's pontificate: 1. Pastoral caregiver; 2. Theologian and opponent of heresy; 3. Heir of St Peter; 4. Administrator of the wider church. While in most cases the existing translations in French, German, English and Italian are exemplary, I hope by presenting these texts according to their chronological order within these four categories to give the reader a sense of Leo's social and historical context, as well as the import of his views on Christology, heresy, ecclesiology and soteriology, and how these developed over time.

After a brief overview of the main events of Leo's life and pontificate, this introduction follows the thematic divisions of the texts translated within. In Part II a brief introduction to each translated text will treat the events that occasioned its production and the textual tradition. I hope thereby to present an accurate picture of the external circumstances and internal pressures which were brought to bear on Leo's pontificate. By taking these pressures into account we gain a more balanced appreciation of the context and contribution of his best-known writings, those that deal with the Eutychian controversy.

1

LEO'S LIFE AND TIMES

Contemporary sources on Leo's life before he entered the pontificate on 29 September 440 are regrettably scarce. A few details are provided by the author of *The Book of Pontiffs* (*Liber Pontificalis*). The earliest recension of this collection of achievements of the bishops of Rome dates to the early sixth century and is thus more than 150 years removed from Leo's own day. *Liber Pontificalis* relates that Leo was born in Tuscany, a dubious claim, and was the son of an otherwise unknown Quintianus. The anonymous author omits to mention that Leo was made deacon under Sixtus III (432–40), in which role he would have received valuable training for the office of bishop. Indeed, this was a common career path in the papal administration. Part of his role as deacon was to undertake diplomatic missions for the imperial government (*legationes publicae*). According to Prosper's *Chronicle*, Leo was acclaimed pope while conducting such a mission in Gaul. He had been sent there to settle a dispute between Albinus, praetorian prefect of Gaul, and the general Aetius.[1]

A *Life of St Leo* composed in Greek conveys the high esteem in which Leo was held by certain parties in the East (van De Vorst 1910: 400–408). The Greek *Life* is preserved in a single manuscript of southern Italian origin.[2] The anonymous author upheld Leo's contribution to Chalcedon but made no mention of the *Tome* by name. In fact the Greek *Life* includes very few verifiable historical facts at all, though it does mention by name Leo's enemies Nestorius (ch. 5), Dioscorus, and Eutyches (ch. 6). The author claims that Leo had monastic training as a youth (ch. 2), a *topos* of the hagiographical tradition, as is his account of Leo's miracles 'in every place and city' (ch. 4). Leo's theological acumen is attributed to the training he received in Greek (ch. 3), a very suspicious claim as Leo himself states that his capacity to understand Greek was limited, and certainly he never wrote in that language.[3] According to the *Life*, it was an

3

orthodox council, presumably Chalcedon, which proclaimed Leo pope, recognising him as a worthy shepherd of the 'divine and first church' (ch. 5). This curious phrase appears to be a plain acknowledgement of papal primacy, a rarity in Greek texts and perhaps explained by its southern Italian provenance. The *Life* does not include the fanciful story recounted in *The Spiritual Meadow* by John Moschus. According to the seventh-century Greek monk, Leo had prostrated himself on St Peter's tomb before sending the *Tome* to Flavian, and prayed that the saint would correct any errors or omissions in the document. After forty days the apostle appeared to Leo, saying 'I have read it and corrected it.' Leo then took up the letter from the tomb and found it corrected by the apostolic hand.[4] This apocryphal story enhances the significance of the *Tome* to a degree that even Leo could not have anticipated at the time of its composition, although one can well imagine him making such a dramatic gesture in an effort to legitimise his claim to apostolic authority. John Moschus, a partisan of Sophronius of Jerusalem, was embroiled in the christological controversy over the number of 'energies', or 'activities' in Christ, and no doubt included this story to affirm the *Tome*'s reputation as a 'pillar of orthodoxy', as it was known after the Fifth Ecumenical Council of 553. In the seventh-century monoenergist and monothelete debates, the *Tome* was frequently cited as the ultimate authority by those who argued for two energies and two wills in Christ, including Sophronius and Maximus the Confessor.

Bishops of Rome as civic leaders

At the time of Leo's accession in 440, Rome was still recovering from the three sieges of Alaric from 408 to 410, and the departure of many of its noble families to the relative safety of their estates in North Africa and other provinces. The Gothic occupation struck a massive blow to the city of Rome's confidence in its invincibility. As Jerome put it plaintively in a letter on the virtues of monogamy to the widow Geruchia, 'What is safe if Rome be lost?' (*ep.* 123.16, Labourt 1949–63 (1961): 93). The peace settlement that was reached between Alaric and Olympius, acting for Emperor Honorius (395–423) after the first siege in 408, included Roman payment of 5000 pounds of gold, 30,000 pounds of silver, and large quantities of silk robes, skins dyed purple, pepper, and hostages.[5] However, Honorius, safely ensconced in his court in Ravenna, did not honour his pledge to hand over noble hostages to Alaric. According to the historian Zosimus, the young emperor was more interested in the fate of his pet pigeons than in the slaughter and capture of many citizens of Rome (Dunn 2009). In vain, Pope Innocent travelled to Ravenna – conveniently escaping the third and final siege – to petition the emperor. Fortunately for the Roman population, Alaric died within the year, before he could fulfil his plans to cross over to North Africa.

Even before Alaric's siege of Rome, the Senate was struggling to maintain its civic institutions, as the dispute over the Altar of Victory demonstrated in 384 CE. Sacrifices at this altar at the beginning of senatorial sessions had been believed to guarantee the security and prosperity of Rome since the time of Augustus. The pagan senator Symmachus appealed in vain to Theodosius I to have the altar restored to the Senate after its removal by Emperor Gratian in 382. Gratian was also the first emperor to refuse the title of *pontifex maximus*, an office that made the emperor the head of the state religion and had been held by emperors since Augustus. Ambrose of Milan was pivotal in the new emperor Theodosius's decision against the Symmachan party (Matthews 1990: 203–9). With the division of the empire between Theodosius I's sons in 395, Arcadius maintained Constantinople as the eastern capital, and the western emperor, Honorius, set up his court in Milan, leaving his general, Stilicho, in effective control. From the time of Alaric's entry into Italy in 401 Honorius vacillated between Rome and Ravenna, and finally in 408 moved his court permanently to the safer city of Ravenna, with its resident army (Gillett 2001: 139–41).

The end of the fourth century saw the 'aristocratisation' – to quote the phrase of Lepelley (1998: 21) – of the episcopal office, and Rome was not exempt. This is obvious from Pope Damasus's inscription at the basilica of St Lawrence *in Damaso*, which echoes the classical love of honour (*philotimia*) without shame: 'I confess I wished to build a new roof for the archives, to add columns on right and left besides, which would keep the name of Damasus intact forever' (*ILCV* 1, 970: 181). In a letter of Innocent I to the bishops who had gathered at the Council of Toledo in 400, we find the pope forbidding anyone to be promoted to the episcopate who had wooed the crowds with spectacles, or who had been ordained to the priesthood of the imperial cult (*ep.* 3, PL 20: 491–2) (Lepelley 1998: 23). Papal properties and their revenues were often donated for the upkeep of churches, even as early as Silvester (314–35), the first bishop of Rome to serve imperial Christianity (*LP* 1: 170–1). Other examples include the *Liber Pontificalis* entries for Damasus, Innocent I and Sixtus III. The inscription in the apse of St Mary Major, 'Bishop Sixtus for the people of God', presents Pope Sixtus as fulfilling a civic function in providing the rich mosaics that decorated the nave and apse.[6] This is indicative of the new levels of largesse required of the incumbent of the see of Rome in the fourth and fifth centuries.

The level of luxury enjoyed by the bishops of Rome was subject to criticism by pagan contemporaries such as the fourth-century historian Ammianus Marcellinus, who accuses the popes of hiding their faults behind the greatness of the city of Rome and urges them to emulate the rustic simplicity of provincial bishops (*Res gestae* 27.3.14–15, Rolfe 1986: 3.20–1).

In the 430s and 440s, the residence of the court was still shifting between Ravenna and Rome. In the absence of strong leadership by the emperor or Senate, the bishop of Rome – like the bishops of other major sees – came to play an increasingly important part in civic affairs in the fifth century (Neil forthcoming). They exercised their civic authority in roles that had traditionally been imperial responsibilities, such as raising tribute for peace treaties, ransoming prisoners of war and other captives, and leading diplomatic representations to emperors and enemy invaders. They were also increasingly involved in patronising the construction of public buildings, now including churches and shrines. In this chapter we consider how Leo fulfilled these four functions. A related civic role, providing for the poor, will be dealt with below (Chapter 2) in relation to almsgiving.

When Leo acceded to the papal throne, both the city and the church were facing an uncertain future. From Sixtus III Leo inherited divisions within the urban population that stemmed from the pontificate of Celestine (422–32), in whose time many had abandoned communion with their bishop. Celestine's predecessor, Boniface, had been ordained on the same day in 418 as a rival, the popular candidate Eulalius, who had the support of the empress Placidia. Both Eulalius and Boniface were expelled from the city by decree of Emperor Honorius, then residing in Milan.[7] Eulalius sneaked into the city to celebrate Easter at St John Lateran in the following year and was evicted by imperial decree. Boniface was recalled and held the see for almost four years. However, when Boniface died in 422 'the clergy and people' (*LP* 1: 227, Davis 2000: 35) requested the recall of the exiled Eulalius, who sensibly refused to return to Rome. Pope Celestine was elected a week after the death of Boniface, while the city was still in uproar, and many refused to accept the new pope. A law of Theodosius II and Valentinian III (425–55) issued at Aquileia three years later subjects those of plebeian rank (*plebs*) who had separated themselves from communion with Pope Celestine to expulsion by the urban prefect (*Codex Theodosianus* 16.5.62, Mommsen and Rougé 2005, SC 497: 328).

Roman food supplies from North Africa had been cut off after the Vandal invasions of this province, beginning in 429 and culminating in the conquest of its major city, Carthage, in 439. The impact on the city of Rome of the loss of this major source of grain and oil was swift and momentous. In the first year of his pontificate, then, Leo would have had to deal with the effects of a shortage of food and an influx of North African refugees, including Manichees, Donatists and Nicene Christians. Each of these groups was fleeing persecution by the Arian king Geiseric in *Africa Proconsularis*, where the majority of Vandals settled (Heather 2007: 139).[8] The two richest alternative sources of grain, the islands of Sicily and Sardinia, were systematically attacked, with Sicily weakened by raids from 440 to 442, and Sardinia falling to Geiseric in the 460s.[9] After 439, the Vandals adopted the Roman system of taxation in North Africa for their own purposes, and the effects of resultant shortfalls in the Roman system show up in legislation from 440 onwards (Wickham 2005: 88–92). It is possible, as Wickham suggests, that Rome was forced to buy supplies of grain and oil from Geiseric for cash. Many of the huge landholdings of the Roman senatorial class in North Africa were also taken over by the Vandals, another lost revenue for the capital. Those who could afford to do so had left the city in droves in the aftermath of 410. The population of Rome was reduced to *c.* 500,000, less than half of its number in the first century CE (Wickham 2005: 33). The demographic trend was not a straightforward decline, however, and the mid fifth century seems to have seen something of a recovery, if we are to trust the findings based on pork rations.[10] The apparent spike in the 450s may well have been due in part to an influx of refugees from North Africa. Added to the Vandal threat from the south, the Hun loomed large on northern Italy's horizons, with the surrender of Milan to Attila and his capture of the wealthy coastal cities of Aquileia and Altinum in 452.

The effects of this economic and demographic crisis on the city come through more clearly in Leo's homilies than in his letters, which present a picture of the church in 'business as usual' mode. In Rome, the imperial government assured the supply of grain and other basic commodities such as pork and oil, but these handouts were available strictly to citizens only, regardless of their financial circumstances. In the food crisis of 383 or 384 the urban prefect had been forced to expel all foreigners from the city to ease the pressure on scanty resources. Ambrose of Milan was outspoken in his condemnation of the banishers for their inhumanity towards those who provided food for the city through their trade (*De offic.* 3.45–52, Davidson 2001: 1,

380–6). Bishops of Rome probably had to step in when imperial food supplies ran short: for example, Pope Gelasius (492–6) allegedly delivered the city of Rome from danger of famine (*LP* 1: 255). By the sixth century total control of the food dole (*annona*) had passed to the bishops of Rome, who also used the produce of their estates to provide for the poor (Humphries 2000: 542).

Barbarian invasions

Rome faced two serious external threats during Leo's lengthy pontificate: the Huns and the Vandals. Attila had been waiting for his opportunity to attack Rome for two decades. Until the accession of Marcian in 450, the eastern emperors had been paying considerable sums to contain Attila's expansion in the East. Marcian decided to take a stronger line against Attila and refused to pay the customary tribute. It was precisely at this time that Attila turned his attention westwards. He decided first to proceed against the Goths and Franks in Gaul. Having suffered a grave defeat at the hands of the combined forces of the Franks, Burgundians and Visigoths under the command of the Roman general Aetius in 451, he proceeded towards Rome from the north in the following year, perhaps at the invitation of Justa Grata Honoria (Mathisen 1996b). Honoria, the daughter of Galla Placidia, was a consecrated virgin who was unhappy in her vocation, one chosen for her by her younger brother, Valentinian III. In *c.* 449, aged around 30, she was discovered *in flagrante* with Eugenius, the manager of her estates. The pair were implicated in a plot to seize power from Valentinian. Her lover was murdered and Honoria, stripped of her royal position, was sent into exile in Constantinople and betrothed to a man of consular rank and good character. From there Honoria sent a desperate missive to Attila, asking for help and sending her ring as a pledge. Attila chose to interpret this signal as a proposal of marriage and accepted with alacrity, demanding half of the western Roman empire as a wedding dowry. Theodosius II, fed up, sent her back to Italy, recommending that Valentinian hand her over to Attila. Theodosius died a few weeks afterwards. Only the petitions of her mother saved Honoria. Attila, using his disappointment as an excuse, decided to invade Italy 'so as to seize Honoria along with her money' (Priscus, *frag.* 15, Gordon 1960: 106).[11]

As part of a Roman delegation that met with Attila in Venetia, Leo was instrumental in the negotiation of a truce.[12] The historian Jordanes claims that Attila's attendants advised him against taking Rome, reminding him that Alaric had not long survived the capture of the city in 410. While Attila was yet undecided, the Roman embassy arrived:

> For Pope Leo himself came to him in the Ambuleian region of the Veneti where the Minucius River is forded at the well-travelled crossing. Attila's violent rage soon settled, and returning whence he had come, he retreated beyond the Danube again with the promise of peace.
>
> (Jordanes, *De origine actibusque Getarum* 223, Giunta 1991: 91)

Priscus suggests that Attila's decision to retire was more influenced by the famine in Italy than by 'the entreaties or bribes of the embassy' (*frag.* 17, Gordon 1960: 108). The exact terms of the treaty are not recorded, but may be comparable with the annual tribute of 6000 pounds of gold payable under the treaty concluded with the Hun in 447, after the invasion of the Chersonese and Thermopylae (Croke 1981: 163). According to Prosper of Aquitaine, the decision to send this delegation 'seeking peace from the most truculent king' was made jointly by the emperor (*princeps*), the Senate and the Roman people (Prosper, *Epitoma chronicon* 1367, Mommsen 1892: 482).

The succinct account of *Liber Pontificalis* omits the imperial commission: 'For the sake of the Roman name [Leo] undertook an embassy and travelled to the king of the Huns, Attila by name, and he delivered the whole of Italy from the peril of the enemy' (*LP* 1: 239, Davis 2000: 39). Leo's role may simply have been to negotiate the ransom of captives (Gillett 2003: 114), a duty that increasingly fell to bishops during the wars of the fourth and fifth centuries (Klingshirn 1985: 184–7). Leo makes occasional general mention of ransoming prisoners in his homilies (e.g. *serm.* 78.4), but the author of *Liber Pontificalis* is silent on the subject. This is a curious omission, as the ransom of prisoners was a chance for an already-powerful bishop to enhance his prestige. Pope Symmachus (498–514), for example, is praised for paying cash ransoms for 'prisoners through the Ligurias, Milan, and various provinces: he gave them many gifts and let them go their way ... ' (*LP* 1: 263, Davis 2000: 48). Perhaps the omission is best attributed to the same reasons as the glossing over of the Vandal disaster in *Liber Pontificalis*: an unwillingness to admit the dire straits of the papacy in this period.

The threat to Roman and Christian civilisation posed by the Hun was averted by Attila's untimely death. In 453, a year after his meeting with Leo, Attila apparently met a sticky end. According to Priscus of

Thrace, on the night of his wedding to the young and beautiful Ildico, Attila fell asleep on his back, drunk and exhausted from the festivities. During the night he suffered a haemorrhage and drowned in his own blood.[13] An even less credible story from the Roman soldier Marcellinus has Attila stabbed with a knife by his wife (*Chronicon*, a. 454, Croke 1995: 21–2). Victor of Tunnuna notes more soberly that Attila died, and that under the reign of his sons the Huns were laid waste and from then on were diminished (*Chronica*, a. 453, Mommsen 1893: 185). Attila's territorial achievements did not outlast the next generation.

Much of Leo's accumulation of power for the see of Rome during his pontificate can be attributed to the weakness of the western emperor, Valentinian III (Mathisen 1996a). Nephew of Honorius and cousin of the eastern emperor Theodosius II, Valentinian was proclaimed Augustus at Rome in 425 at the tender age of 6, through the machinations of his mother Galla Placidia and after the collapse of the pretender John. Until his marriage to Licinia Eudoxia, daughter of Theodosius II, in 437, real power was held by Valentinian's mother as regent. After his marriage it was transferred to the hands of Aetius, patrician and *magister militum*. Valentinian III died on 16 May 455, murdered by two of his bodyguards, former partisans of Aetius, the general whom he had killed in the previous year. Valentinian's death brought to an end the relative stability imposed by the dynasty of Theodosius I.

Three emperors followed in quick succession, the so-called 'shadow' emperors. The first was Petronius Maximus (17 March–22 May 455) who had allegedly instigated the murder of his rival Aetius. By John of Antioch's account, the murders of Aetius and Valentinian were part of Maximus's revenge for the emperor's seduction of his wife. The new emperor then compounded his sins by forcing Valentinian's widow, Eudoxia, to marry him in order to consolidate his claim to legitimacy.

Petronius Maximus's rule was brought to a premature end by the Vandal invasion of Rome. Upon the death of Valentinian, Geiseric seized his chance and laid siege to Rome in May 455. Just as Valentinian's sister Honoria was said to have summoned Attila three years earlier, some sources blamed Eudoxia for inviting Geiseric to Rome. Eudoxia, like Honoria, suffered from a broken heart, forbidden to grieve for her husband and forced to marry his murderer. The Byzantine chronicler Malchus reports that Geiseric carried Eudoxia off to Carthage together with two of her daughters, Placidia and Eudocia. The Vandal king later brought Eudocia into his family through marriage to his son Hunseric. Maximus was killed and Geiseric's forces laid siege to the city. Leo proved unsuccessful in averting the Vandals, although Prosper maintains that his supplications softened the blow, so that the invaders restrained themselves from fire, slaughter and punishments, and contented themselves with emptying Rome of all its remaining wealth. The subsequent siege, lasting fourteen days, took a severe toll on the city's already scanty resources. Prosper reports that Geiseric took 'many thousands' of prisoners, chosen for their age and their skills (Prosper, *Epitoma chronicon* 1375, Mommsen 1892: 484), thus further reducing the population.

Valentinian's rule and connection with the old regime in Constantinople had been the last unifying force in the West, and after his death the Germanic tribes quickly gained the ascendancy. Petronius Maximus's successor, the former Gallic general Avitus, lasted only a year as emperor (455–6) before he was deposed in the revolt of generals Majorian and Ricimer in October 456. Majorian (457–61) succeeded Petronius but never lived in Rome, residing in Ravenna before moving to Arles for campaigns against the Vandals and Burgundians (Gillett 2001: 148–51).

It is easy to be misled by the letters and homilies of Leo himself as to the stability of his domain. Their tone is one of unshakeable confidence in God's providence, even an arrogant complacency, based on his belief that the Roman empire had been chosen as God's special agent to bring Christianity to the world and nothing could stand in its way. By the end of Leo's pontificate, the rule of the western Roman emperors, which had lasted almost half a millennium, was all but over. Odovacer's deposition of Romulus Augustulus in Ravenna fifteen years later was the final nail in the coffin. Felix (483–92) was the first pope to serve under Gothic kings, Odovacer and then Theodoric. With the decline of the western Roman empire, however, came the rise of the western bishop. We have seen how Leo fulfilled the civic roles of raising tribute, ransoming slaves and undertaking diplomatic missions to barbarian invaders. Let us turn now to a fourth civic function, already adopted by popes in the fourth century, but greatly increased in the fifth: urban building programmes.

Building the church

Both Sixtus III and Leo accepted aid from the western emperors for new church constructions and the repair and adornment of existing churches in the city. Sixtus III's ambitious building programme was largely undertaken at imperial expense: Valentinian III contributed more to the provision of churches in Rome under Sixtus III than any emperor before him except Constantine I (Gillett 2001: 145).

Valentinian's wife, Empress Licinia Eudoxia, donated funds for the building of the new church St Peter in Chains. In cooperation with Leo, Galla Placidia contributed to repairing damage caused by lightning at St Paul's Outside the Walls, which was also adorned with fresco medallions of all the popes up to Leo (see cover illustration).[14]

However, the money available to Leo from the imperial purse for the building and refurbishment of churches was steadily decreasing from the mid fifth century. The level of Valentinian III's fiscal difficulties is indicated by the levying of a new sales tax in 444, which required one-twenty-fourth of the value of the sale to be paid as a tax, half by the vendor and the other half by the buyer (*Nov. Val.* 15). This tax, called the *siliquaticum*, was retained in Italy until the following century (Moorhead 2001: 40–1). No great expenditures on new church buildings or furnishings are attributed to Leo, and no emperors or empresses are mentioned as benefactors of the church in *Liber Pontificalis'* entry for Leo.

Leo apparently established a monastery at St Peter's basilica, one later dedicated to 'Saints John and Paul'.[15] Roman monasteries at this time were limited to a few private foundations.[16] No archaeological evidence survives for a monastery at St Peter's, but there may be literary confirmation in Gregory the Great's *Dialogues* 4.13, where he asserts that 'in the time of the Goths', i.e. after 476 CE, the monastery at St Peter's housed the widow Galla, daughter of the consul Symmachus. Pope Gregory heard this story from nuns who were living in the same monastery in 593.[17] The apse-vault in St John Lateran that is attributed to Leo (*LP* 1: 239) actually dates to the time of Pope Celestine.[18] No donations of precious stones or gold or silver are attributed to Leo.

Prominent citizens continued to make significant contributions to the Roman church and city under Leo, as they had done in the past. Under Sixtus III, the future emperor Petronius Maximus, while urban prefect – a position he held twice (420–21; and 421 or 439) – restored St Peter's basilica. Under Leo, he built a new forum on the Caelian Hill in 443 or 445 (*PLRE* II: 749–51). The ex-consul Marinianus helped fund Leo's restoration of St Peter's after it had been damaged by fire (*PLRE* II: 724).[19] In the 450s, the wealthy virgin Demetrias Anicia dedicated a shrine to St Stephen on her estate on the Latin Way, in payment of a vow to Leo.[20] The dedicatory inscription shows that the classical form of public giving in return for social recognition was alive and well in mid fifth-century Rome.[21]

After 'the Vandal disaster' in 455 Leo had to replace all the consecrated silver services throughout all the endowed churches (*tituli*) by melting down six silver water-jars: two each from St Peter's, St Paul's and St John Lateran.[22] These had been donated by Constantine the Great, and amounted to 600 pounds of silver. The fact that the bishop of Rome was forced to melt down large silver plate for this purpose points to what we might call a severe 'cash-flow problem', exacerbated by the necessity of paying ransom and tribute to barbarian invaders. Apart from this single mention of the Vandal disaster, *Liber Pontificalis* gives no further details of the threatened invasion of the Hun or Geiseric's siege. It seems that such low points in the city's history were not considered fit for inclusion in a triumphalist account of the achievements of the papacy.

Leo's building campaign may have been limited by straitened finances, but the modest foundations he made show a sharp appreciation of the symbolic significance of maintaining visible shrines, especially in relation to the apostles Peter and Paul, and Pope Cornelius (251–3). Leo is said to have dedicated a shrine to Cornelius on the Appian Way at the catacombs of St Callistus.[23] Leo instituted a round-the-clock guard of the tombs of Peter and Paul by clerical wardens (*cubicularii*), on the model of the imperial eunuchs who served the emperor's bedchamber. In his homilies and letters Leo tirelessly championed the cult of St Peter, with which emperors and leading families of Rome strongly identified themselves, beginning with Constantine the Great's construction of a great basilica around St Peter's tomb.[24] Emperor Honorius, too, had built a mausoleum for his family next to St Peter's, in which Galla Placidia reinterred the body of her first child, Theodosius, her son by the Gothic leader Athaulf. Both Leo and the Roman senate attended the public ceremony accompanying Theodosius's reburial in 450 (Gillett 2001: 147). Gothic blood was no impediment to imperial honours or papal respect. The ex-consul Sextus Petronius Probus, patriarch of the fabulously wealthy Anician clan, built a mausoleum next to St Peter's where he and his wife were laid in the late fourth century.[25] Finally, Leo himself was buried in the portico of St Peter's basilica.

The Leonine corpus

Leo was a prodigious preacher and correspondent, leaving ninety-seven extant sermons and 143 surviving letters. He preached some fifteen times each year on significant occasions throughout the annual liturgical cycle (Green 2008: 97): the anniversary of Leo's ordination (29 September), the solemn fasts, Christmas, Epiphany, Easter, the Feast of the Ascension, Pentecost, the anniversary of Saints Peter and Paul. Of these sermons, about twelve were chosen from each year and put together in an edited collection for circulation in Leo's lifetime, soon after 445 (CCSL 138: cxciii). These fifty-nine sermons from 440 to 445 formed the basis of Leo's first sermon collection (CCSL 138: clxxvii). The second collection comprises revisions of eleven sermons of the first collection (*sermones* 22, 33, 34, 39, 40, 42, 58, 59, 61, 76 and 90) and several new sermons from 446 to 461, the principal texts being preached between 452 and 454 (CCSL 138: clxxvii, cxcix). Most of these concern the Eutychian controversy. A ninety-eighth sermon, the *Preface to the Creed* addressed to catechumens and contained in the *Gelasian Sacramentary*, was included in Dolle's edition of the sermons (SC 200, Dolle 1961–2003 (1973): 294–300).

The 143 letters attributed to Leo in PL 54 are generally accepted as genuine,[26] making the corpus the largest surviving papal letter collection before the time of Gregory the Great. In addition to these, thirty letters not written by Leo are included in the Leonine epistolary corpus in PL 54. Nineteen letters were addressed to Leo by some of the most significant figures of the age, including the eastern emperors Marcian and Theodosius II, Theodosius's sister Pulcheria and Valentinian's mother Galla Placidia, as well as Eutyches (*ep.* 21), Flavian (*epp.* 22 and 26) and various other bishops. The epistolary corpus includes two edicts of Valentinian: his edict of 445 on the punishment of Manichees (*ep.* 8), and a *Constitution* addressed to Aetius *magister militum*, supporting Leo's decision against Hilary of Arles (*ep.* 11). A further nine letters consist of exchanges between other parties: Peter Chrysologus to Eutyches (*ep.* 25), Hilary the deacon to Pulcheria about the Robber Synod (*ep.* 46), four letters from the western imperial family to Theodosius II requesting a new council (*epp.* 55–8), and three polite refusals from Theodosius (*epp.* 62–4). In 431 Cyril sent another letter, now lost, in which he sought help from Leo against the pretensions of Juvenal of Jerusalem.[27] From his wide network of correspondents it seems that Leo was a person of considerable influence, in both ecclesiastical and imperial circles.

Apart from the body of dogmatic letters concerning the Eutychian controversy, most of Leo's surviving letters have to do with matters of discipline and ecclesiastical jurisdiction, and have thus been preserved in canon law collections (see the final section, below). As *Liber Pontificalis* notes, 'Again the blessed archbishop Leo dispatched many letters on the faith, which are kept safe today in the archive' (*LP* 1: 238). Leo's letters were not the first to be consciously preserved in papal archives: the decretals of Popes Siricius, Innocent, Zosimus, Boniface, Celestine and Sixtus III had been similarly archived, but the preservation of Leo's letters for posterity bears witness to the value that was placed on this bishop as an ecclesiastical lawgiver. There must have been numerous personal letters that were excluded from these dedicated letter collections by the narrow purview of the compilers. It is most regrettable that no personal letters have survived, as they would have helped to round out our picture of Leo's episcopal activities beyond his canonical pursuits.

Leo's literary style

Much ink has been spilled on the subject of Leo's literary and rhetorical style, largely in connection with the ongoing debate about Prosper of Aquitaine's contribution or influence on Leo's homilies and letters, especially the *Tome*. The stylistic similarities between the two authors have attracted much comment, especially when Leo's style is compared with that employed in the tract *On the Calling of all the Nations*, a work once believed to have been written by Leo but now more firmly attributed to Prosper (Cappuyns 1927). Within two decades of Leo's death, Gennadius of Marseilles noted that Prosper was said to have drafted certain letters of Leo against Eutyches (*De viris inlustribus* 85, Herding 1924: 106). In 1678 Canon Joseph Antelmi of Fréjus attributed the whole Leonine corpus to Prosper, on the grounds that Leo would not have had time to write his own work and that Prosper had simply imitated Leo's style. Gaidioz (1949) advanced the more measured claim that Prosper had a hand in Leo's earliest homilies and in much of his later correspondence during the Eutychian controversy. Gaidioz's conclusions were based on the assumption that Prosper, acting as Leo's secretary, had been a superior source of theological knowledge for the pontiff, who was no great shakes as a theologian. Green reviews the evidence and concludes that Gaidioz's conclusions were based on flimsy arguments, and that James (1993) failed to prove that Prosper was responsible for anything that has come down to us under Leo's name (Green 2008: 195–201).

Leo's homiletic style is not overly showy or elaborate but concentrates rather on clarity and simple eloquence. Typical of Leo's style is the use of balanced phrases, e.g. 'Let us spend on virtue what we take away from luxury; let the abstinence of the faster become the refreshment of the poor' (*serm.* 13, CCSL 138: 54) (Green 2008: 134). To reinforce a particular point he often layered adjective-noun pairings, especially in groups of three: e.g. abstinence from food produces 'chaste imaginings, rational wills and sounder counsels' (*serm.* 13, CCSL 138: 154). Leo makes frequent recourse to stark contrasts such as 'flesh/spirit', 'human/divine', and 'piety/impiety' to drive home his doctrinal points, e.g. ' … because [Christ's] perfect humanity is shown by the hunger of the body and his manifest divinity was shown by the ministering angels' (*serm.* 40.3a, CCSL 138a: 227). Contrasting pairs of nouns are also often grouped in threes, e.g. 'let severity be transformed into mildness, indignation into meekness, and discord into peace' (*serm.* 42.6, CCSL 138a: 249). Leo had no intention, however, of elevating style over substance (Halliwell 1939: 92). He favoured 'a direct and positive mode of presentation without the artificiality of devices better suited to the professional rhetorician' (Halliwell 1939: 94). The most conclusive evidence of this is the complete absence of allegory and the infrequency of metaphor. This distinguishes him from other, more popular patristic writers like Augustine, Ambrose, John Chrysostom and Basil of Caesarea. Leo's figures of comparison are plain and informative without any of the ornamentation common to more elaborate forms of comparison (Halliwell 1939: 94–5). This lack of the picturesque can make Leo's writing seem quite dull and pedestrian. One must in this case remember the audience: Leo was not writing for his own amusement (or ours!) but for the spiritual edification of his readers. Leo did not consider the allegorical interpretation of scripture appropriate to the elucidation of doctrine.[28] This hermeneutical position is quite unusual among the Late Antique fathers, and has implications for Leo's understanding of heresy, as we will see.

In the letters, the style is much the same, unsurprisingly, since many of them treat similar christological subject matter or matters of discipline, or both. Such addresses as the *Tome to Flavian* (*ep.* 28), Leo's *Letter to the Palestinian monks* (*ep.* 124), as well as his *Second Tome to Emperor Leo* (*ep.* 165), may be more accurately described as 'treatises' written for public consumption to deliver doctrinal guidance. In Leo's letters to individuals on matters of discipline we find him using the lofty language of Petrine succession, which was designed to impress the full weight of his authority. Leo's use of set rhythmic patterns in his letters for short clauses (*clausulae*) was a typical device of Latin oratory (di Capua 1934: xxiii–xxxii). His use of honorific titles (e.g. 'Your Beloved', 'Your Charity', 'Your Brotherhood') conforms closely to established usages in official civil and ecclesiastical discourse.

A study of the vocabulary used in the sermons and letters of Leo revealed that he was not a great innovator in language (Mueller 1943: 242). His use of Latin theological terms drew heavily from the terminology developed by Hilary of Poitiers, Ambrose, Jerome and Augustine. Leo was fond of Ciceronianisms, that is, nouns, adjectives and adverbs that were common in the writings of Cicero, but rare before Late Latin. While the sermons adopt a more familiar tone, the variance in vocabulary in the letters and sermons is due more to differences in subject matter than to stylistic differences determined by genre. The vocabulary of the sermons includes more Christianisms, i.e. instances of semantic change that are limited to a Christian literary context, than do the letters, due to their greater amount of specifically Christian content (Mueller 1943: 240–2).

Much less work has been done on the sources of and influences on Leo's literary output. Leo did not aim to be original or speculative in his theology, and freely drew on the western and eastern patristic traditions in his efforts to persuade readers that his doctrine was in strict accordance with tradition. The florilegium of patristic testimonies attached to *Letter* 165, for example, included excerpts from Hilary of Poitiers' *On the Trinity*, Athanasius's *Letter to Epictetus*, Ambrose's *Concerning the faith* and *On the incarnation of the Lord*, Ambrose's *Letter* 46 (not in all manuscripts), Augustine's *Letter* 137, *Letter* 187 and *Homily* 78, John Chrysostom's *On the Ascension* and *Homily on the Cross*, Theophilus of Alexandria as quoted by Jerome in *Letter* 98, Cyril of Alexandria's *Commentary on the Incarnation* and *Second Letter to Nestorius*, and Gregory of Nazianzus's *Oration* 13.[29] As well as the established influence of major western theologians like Hilary of Poitiers, Ambrose and Augustine, the lesser-known figures of Nicetas of Remesiana and Gaudentius of Brescia seem likely to have had an influence on Leo's *Tome* (Granata 1960: 263–82). These influences will be discussed in relation to the relevant texts within.

2

PASTORAL CAREGIVER

Leo's concern for the spiritual direction of the general Roman congregation is a somewhat neglected aspect of his pontificate. It is most readily discovered in his homilies. Leo's homilies offer advice on a broad range of themes relating to the spiritual life, including fasting and almsgiving, the proper relation between Christian and Jew, and correct attitudes towards astrology and other 'pagan' religious practices. These homilies span the whole liturgical cycle and give us some insight into Leo's concern with liturgical uniformity within the city of Rome.

Fasting and almsgiving

Leo's surviving homilies are organised around major liturgical feasts, many of them fasts that were accompanied by a call to almsgiving. These included the fasts of September, December and Pentecost. The fasts are dealt with further on in this chapter (see 'Importance of the Christian calendar'). Other important occasions for almsgiving were the Collects of November, and the feast of St Peter and St Paul. Almsgiving is listed alongside 'the waters of baptism' and 'tears of repentance' as an equally effective means of blotting out sins (*serm.* 49.6, CCSL 138a: 290).

Leo was the first bishop in the West to institutionalise giving to the poor through a series of collections throughout the seven regions of the city (Neil 2007: 148). The distributions of the funds collected and gifts of food and clothing were supervised by deacons or 'overseers' (*praesidentes*). In *Homily* 11.2 Leo refers to 'a holy collection from the resources of many, which would provide the necessary expenses through the care of the overseers' (CCSL 138: 46). This system had been introduced in the West by John Cassian, following the model of large eastern churches, such as those of Constantinople and Antioch.

Already in the fourth century, we find the implementation of 'poor roles' (*matricula pauperum*) to support the poor – particularly widows and orphans – of the diocese of Milan in the time of Ambrose, and later in Hippo under Augustine.

All of Leo's homilies on almsgiving place a great emphasis on mercy (*misericordia*) as a divine quality instilled in all human beings by virtue of each being made in the image and likeness of God (Gen. 1: 26). Mercy to the poor is an imitation of God's mercy towards all human beings. The same idea is found in Gregory of Nazianzus's *Homily* 14, *On love for the poor* (PG 35: 892C), and in Gregory of Nyssa, *On benevolence* (van Heck 1992: 102.15–16). Leo was the first bishop of Rome to develop a thorough theology of self-interested giving aimed primarily towards the aristocracy, offering the standard advice to give from their surplus, without requiring the degree of renunciation embodied in voluntary poverty, as espoused by Melania the Younger and her husband Pinianus in the aftermath of Alaric's sack of Rome. In *Homily* 78.4, Leo advises that whatever is spent on acts of mercy is laid up for the giver's eternal reward: 'For whatever is spent on food for the poor, on care for the sick, on the price of captives, and on any kind of piety is not decreased but increased … ' (CCSL 138a: 496–7). *Homily* 95, on the Matthean Beatitudes, gives a similar message (CCSL 138a: 582–90).

The theme of divine accounting, whereby material loss is transformed into spiritual gain, is a favourite of Leo (Armitage 1997: 204). In *Homily* 9.2 Leo states the case plainly: 'Food for someone in need is the cost of purchasing the kingdom of heaven, and the one who is generous with temporal things is made heir of the eternal' (CCSL 138: 35). While redemptive almsgiving is common among other, earlier western preachers, such as Cyprian of Carthage, Augustine of Hippo, and Ambrose of Milan (Ramsey 1982), it is also a characteristic doctrine of some eastern preachers on poverty and almsgiving, including the Cappadocians. Almsgiving aids the salvation of the giver, and gifts given in this life are a deposit made, with interest, for eternal life. In *Homily* 17.2 Leo also ascribed to the almsgiver the role of creditor in respect to God, who would repay money given to the poor with interest after death (Armitage 2005: 178–81). This was 'holy usury' (*sanctum fenus*), as distinct from ordinary usury, which was universally condemned in patristic writings, eastern and western. Leo had taken the opportunity to condemn the practice of usury by any clerics or laypersons in *Letter* 4 (PL 54: 610–14). The notion of holy usury was common to others, such as Ambrose and Augustine. Christ, who voluntarily made lowly human nature his own, rewards those who give

19

to the poor as if they gave to him (*serm.* 9.2). Christ is the face of the poor. As Leo puts it in *Homily* 9.3, 'Rightly in the needy and poor do we recognise the person of Jesus Christ our Lord Himself ... ' (CCSL 138: 36). This was an argument used by many preachers before him, including Basil of Caesarea (*ep.* 150.3, Courtonne 2002: 75.27–9) and Gregory of Nazianzus in his *Homily* 14 (PG 35: 909B). The roots of the doctrine of self-interested giving are found in the Hebrew scriptures, e.g. Psalm 41: 1: *Blessed is he who considers the needy and the poor, God will set him free on the evil day,* cited by Leo in *Homily* 6 (CCSL 138: 28), where he again identifies the needy with Christ. In *Homily* 16.2, delivered during the winter fast of December, Leo uses Proverbs 11: 17 to spell out the doctrine of self-interested giving most explicitly (CCSL 138: 62). Inverting the traditional Roman model of patronage, Leo promises in *Homily* 10.4 that not only will God know of the almsgiver's good works, but also the alms themselves and their beneficiaries will intercede for the giver in heaven (cf. Sir. 29:15). Leo interpreted the injunction to show mercy to one's neighbour as a common Christian obligation in a concrete and financial sense. While the pagan philanthropist could legitimately expect to be honoured for his largesse, the Christian giver of charity should ideally remain anonymous to the recipients of his or her alms, content with the knowledge that such deeds were known to Christ (cf. Finn 2006: 182). *Homily* 10.2 condemns the useless largesse of the rich, instructing that generosity should now be directed where it is needed most, among the poor. Of those wealthy citizens who give only to gain glory for themselves and without regard for the need of the recipients, Leo warns: 'they feast on no food of justice, no sweetness of mercy' (CCSL 138: 40–1).

The language of justice and mercy is reminiscent of the appeals of the Psalmist, whose invocations of God's justice and mercy for the poor were typical of what Bolkestein called the 'oriental' model of social relations in Egypt and Israel, whereby the weak had a right to rely on protection from the wealthy and powerful. In contrast, the Greco-Roman model was based on the power of the Assembly, where the plebs who held the majority could compel the wealthy to support them in times of need, such as a shortage in grain supply. According to Bolkestein, this was the reason why the Greek state did not undertake poor relief. Private charity was not encouraged or even considered an important virtue (Bolkestein 1958: 102–3). Public largesse, on the other hand, was a virtue to be undertaken by public office holders, in return for public recognition of their generosity. Leo's challenge to the normal rules of Greco-Roman civic philanthropy is most apparent in his many homilies on almsgiving.

Contrary to some earlier Christian authors, such as Ambrose, Leo does make a distinction between those more and less deserving of alms, showing a strong preference for giving alms to the faithful, as in *Homily* 10.2, where he cites Galatians 6: 10: *While we have time therefore*, as the Apostle says, *let all our actions be for the good of everybody, and especially of those who belong to the household of faith* (CCSL 138: 43). Particularly deserving are those poor who disdain to confess their neediness, and prefer to suffer deprivation than the shame of a public appeal (*serm.* 9.3).

Condemnation of astrology, and other 'pagan' religious practices

Pluriform religious practices were found even among Christians in fifth-century Rome, as the aristocracy began to convert in large numbers and the status of traditional civic religion was under review. In 391 Theodosius I had sanctioned the destruction of the Serapeum, the most famous pagan temple in Alexandria. In the Theodosian decrees of 391 he also outlawed blood sacrifices, the adornment of pagan statues, and visits to pagan temples. Many temples were subsequently destroyed or converted into Christian churches. The practice of witchcraft and the taking of auspices to predict the future were also outlawed. Personal religious practices such as the wearing of amulets and commissioning of spells and curses were treated as demonic activities by such reformers as John Chrysostom, although he allowed the wearing of a cross and making the sign of the cross to ward off evil. Astrology, or consulting the stars to discover an individual's destiny, was also subject to attack by Christian preachers, especially Augustine and Leo. The need for such pastoral rebukes is obvious from the reports that even Valentinian III was apparently much influenced by sorcerers and astrologers (Mathisen 1996a), like other emperors before him. For Leo, such magical practices were deceits of the devil and had no place in the life of the Christian (*serm.* 27.3):

> By their agency remedies for illness are guaranteed, as well as predictions for the future, placations for demons, and the removal of ghosts. Added to these are those who pretend that the whole condition of human life depends on the effects of the stars, and they call the inevitability of fate that which is either the will of the divine, or our own.
>
> (CCSL 138: 135)

At stake was no less than the Christian understanding of providence. Astrology and magic, in Leo's view, denied God's role as the sole determinant of human destiny. To try to predict or alter the future, or to play with the fates, was a refusal to accept one's place in God's divine plan, and an abdication of one's own moral responsibility. It is no surprise, then, that magic and astrology turn up in association with all the worst heresies. Manichean astrology dictated the worship of the sun and the moon in their soteriological function as 'Vessels of Light', the mapping of the twelve signs of the zodiac onto different parts of the body. This led to a certain degree of fatalism, but the followers of Mani accepted that all people would be held accountable at the Final Judgment, *contra* Leo, who accused them of a total denial of human responsibility for moral conduct.[1] Priscillianists in Spain were also accused of practising weather magic to control the sun and moon (Chadwick 1976: 51–6).

Quite apart from these 'popular' religious practices, Hellenistic cosmological religion continued to be prevalent among educated converts. The Jewish philosopher Philo addressed such beliefs in first-century Alexandria in his work *On the confusion of languages*. While a direct link between Philo and Leo has not been established, Leo certainly had access to the works of Ambrose, who took up many ideas from Philo and communicated them to the West. In *Homilies* 22 and 27, Leo protests against those Christians who carry out obeisance on the stairs of St Peter's before going inside for worship on the feast of the Nativity. These homilies show that the pagan tradition of celebrating the 'new sun' (*sol novus*) on 25 December, the feast of Saturnalia, was still fully intact at that time (Wallraff 2001: 187). The feast of the Nativity, which assumed a greater importance in the fifth century, was timed precisely to coincide and eclipse the feast of the winter solstice. This is discussed further in the introduction to *Homily* 27, below.

Importance of the Christian calendar

Leo was concerned to forge a Christian civic identity that was distinct from both the Roman pagan and Jewish traditions. One way of doing this was through the implementation of a distinct Christian calendar, which divided civic time according to the liturgical cycle rather than according to secular festivals (Markus 1990: 126–31). In particular, this meant reinforcing Constantine the Great's introduction of Sunday as the Lord's Day rather than Saturday – the day of the Jewish Shabbat – and replacing other Jewish and pagan festivals with Christian ones, such as the solemn fasts. Some pagan feasts, whose religious content had all but disappeared, were allowed to stand. For example, the festival of Lupercalia (15 February) appears in the calendar of the Roman Christian Polemius Silvius in the year 448/449 (CIL 1, Mommsen 1863: 337). The pontificates of Sixtus III and Leo I mark the high point of the partnership between the papacy and the Christian aristocracy of Rome, a partnership that ended with the papal attack on the feast of the Lupercalia by Felix III, or his successor Gelasius, later in the same century (Markus 1990: 133). In terms of the number of ordinations he performed, Leo far outstripped any other bishop of Rome in the fifth century. He is said to have ordained eighty-one priests and thirty-one deacons for Rome, and 185 bishops for 'various places' (*LP* 1: 239). Even if the latter figure is simply implausible (Davis 2000: xxi), this account points to the great emphasis Leo placed on the clerical orders.

Solemn fasts

Four fasts were celebrated in the time of Leo: the September fast, the December fast, the Lenten fast, and the fast after Pentecost. The three solemn fasts of September, December and Pentecost were probably instituted in Rome as early as the late second or early third century. Callistus (217–22) established this practice, according to *Liber Pontificalis*: 'He decreed that on Saturdays, three times a year, there should be a fast from corn, wine and oil according to the prophecy'[2] – an interpolator has added that the fasts were held in the fourth, seventh and tenth months (*LP* 1: 141, Davis 2000: 7). By Leo's time a fourth fast had been added, that of Lent.[3] In his twenty-two homilies on the fasts, Leo highlights the great apotropaic power of collective fasting (Stökl Ben Ezra 2003: 265). Fasting by the community, in association with almsgiving, was meant to ward off evil and to placate God (e.g. *serm.* 88.2–4). In *Homily* 89 Leo is concerned to emphasise the differences between the Christian fast of September and the Jewish fast of Yom Kippur, which fell in the same month. Leo apparently had real experience of Yom Kippur in Rome in his day, as opposed to a merely academic knowledge. His references in *Homily* 89.1 to barefoot processions, complete abstinence from food and cessation of all work give an accurate portrayal of contemporary Jewish customs in association with the festival (Stökl Ben Ezra 2003: 274):

> When, therefore, dearly beloved, we encourage you on to certain matters set out even in the Old Testament, we are not subjecting you to the yoke of Jewish observance, nor are we

suggesting to you the custom of a worldly people. Christian self-denial surpasses their fasts, and, if there is anything in common between us and them in chronological circumstances, the customs are different. Let them have their barefoot procession, and let them show their idle fasts in the sadness of their faces. We, however, show no change in the respectability of our clothes. We do not refrain from any right and necessary work. Instead, we control our freedom in eating with simple frugality, so that in our consumption of food, moderation is chosen but creation is not condemned.

(CCSL 138a: 551.9–19)[4]

Another homily on the September fast is translated below (*Homily* 87).

Easter

Also important was the distinguishing of Easter from the Jewish Passover feast. This explains the Roman concern to devise a system for calculating the date of Easter that was independent of Jewish *Nisan*, the formula used in Alexandria and elsewhere in the East. The different methods are discussed in *ep.* 137, translated below. The various systems necessitated frequent enquiry by bishops of the West for the proper date in any given year: compare *ep.* 3 in which Paschasinus, bishop of Lilybaeum, enquires about the date of Easter in 444, and *ep.* 88 of Leo to the same Paschasinus in 451, asking him to verify the western date for Easter in 455, four years later. Even the emperor consulted Leo about the date of Easter in 455 (*ep.* 137). On that occasion Leo decided to follow the emperor's preference and celebrate according to the Alexandrian calculation on 24 April. He instructs the bishops of Gaul and Spain that they should do the same, for the sake of unity and peace (*ep.* 138). In this case, Leo's desire for ecclesiastical peace and liturgical uniformity won out over his desire to uphold local custom:

Since it is proper that the bishops have a unified practice in carrying out prescribed regulations, we must be particularly cautious above all that no fault occurs in observing the Easter festival on different dates, out of ignorance or presumption.

(PL 54: 1101–2)

Leo's concern with liturgical uniformity also extended to the performance of the rite of baptism. A practice had arisen in southern Italy of baptising on saints' days. According to Leo, writing to the bishops of Campania, Samnium and Picenum in 459, baptism should only be performed in the Easter Vigil and on Pentecost Sunday (*ep.* 168). Here again, he cites apostolic tradition in his favour (PL 54: 1210A). He also censured the practice of delaying one's baptism until death was at hand so as to avoid defiling one's pristine state by sin. While infant baptism became the norm in the West in this century, Leo's warning about the risks of leaving one's baptism so late that one might not be able to receive it in full consciousness indicates that adult baptisms were still a common practice.

The Collects

Leo's concern to stress the triumph of Christianity over Rome shows the need to break with that city's proudly held pagan traditions. In *Homily* 9, he explicitly links the relatively new 'apostolic' tradition of collections for the poor with the effacing of pre-Christian civic traditions. Likewise in *Homily* 8 (November 442), Leo claims that the date for the church Collects was deliberately chosen in order to destroy 'the snares of the ancient enemy on the day on which the impious used to serve the devil in the name of their idols' (CCSL 138: 31). The traditional dating of the homilies to 29 June, the feast of St Peter and St Paul, has hindered the correct interpretation of the five sermons on the Collects. The incorrect dating led several commentators to read Leo's remarks on ancient pagan festivals as referring to the *Ludi Apollinares*.[5] These games, dedicated to Apollo and comprising contests in literature, music and dance, were celebrated over eight days from 6 to 13 July. Chavasse has restored sermons *Homilies* 6, 7, 8, 9 and 10 to their original context in November (CCSL 138: 26).

On two occasions (*serm.* 9.3 and *serm.* 10.1) Leo refers to the November collections as an apostolic institution, i.e. initiated by Peter and Paul themselves, but elsewhere he modifies such lofty claims for their beginnings (*serm.* 7 and *serm.* 11.2). The purpose of the offering of alms was to protest 'against the unholy victims of the wicked', Leo declares in a homily delivered in the same year as the investigation against the Manichees was to take place (*serm.* 9.3, CCSL 138: 35–6). Later in the same homily (*serm.* 9.4), Leo asked the congregation to denounce to their priests the Manichees hiding in their midst.[6] The 'unholy victims of the wicked' can thus be read both as the sacrifices that accompanied pagan games, as well as the contemporary sacrifices of the Manichees in their immoral rituals (cf. *Homily* 16.4 below). Alms are an effective remedy against the sin of heresy.

Penance

Leo was also concerned to standardise the rules for the implementation of the sacrament of penance, as we find in his correspondence with two bishops of Gaul (*ep.* 108 to Theodore of Fréjus and *ep.*167 to Rusticus of Narbonne, both translated below). The sacrament of penance was usually undertaken publicly in this period,[7] and involved physical separation from the rest of the congregation in church as well as abstinence from communion for a fixed period, until the bishop was satisfied that amends had been made and offered the penitent absolution. As yet, there was no permanent opportunity in Rome to receive the sacrament of penance: this would come later in the fifth century, when Simplicius (468–83) arranged for there to be bishops on hand round the clock at the great churches of St Peter's, St Paul's and the Lateran for penance and baptism in cases of emergency, where death seemed imminent. This change in practice would have required a greater number of clergy than had previously sufficed. The penitents who had fulfilled their obligations of frequent repetition of prayers and assiduous attendance at mass, and often the payment of a fine, while observing celibacy and withdrawal from public office, were received back into communion at Easter. It was the deacon's duty on Holy Thursday to request that the bishop grant absolution to the penitents, a duty that Leo himself would have performed many times as archdeacon (Uhalde forthcoming).[8] Leo's leniency in adapting the laws of penance to fit individual cases is often cited as a watershed in implementation of the sacrament. Even in the late fourth century, Pope Siricius imposed rigorist requirements on public penitents for the remainder of their lives.[9] By the early fifth century, however, such rigorous discipline was already being tempered. In 405 Pope Innocent I instructed that deathbed reconciliation could now be offered to those who had lived a dissolute life after their baptism until death was upon them (Hoyce 1941: 23). In the days of persecution, i.e. the second, third and early fourth centuries, such people had been accepted into the ranks of penitents but the reconciliation of communion was refused, but later a milder rule was adopted (*ep.* 2, PL 20: 498). Leo addresses similar difficult cases in *Letter* 167 (Questions 7 and 8).

3

THEOLOGIAN AND OPPONENT OF HERESY

Leo's letters and sermons denouncing Manichees, Nestorians, Pelagians and Priscillianists reflect some of the many diverse Christian beliefs and practices that were current during his time. Leo's best-known intervention against a new 'heresy' (the criteria for which identification are discussed below) was his involvement in the Eutychian controversy, which was debated at the Council of Constantinople (448), the so-called 'Robber Council' at Ephesus (449) and the Ecumenical Council of Chalcedon. This christological controversy occasioned his famous *Tome to Flavian*, bishop of Constantinople, which became the touchstone of Chalcedonian orthodoxy. The most important elements of Leo's christology as outlined in the *Tome* will be presented in the introduction to *Letter* 28, below. A brief treatment of Leo's soteriology is included here to broaden our understanding of his theology as positive and constructive rather than simply 'reactive'.[1]

Leo's soteriology and christology

As the late Basil Studer astutely observed, Leo's christological doctrine is too often examined in isolation rather than as part of an overarching soteriology (Studer 1986: 765). The importance of this observation has been reinforced by two studies of Leo's understanding of the economy of salvation, those of Armitage (2005) and Green (2008). Armitage focused his discussion on the concept of 'twofold solidarity', that is, Christ's sharing of the same substance as Mary, his human mother, and God, his divine father. This idea was summed up in the Nicene Creed by the attribution to Christ of the adjective 'consubstantial' (Greek *homoousios*).

Leo's concept of 'substance' (*substantia*) perhaps needs some explanation. The noun 'substance' was originally used by Tertullian in his discussion of Trinitarian doctrine. It could be made to stand for two

Greek concepts: those of 'essence' (Greek *ousia*), and 'nature' (Greek *physis*). The orthodox Trinitarian doctrine endorsed by the first two ecumenical councils accepted that the Trinity was one essence (*ousia*) in three persons, namely the persons of God the Father, Jesus Christ the Son, and the Holy Spirit. The next question, arising in the fifth century, was how a Christian should understand that essence in the one person (*prosopon*) of Jesus Christ. Christ's essence was necessarily both human and divine, since Christian councils had defended his true humanity already against the teaching of the Docetists and his true divinity against the teaching of Arius. Did that make it divided? Could the human really be separated from the divine, or were they mixed together in Christ in such a way as to be indistinguishable? Leo's solution was to understand them as 'twofold' (*duplex*). He occasionally used the phrase 'consubstantial with the Father, consubstantial with the mother' to express this idea (e.g. *ep.* 30.6). Leo maintained that acceptance of this doctrine was essential for salvation: 'For it does no good to call our Lord, the son of the blessed virgin Mary, a man, if he is not believed [to be] a man of the same race and seed, of whom it is preached in the beginning of the Gospel' (*ep.* 30.1, PL 54: 787B). In a letter sent to Theodosius II on the same day as Leo sent the *Tome to Flavian*, he describes the *Tome* as 'a rather full treatment of what the Catholic Church everywhere believes and teaches concerning the mystery of the Lord's incarnation' (*ep.* 29, FOTC 34: 107). In the *Tome*, Leo presumed to speak for the whole church. He did not see it as presumption, of course, merely his natural prerogative as the incumbent of the see of St Peter.

When discussing the nature of Christ, Leo usually used two terms interchangeably: 'substance' (*substantia*), and 'essence' (*essentia*). Both had to do with that essential part of Christ's being that was both human and divine, more than a soul and more than his personhood. The term 'nature' (*natura*) was, however, preferred in the *Tome to Flavian* and in other letters of 449, with the exception of *Letter* 31.[2] The implications for Leo's soteriology of the idea of twofold consubstantiality were serious. Like other fathers influenced by the teachings of the second-century Irenaeus of Lyons, Leo believed that 'what is not assumed is not healed but what is united to God is saved', in the words of Gregory of Nazianzus.[3] That is to say, what Christ did not take up from human existence in his incarnation could not be saved by his death and resurrection. The idea was that if Christ were not fully human, as we are fully human, then all of humanity would not be redeemed by his sacrifice on the cross. This was the only way for Christ to defeat the devil and vanquish his demonic power over human beings. A novel theme in Leo's homilies and dogmatic letters is the devil's right to power over humanity: the basis of the devil's dominion over human beings before Christ's saving act was Adam's voluntary enslavement to sin. By causing suffering and pain for the sinless Christ, the devil exceeded his rights and thus forfeited his power over human beings.[4] Leo is a biblical theologian rather than a speculative one, and so is concerned to show how Christ fulfilled the predictions of the Hebrew prophets, and how Christ's personal history had been anticipated in the lives of the Old Testament saints (*serm.* 30.3–4) (Armitage 2005: 64–70).

Leo's understanding of how Christ fulfils the old covenant between God and Abraham is also important. Christ instituted a new law by which all nations could be saved and become the 'true Israelites' (*serm.* 30.7) (Armitage 2005: 25–42). Leo's idea of salvation was universal and communal: it was not for individuals but for the community as a whole. A new social contract had been implemented for those who followed Christ. Leo saw Rome as a Christian community, albeit a nascent and imperfect one. This ideal embraced both the city of Rome and its inhabitants, and Rome in a larger sense as standing for the civilisation introduced by the first Christian Roman emperor, Constantine the Great. Like Ambrose and the poet Prudentius in the fourth century, Leo believed that the Roman peace introduced by Augustus was the necessary precondition for the new dispensation. This notion contrasts sharply with the negative view of the pagan Roman empire expressed in Augustine's *City of God* (McShane 1979: 68). The expansion of Roman territory in pre-Christian times and the imposition of the 'Roman peace' had allowed Christians the opportunity to spread their gospel far and wide and also to impose the faith on subject peoples. Forcible conversion, like that of the Goths, posed no moral conflict for Leo. What mattered was that the faith embraced was orthodox Christianity and not the Arianism of the Goths and Vandals, or any more heretical persuasion. Leo sought to make Christianity a truly civic religion.

The struggle against heresy

Heresy, for Leo as for other church fathers of the Late Antique period, was a serious matter because it threatened the fabric that held society together. A common faith was necessary for social harmony. An orthodox faith was essential for communal safety and prosperity. Leo is not slow to remind his imperial correspondents of the basis of their power and peaceful rule, as for instance in *Letter* 31.1 to Pulcheria:

'And whatever the industry of the priesthood obtains in our times against those who attack the catholic truth redounds to your utmost glory, as long as in all things, as you have learned from the Holy Spirit's teaching, you submit your power to Him by whose help and protection you rule' (PL 54: 789C–90B). Any aberration from orthodoxy threatened the delicate balance between God and his favoured people. Thus, heresy and schism, which were often difficult to distinguish in patristic rhetoric – although some, like Cyprian, maintained a clear distinction – had to be stamped out at all costs, even by use of imperial forces if necessary. For Leo, as for every bishop of his era, faith was a corporate, not an individual, affair. Leo often describes heresy as an assault against the integrity of the faith. Just as the efforts of the church to maintain orthodoxy contributed to the emperor's glory and helped him maintain peace and unity, an emperor's failure to pursue such infringements was seen as a dereliction of his Christian and imperial duty.

Leo's aversion to allegory in his doctrinal exegesis explains in part why he was so averse to speculation on the nature of the relationship between the human and divine in Christ. For Leo all the necessary data on this question had been given in the scriptures and in the writings of the fathers preceding him. He did not question why those patristic writings were accepted as canonical; that was a given. Even though the christological controversy over the number of natures in Christ was breaking new ground in his day, Leo understood this as a question that was not new and had already been dealt with most adequately. In a similar fashion, he sought to explain heresies not as innovations but as new versions of old errors. This was the case with Eutychianism, which Leo described as combining the errors of the Manichees with those of the Gnostic Marcion (*ep.* 124) or of Valentine (*ep.* 165). According to Flavian, Eutyches had adopted the errors of Apollinaris and Valentine. Priscillianism was a new form of Manicheism. Nestorianism was derived from Pelagianism and Apollinarism. The genealogy of heresy could be used against Leo, however, as when the anti-Chalcedonian monks of Palestine accused him of Nestorianism.

The inadequacies in Leo's definition of heresy become glaringly obvious in his persecution of Priscillianism, named after its originator, Priscillian, bishop of Avila (381). Priscillian had been sentenced to death as a sorcerer and a heretic in 385 or 386, together with several of his followers, by the new emperor and zealous defender of the faith, Magnus Maximus (CFML 1: 3). Even orthodox bishops censured the emperor's radical action at the time. Priscillianism refused to be put down, however, and the cult of its 'martyrs' added to its growing appeal in Spain. Orosius of Braga addressed Augustine of Hippo on the matter in the early fifth century in his work *Commonitorium*. In the 440s Priscillianism resurfaced in the Iberian Peninsula, causing the bishop of Astorga to consult Leo for advice. Leo's reply is translated below (*ep.* 15). While Leo certainly exaggerated the similarities between Priscillianism and Manicheism, the Priscillianists shared with Manichees certain doctrines. These included the consubstantiality of the human and divine – namely, that the human soul is made of divine substance – and the independent existence of evil, as well as a negative attitude towards the human body arising from their dualistic doctrine of the existence of two powers, one evil and the other good (CFML 1: 4). Some aspects of Priscillianist practice also revealed Manichean influence, such as fasting on Sundays and rejection of marriage and procreation. In spite of these similarities, one is inclined to agree with Schipper and van Oort that Priscillianism was not a true heresy: 'In retrospect, Priscillianism creates the impression of a dissident move-ment within the Catholic Church, marked by a strong preference for asceticism and esotericism' (CFML 1: 19). Priscillian himself was keen to disavow the 'pseudo-bishops and the Manichees' (*tract.* 2.50, Schepps 1889: 40–1).[5] This made no impression on Leo the Great, however. The slightest whiff of Manicheism was enough for him to declare a marginal group like the Priscillianists beyond the pale of orthodoxy (*epp.* 15.4 and 15.7, below). According to Leo, Manichees and Priscillianists were 'different in name alone' and guilty of the same sacrileges. Pretending to be Catholics, they came to mass in order to convert churchgoers. They both accepted apocryphal books while rejecting the canon of the Old Testament as well as some New Testa-ment texts, and practised rituals that were, at best, unorthodox, at worst, depraved (*ep.* 15.16, CFML 1: 72; translated within). Let us now consider why Leo believed that the Manichees posed a serious threat to Roman orthodoxy, and the Leonine solution to the Man-ichean problem.

Inquiry against the Manichees

The investigation into Manicheism in Rome is a good example of Leo's successful appeal to imperial power to stamp out a spiritual problem. Manichees were first discovered in Rome in the time of Pope Anastasius (399–401/2), who required that any cleric coming from overseas bring five letters of recommendation to prove that he was not a Manichee (*LP* 1: 218). An imperial edict of 425 expelled 'Man-ichean heretics or schismatics or astrologers and every sect opposed to the Catholics' from the city of Rome.[6] In late 443, Leo convened a commission of bishops, senators and other leading citizens to investigate and condemn Manicheism. Their numbers in the city had grown in the previous five years (*ep.* 7.1, PL 54: 620A) since the Vandals had expelled many North Africans from their homes (*serm.* 16.5, CCSL 138: 65). Their rejection of the eucharistic sacrament of the cup made them obvious in liturgical contexts, as did their custom of fasting on Sundays and Mondays, in honour of the sun and the moon (*serm.* 42.5, CCSL 138a: 247). Leo accuses them of the worst kind of depravity, abusing children in debauched sexual rituals masquerading as religion (*serm.* 16.4 below). A young girl was allegedly groomed by two women and set aside for this ritual role. Her violation by a youth was presided over by a so-called 'bishop'. Some corroborating evidence for such practices exists from another hostile witness, Augustine (*De haeresibus* 46.9, van den Hout et al. 1969: 314–15). Augustine describes a trial of Manichean Elect that took place in Carthage some years earlier, involving a case where a girl of less than 12 years of age was allegedly abused in similar circumstances. That trial was presided over, and the accused charged, by the tribune Ursus. Leo's tribunal, on the other hand, was made up of both secular and ecclesiastical judges, and presided over by the bishop himself.

Whatever the truth of the matter, followers of this religion were condemned outright by Leo's tribunal. He proudly announced to his fellow bishops in Italy in 444 (*ep.* 7.1) that the Manichees had been extinguished in Rome and restrained by his authority and judgement, and warns them to be vigilant lest its shady roots be seeded among them (PL 54: 620B–C). The emperors Valentinian III and Theodosius issued a constitution on 19 June 445 making Manicheism a public crime. The penalties were severe: Manichees were forbidden to enrol for military service, to live in cities, to receive or leave inheritances. These were the same penalties applied to others found guilty of sacrilege: 'For nothing seems to be too severe to be decreed against those persons whose incestuous perversity in the name of religion commits deeds that are unknown and shameful even in brothels.'[7] Lay people were encouraged to denounce suspected Manichees with impunity, a policy of public outing that Leo also endorsed in several sermons of 443 and 444 (e.g. *serm.* 16.5 below).[8]

While Leo was satisfied that Manicheism had been extinguished in Rome, due to his and Valentinian's combined intervention, the group persisted into the next century in Rome. Gelasius (492–6) and Symmachus (498–514) were both required to take strong action against them, burning their images and books outside church doors and sending them into exile (*LP* 1: 255 and 261). In Symmachus's case, the purge was undertaken in reaction to Emperor Anastasius's accusations that Symmachus himself was a Manichee (Davis 2000: 130). His successor, Pope Hormisdas (514–23), implemented another investigation into Manicheism, this time resorting to trial by torture (*LP* 1: 270–1).

Pelagianism

The suppression of Pelagianism became the focus of Leo's efforts even before his ordination as bishop. In the early fifth century Pelagius had found an enthusiastic body of supporters among the Roman aristocracy, with his doctrine of perfection by works. With their denial of original sin, strong emphasis on the freedom of human will and the ascetic way of life, as well as their endorsement of the total renunciation of private property, Pelagius's teachings posed a threat to the social fabric of the Roman senatorial class. Among Pelagius's chief supporters was the prominent advocate and aristocrat Caelestius. Pelagius is known to have corresponded with Melania the Younger and with Demetrias Anicia. To some, especially Augustine, the Pelagian doctrines of justification by faith and the human capacity to achieve perfection through acts of virtue appeared to undermine the doctrine of salvation by divine grace. Pelagius was first condemned by the synods of Carthage and Milevis in 416, and the findings of these two African councils were endorsed by Pope Innocent I. Pelagius then appealed to Innocent for protection and approval of his teachings. Upon the death of Innocent, the Greek pope Zosimus (417–18) took up the joint cause of Pelagius and his associate Caelestius and pronounced both men innocent of deviation from the Catholic faith. The outraged African bishops, led by Augustine, held another synod at Carthage in 418 and reinforced their condemnation of both men and their teachings. Zosimus changed his tune, endorsed the Synod of Carthage and declared Pelagian doctrine a heresy.

Pelagians were expelled from Italy by an imperial rescript of Honorius in 418. Under Zosimus, the future pope Sixtus III had vacillated in his attitude to Pelagius, first finding for him and later against (cf. Augustine, *ep.* 191, PL 33:867–8; *ep.* 194, PL 33: 874–91).[9] The Pelagian cause was taken up in Italy by Julian of Eclanum. Julian attacked the anti-Pelagian camp, led by Augustine, as enemies of marriage and holding 'Manichean' views. In 429 Julian took refuge, along with Caelestius, in Constantinople in the court of Patriarch Nestorius. The following year Theodosius expelled all Pelagian clergy from the East and Julian returned to Italy. Pelagianism was condemned at the

Ecumenical Council of Ephesus in 431 and ceased to be a problem in the East. However,trouble with Pelagians continued to brew in the West. In Italy, according to Prosper,[10] Leo was instrumental in Sixtus's opposition to Julian in 439 and in preventing him from regaining his former see of Eclanum. Around 440, the year of Leo's accession, a book was published in Rome by the circle of Julian of Eclanum under the title of *Praedestinatus*. Although it contained a nominal condemnation of Pelagius it was in fact a Pelagian or semi-Pelagian defence of free will and a condemnation of Augustine's teachings on grace and predestination, which it presented in a much distorted version.

Semi-Pelagianism, a modified form of Pelagianism whose tenets differed in crucial respects from the teachings of Pelagius on free will and original sin, was introduced by John Cassian and taken up by the monks of Marseilles. The term semi-Pelagianism is in fact anachronistic. Those to whom it is today applied were simply trying to come to terms with Augustine's somewhat extreme views on predestination and the role of free will in human salvation. Near the end of his life, Augustine dedicated two works to defending his doctrine of an arbitrary election, i.e. that people are chosen by God regardless of their own will, and his doctrine of a human will determined wholly by grace rather than a grace dependent on human will (*On grace and free will*, and *On correction and grace*). Two final works of Augustine were dedicated to refuting the revival of Pelagianism in Gaul.[11]

One of the first problems Leo had to face during his pontificate was the rehabilitation of clergy who had supported Pelagius or Caelestius and now wished to return to the mainstream church. There are only two references to Pelagianism in Leo's surviving letters: *Letter* 1 to the bishop of Aquileia, and *Letter* 2 to Septimus of Altinum (Pietrini 2002: 85–8).[12] Neither letter makes mention Julian of Eclanum, who is thought to have returned to Italy and remained there until his death in Sicily *c.* 455. Leo sent similar letters to the metropolitan bishop of Venice, to which the Church of Altinum belonged, and asked Bishop Septimus to cooperate with his metropolitan bishop to implement his instructions in that province (*ep.* 2.1).

In his polemic against Pelagianism, and in his views on the role of human free will in salvation, Leo was strongly influenced by Augustine's works on grace (Pietrini 2002: 283). Augustine's influence is evident in *Homily* 19, delivered in 452:

> For, if our will is God's will, our weakness will receive strength from God, from whom the will came; *for it is God*, as the Apostle says, *who works in us both to will and to act for*

[God's] good pleasure (Phil. 2: 13). And so no one will be puffed up with pride, or crushed with despair, if he uses the gifts which God gave to God's glory, and withholds his inclinations from those things, which he knows will harm him.

(*serm.* 19.3, CCSL 138: 79)[13]

However, in contrast to Augustine's picture of 'a God whose saving love did not reach out to all humanity' (Green 2008: 78), Leo constantly emphasised that grace was offered to all peoples.[14] Nor was he drawn to the theories of the monks of Marseilles. Leo rejected the semi-Pelagian idea of 'the beginning of faith' as a point of commitment to God before grace started to act, reiterating in *Letter* 1.3 that, 'Whatever is not given freely is not grace but the reward and recompense of what is deserved' (PL 54: 595).[15] Leo's insistence on the universal possibility of grace and salvation is one of the most attractive aspects of his theology, and reveals his awareness of the pastoral dangers of preaching a God whose salvation was not offered to everyone.

Pelagianism persisted in the West well after the time of Leo: the letters of Gelasius lament recurrences in Dalmatia and elsewhere at the end of the fifth century.[16] Pelagian and semi-Pelagian ideas continued to flourish in Gaul, Britain and Ireland until their ultimate condemnation at the second Synod of Orange in 529.

Nestorianism

Nestorius, a Syrian monk and disciple of Theodore of Mopsuestia, came to the patriarchate of Constantinople in 428 ill prepared for the political intrigues in which he was about to be embroiled. The rivalry between the sees of Alexandria and Constantinople had been sharpened by the elevation of New Rome as second in honour to Old Rome by the second Ecumenical Council, held at Constantinople (381). Theophilus of Alexandria had taken a big stick to another Antiochene patriarch of Constantinople, John Chrysostom, and forced him into exile, first in 403 and again in 404. Theophilus's nephew and successor to the patriarchate, Cyril of Alexandria (412–44), was unimpressed by the choice of another Antiochene candidate in 428, the monk Nestorius. Nestorius did not help himself by quickly getting several Christian factions offside in his own see: the Arians, Quartodecimans, Novatianists and Macedonians were all violently evicted from their churches in Constantinople as part of his attempt to root out 'heresy'.

Nestorius added fuel to the fire being prepared for him by endorsing the preaching of a young priest in his see against the application of the title of 'mother of God' (Greek *theotokos*, literally 'the God-bearer') to the Virgin Mary. The historian Socrates reports that in the course of a sermon Nestorius's protégé Anastasius made the following incendiary pronouncement: 'Let no man call Mary "the mother of God", for Mary was human and it is impossible that God could be born from a human being.'[17] Given that the term 'God-bearer' had been used of Mary by such authorities as Origen, Athanasius, Eusebius of Caesarea and Gregory of Nazianzus, Nestorius's support for Anastasius was bound to cause a scandal. Cyril seized the opportunity and greatly exaggerated the offence of Nestorius, falsely accusing him of Apollinarianism and Pelagianism. In his work *Book of Heraclides* 228 (Nau 1910: 138), Nestorius claimed that he could not understand what Cyril meant by the term 'hypostatic union' in relation to the incarnate Christ, since Nestorius interpreted 'hypostasis' in the outdated Nicene sense of 'real being', the equivalent of *ousia*. Cyril, on the other hand, was using *hypostasis* in the new sense adopted by the Council of Constantinople in 381 to mean 'differentiated subject' (McGuckin 1994: 148–9). Nestorius's theological position on the divinity and humanity of Jesus Christ was informed by the teaching of Theodore of Mopsuestia, that there was not a personal union in Christ but 'a union of different things in close relation' (*henōsis schetikē*), a position that came dangerously close to the division of Christ into two *hypostases* or persons.[18] The matter was brought to trial at the Council of Ephesus in 431 and Nestorius was convicted and exiled.

A year after Nestorius's ordination as patriarch, and just as the storm of accusations of heresy was about to break over his head, Caelestius, Julian and several other Pelagian bishops sought refuge in the imperial court in Constantinople. How far Nestorius was influenced by their views cannot be determined – Nestorius certainly never mentioned Pelagius by name, but he may well have regarded his enemies' enemies as his friends. This certainly seems to be the case for Caelestius, to whom Nestorius wrote a letter of consolation upon his forced departure from Constantinople. A Latin translation of this letter formed part of a dossier of anti-Pelagian texts made by Marius Mercator, the fifth-century disciple and correspondent of Augustine (*ep.* 35, ACO 1.5.1, Schwartz 1925: 65). For Mercator, a staunch opponent of Pelagius, it was a case of his enemy's friends (the Nestorians) becoming his enemies. It was Nestorius's support for Pelagius rather than his doctrinal aberrations that earned him the opprobrium of Pope Celestine (Bark 1943; Dunn 2001a). Nestorius and Caelestius were condemned together in the *Acts* of the Ecumenical Council of

Ephesus, though neither is mentioned by name. As Bark puts it, at this council, 'Celestine sacrificed Nestorius to Cyril and Cyril agreed to the condemnation of the Pelagians, in whose teachings he had previously shown no interest at all' (Bark 1943: 215). Leo was much influenced in his early years as a deacon by the monk John Cassian (c. 360–435), and commissioned from him the work *On the incarnation of Christ*, directed against Nestorius. However, Cassian's work proved disappointing and was not taken up in Rome or elsewhere. In it, Cassian accused Nestorius of adopting the errors of Pelagius, without much justification.[19] Both Cyril and John Cassian saw a link between what they perceived as Nestorian 'adoptionism' – i.e. the doctrine that God the Father merely adopted the human Jesus as His son, having foreseen his merits – and the Pelagian theory that Christ was simply a moral example for humankind, rather than its saviour.

Whenever Leo mentions Nestorianism it is in association with Eutychianism, as the opposite side of the same heretical coin. Both Nestorius and Eutyches were guilty, in Leo's view, of the same error, but in different directions. Nestorius, in emphasising the human person of Christ, failed to acknowledge his full divinity. Eutyches, in emphasising the 'one incarnate nature of God the Word' – a quotation from Cyril of Alexandria – erred in denying Christ's full humanity. Leo was outraged to hear that, due to malice or a misreading of his *Tome*, he himself had been accused of Nestorianism (*ep.* 124 to the monks of Palestine). The *Tome to Flavian* was the sole comfort of Nestorius in the last two miserable decades of his life spent in exile, since Nestorius believed that the *Tome* was his theological vindication (Pásztori-Kupán 2006: 12). It is unlikely that Leo would have concurred with this view.

Eutychianism

The monk Eutyches, an abbot or archimandrite of Constantinople, first crops up in Leo's letters in a very favourable light. The pope had received information from the abbot concerning his attempts to suppress Nestorian resistance to his own heretical views on the incarnation. Leo, unaware of what these views were, congratulated 'his dearest son' Eutyches for his concern in this matter, and promised to pursue the elimination of the 'heinous poison' of Nestorianism (*ep.* 20, 1 June 448). In December of the same year, Eutyches, by now condemned by a council held in Constantinople in November, appealed to Leo for help (*ep.* 21). Leo wrote at once to Flavian in some embarrassment, asking why he had not been fully informed of the scandal (*ep.* 23). Flavian had indeed informed the pope at the end of 448 (*ep.* 22), but his letter was delayed in transit and crossed paths with Leo's own complaint. Thereupon Flavian sent a second letter to Leo (*ep.* 26) outlining again Eutyches's double error, which was derived from the heresies of the Syrian Apollinaris and the Roman Gnostic Valentine, according to Flavian. The first error was his belief that before the incarnation Christ had two natures, and afterwards only one. Eutyches's second erroneous doctrine was that the body that Christ took from the Virgin was not of the same nature as a human body. Since it was not of human substance it was consubstantial neither with us nor with the woman who bore him according to the flesh (PL 54: 743B–45B).

In response to Flavian's second letter, Leo promised a full reply (*ep.* 27). This came in the form of the *Tome to Flavian*, composed on 13 June 449 (*ep.* 28, translated below). Around the same time as the arrival of Flavian's second letter to Leo, in May 449, Theodosius II requested Leo to attend a council to be convened in Ephesus to settle the dispute. It was to be presided over by Dioscorus of Alexandria, a Eutychian supporter and opponent of the patriarch of Constantinople. Refusing the invitation, Leo agreed to send two delegates along with the *Tome to Flavian*, which was supposed to be read out to the gathering of bishops. Dioscorus, however, prohibited its presentation at the Council of Ephesus in August 449. Flavian was deposed as patriarch of Constantinople, and mauled so badly that he died on his way to exile. Leo was furious at this insult and at the outcome of the council, denouncing it as 'a den of thieves' (*Latrocinium*). The appellation 'the Robber Council' was quickly adopted by the losing side. The *Tome to Flavian* had to wait another two years for its 'day in court'. Another council was convened in October 451 by the new emperor, Marcian. Again, Leo declined to attend. This time, however, his legates Julius, bishop of Puteoli and the deacon Hilary, who would succeed Leo as bishop, were successful in bringing the *Tome* to the notice of those present. To certain factions in the dispute, the *Tome* seemed to contain a partial solution to their impasse. In particular the phrase 'in each nature' was seized upon as being sufficiently vague to admit a broad spectrum of interpretations. Leo's second major christological statement, the letter written to the monks of Palestine in 453 (*ep.* 124, translated below), was 'effectively a replacement and emendation of the Tome' (Green 2008: 236). It was reprised in *Letter* 165 to Emperor Leo, the document known as 'the second Tome', and had a significant impact on that emperor's approach to the ongoing christological disputes in the East.

4

HEIR OF ST PETER

Leo's views on the primacy of the bishop of Rome prepared the ground for future papal leaders' tendentious relations with other sees, especially that of Constantinople. Leo's rejection of *Canon* 28 of the Council of Chalcedon, which claimed equal dignity for the see of Constantinople, created a lasting cloud over relations between Rome and the churches of the East (*ep.* 114).

Leo has often been cited as the first bishop of Rome to have a strong sense of Roman primacy. He saw himself as the 'heir of St Peter' not as an individual person but in virtue of his office as leader of the Church of Rome that had been founded by the apostle Peter. Rome's claim to apostolic status was doubled by the tradition that Paul had also been martyred in Rome, like Peter, during the reign of Nero. The historical basis for this line of succession was the *Letter of Pope Clement I to James the brother of the Lord*, in which Clement claimed to have been personally anointed as the third (or fourth) bishop of Rome by the apostle himself. This forgery was written in the late second or third century, and had been translated into Latin by Rufinus of Aquileia in the first decade of the fifth century (Neil 2003: 38). Leo was not the first bishop of Rome to describe himself as the heir of St Peter, basing his claim to authority on the Petrine commission in Matt. 16: 18–19: *You are Peter, and on this rock I build my church*, etc. On the other hand, Leo may have been the first to use the term 'the unworthy heir' (*indignus heres*), a phrase that Ullmann regarded as a deliberate borrowing from Roman legal terminology.[1] However, in Roman law the 'unworthy heir' was one who was legally unable to claim an inheritance. The legal meaning of this phrase fits ill with Leo's understanding of himself as Peter's successor, inheriting from the first apostle the keys to the kingdom of heaven and the spiritual powers of binding and loosing. Leo's declaration of 'unworthiness' was intended only in a moral sense. Having inherited the leadership of the Roman see via an uncontested election, Leo believed it was his right and responsibility to offer leadership not just to the Church of Rome but also to the wider church. Leo's commitment to the theory of Roman primacy was usually tempered in practice by the strong sense of collegiality that informed most of his dealings with other bishops. On matters of local custom, Leo did not always insist on imposing the Roman way: for example, he agreed to adopt in the West the Church of Alexandria's calculation of the date of Easter in 455.[2]

A notable exception to Leo's usual collegiality was his disciplinary action towards Hilary of Arles (James 1984: 226). One might expect to see some difference in Leo's treatment of those churches outside his patriarchate, but geography alone cannot explain the particular vehemence of Leo's dispute with Hilary. That dispute will be dealt with in the next chapter. Here we are concerned with just what the Petrine succession meant to Leo, and what it meant to other sees. These are questions that we can only approach through Leo's writings and those of his episcopal correspondents.

Primacy of the bishop of Rome

The sources containing Leo's most explicit claims to primacy over the wider church are his homilies on the anniversary of his succession and on the Feast of Saints Peter and Paul. Two of these are translated within this volume (*serm.* 4 on his anniversary, and *serm.* 82 on the Feast of Peter and Paul). Their rhetoric is somewhat overblown, in keeping with the occasion and the audience. Leo's authority was strongest in suburbicarian Rome, and within the borders of Italy. As geographical distance from the Eternal City increased, so the pope's reach weakened. In Gaul and Spain, results of Leo's attempts to interfere in local ecclesiastical governance were variable. In Africa they were least likely to be successful, given the strong sense of collegiality cultivated by the North African bishops through frequent local synods, headed by the bishop of Carthage. The African bishops had contested Roman authority since the mid third century, when Cyprian of Carthage first challenged Stephen of Rome's ruling on the issue of rebaptism for those who had lapsed in the persecutions. Even within Italy, Leo encountered resistance to his authority on the use of saints' days for baptism, of which he disapproved (*ep.* 168, PL 54: 1210) and, in Sicily, the refusal to follow the Roman formula for the dating of Easter (*ep.* 3) (James 1984: 214). In spite of this, or perhaps because of it, Leo took the opportunity at least twice a year to present a vision of the bishop of Rome as the divinely commissioned ruler of the church.

The first of these liturgical occasions was Leo's ordination on 29 September 440. The first four anniversary sermons (*sermones* 1–4) were transmitted in the manuscripts as a group (CCSL 138: 3), and were delivered over the first four years of Leo's pontificate – there is no anniversary sermon for 442. The opening sentence of *Homily* 4 reveals one of Leo's key concerns: the unity of the Christian community, which he further specifies as 'unity of faith and baptism'. Leo cites the apostle Peter twice, in verses from the first epistle of Peter: *And you yourselves like living stones will be built up into spiritual homes, a holy priesthood, making spiritual sacrifices acceptable to God through Jesus Christ* (1 Pet. 2: 5); and later: *But you are a chosen people, a royal priesthood, a holy nation, a people belonging* [to God] (1 Pet. 2: 9). He then turns his audience's attention from the glorious occasion of his own ordination to its source: this day should be celebrated chiefly for the glory of Peter (*serm.* 4.2). Peter 'is placed over the calling of all peoples, and over all the apostles, and all the Fathers of the church: so that although there are many priests in the people of God and many shepherds, yet Peter properly reigns over all whom Christ rules first of all' (*serm.* 4.2). The reason for Peter's leadership in 'apostolic dignity' was the fact that he was the first among the disciples to confess Christ as 'the Messiah, the Son of the Living God' (Matt. 16: 16–17) (*serm.* 4.2). The first confession as the foundation of Peter's powers is also cited in *Homily* 3.3 (CCSL 138: 13) and *Homily* 83.1 (CCSL 138a: 519).

Homily 84 on the anniversary of the sack of Rome by Alaric provides an interesting glimpse into Leo's understanding of the destiny of Christian Rome. Leo attributes the sparing of citizens during the sack of Rome to the protection of the saints in whose shrines Christians and others took refuge. This is not an appeal to a new kind of Roman triumphalism – after all, Alaric's sack of Rome was an ignominious defeat for the city – but a plea to honour its new patrons, the martyr saints who had proved more powerful than the pagan gods. The cult of St Lawrence also received a significant boost during the pontificates of Sixtus and Leo, as *Homily* 85 (below) illustrates.

It is interesting to note that *Liber Pontificalis* does not mention Leo's contribution to the debate on Roman primacy, but does assert that his successor Hilary 'condemned Eutyches and Nestorius and all their followers, and all heresies, and confirmed the dominion and pre-eminence of the holy and apostolic see' (*LP* 1: 242, Davis 2000: 40). Pope Hilary is also said to have issued a 'decree about the church' on 16 November 465. This probably refers to a letter – of which only a fragment survives – preserved in the *Thessalonica Collection*, a collection of decretals compiled to bolster Roman claims to jurisdiction over the ecclesiastical province of eastern Illyricum (Jasper 2001: 82).

Old Rome versus New Rome: conflict with the church of Constantinople

The relationship between the sees of Constantinople and Rome had been fraught since 381, when the bishops present at the Second Ecumenical Council of Constantinople declared that New Rome should be second only to Old Rome in primacy of honour (*Canon* 3). After the Robber Synod of 449, Leo decided to take action against the unorthodox behaviour of Emperor Theodosius II, who had upheld the decisions of the Robber Synod and refused to reopen the matter. In a diplomatically worded letter to Theodosius, Leo requested that the emperor make a statement of orthodox belief and circulate it among the churches. He also asked that an ecumenical council be held in Italy to resolve the question of so-called 'monophysitism'. For, Leo pointed out in *ep.* 69, 'It will benefit the universal Church as well as your government if, in a single profession of faith by the whole world, there is adherence to belief in one God, one faith, one pledge of man's salvation' (PL 54: 892B, FOTC 34: 140). Who knows what hell would have broken loose from Constantinople if fate had not intervened? Before he received Leo's letter, Theodosius met his death in a riding accident while hunting, in mid 450. With Theodosius's death, a new era of rapprochement between East and West seemed on the verge of dawning. The new emperor, Marcian, and his wife Pulcheria, sister of Theodosius, were initially very well disposed towards Rome, and Leo in particular, and wished to uphold his condemnation of Eutyches through the convening of a new council in the East.

Letter 73, from Valentinian and the very new Emperor Marcian, offered formal recognition of the pope's primacy among bishops. Written in Constantinople at the end of August or the beginning of September 450, and addressed to 'the most revered Leo, archbishop of the glorious city of Rome', it merits inclusion in full here:[3]

> We have come to this greatest rule by the providence of God and through election by the most excellent Senate and the whole army. Whence, on behalf of the revered and catholic religion of the Christian faith, by whose aid we trust the power of our rule is governed, we believe it is right for your Holiness, *as the bishop pre-eminent in the divine faith*, to be addressed in sacred letters at the outset. We invite and

beseech [you] that your Holiness would pray to the eternal Deity, for the solidity and standing of our rule; because it is also our intention and desire, that, after every impious error has been removed through the celebration of this synod, *with you as author*, the greatest peace may hold around all bishops of the catholic faith, being purified from every spot and stain. Made at Constantinople, in the seventh consulship of our lord Valentinian ever Augustus and with Avienus as consul.

(PL 54: 900A–B)

The key phrase 'with you as author' indicates that Leo was invited to play a leading role at the synod, even while Theodosius insisted that it be held in Constantinople rather than Rome. In this letter, the imperial rulers of East and West acknowledged that Leo held the headship among bishops, and by that acknowledgement brought it a little closer to reality. In May of the following year Marcian and Pulcheria sent out a summons to all bishops of major sees to attend the Council of Chalcedon. The imperial couple repeatedly requested Leo's attendance at the synod, but to no avail. With Attila on the horizon after his invasion of Gaul, Leo unsuccessfully sought postponement of the council until 'a more opportune time'. In the end, he agreed to send legates, since 'present difficulties' did not allow him to travel so far from home (*ep.* 89).

Although the majority of bishops at Chalcedon agreed that 'Peter has spoken through Leo', in an acclamation of support for the *Tome*, the same council ratified a canon which caused great contention with the bishop of Old Rome. This was the infamous *Canon* 28, added to the original twenty-seven canons after a final additional session of the Council, which declared that Constantinople was equal to the Church of Rome, which held 'primacy of honour'. The basis for New Rome's privileges was the city's status as an imperial capital. The reiteration of this claim at Chalcedon was really an attempt to contain the ambitions of the patriarchate of Alexandria vis-à-vis Constantinople by asserting the authority of the emperor over all the churches apart from Rome. In contrast to the deferential tone of *Letter* 98, in which the bishops assembled at Chalcedon sought Leo's ratification of the council's *Acts*, *Canon* 28 smacked of imperial hauteur. Leo refused to ratify the *Acts* while they contained this canon. In 454 Leo sought the support of Proterius of Alexandria, 'the successor of St Mark', against Constantinople's 'unprincipled ambition', which had 'injured the dignity' of the other great sees in the so-called twenty-eighth canon (*ep.* 129). Leo deliberately emphasised the relation of Mark the Evangelist to St Peter as one of disciple to teacher.[4] In another letter to Emperor Marcian in 452, he pointed out that the see of Constantinople's claim was not based on any apostolic foundation but on secular power (*ep.* 104.3) (McShane 1979: 160–3). This was the germ of the 'two powers' theory that was to be developed to great effect by Pope Gelasius at the end of the fifth century. The eastern emperor was head of his church in a way that was never possible in the West, largely due to the claims of the bishop of Rome. This difference in structure and ideology was to bring the eastern and western churches into schism in the late ninth century and again, permanently, in 1054.

5

ADMINISTRATOR OF THE
WIDER CHURCH

Leo's leadership among the bishops of suburbicarian Rome was undisputed, and followed the precedent of all archbishops in major cities. Within Italy, too, he had a good claim to the last word, although he encountered resistance, as we have seen, even among the bishops of Sicily, over the dating of Easter. However, his command over the broader church was much more subject to debate, especially when it came to the disputed provinces of Illyricum and his relationship with Constantinople.

The dispute with Hilary of Arles

The difficulties inherent in any Roman bishop's attempt to impose his authority on wider church are well illustrated by Leo's dispute with Hilary of Arles and the bishops of Gaul. The bishops of Gaul had long recognised Arles as their most important see, even though the supremacy of the bishop of Arles was contested by rivals such as the bishops of Vienne. In the mid 440s Leo saw that the bishop of Arles was overreaching his powers by ordaining bishops throughout all of Gaul, and decided to intervene on behalf of two appellant bishops. The first of these, Bishop Celidonius of Besançon, had been falsely accused of marriage to a widow, and had been deposed by a Gallic council convened by Hilary. The accused brought his case to Rome and Hilary was forced to put in an appearance. Leo decided that Celidonius had been falsely charged and wrongfully deposed, since Hilary was not a vicar and had no metropolitan powers over Besançon. The second appeal to Rome was brought by Projectus, whom Hilary had replaced by another bishop after he had fallen ill and seemed likely to die. Apart from the illegality of consecrating a new bishop in place of one who was still living, Hilary had no formal rights of jurisdiction over Projectus's province, probably that of Narbonne. *Letter* 10 (*c.* 1 July 445) announces the pope's intention to bring Hilary and his supporters to heel. Leo had to tread quite carefully in relation to the bishops of Vienne, when recommending a course of action against another Gallic bishop that it was not in his power to enforce. In reporting on the two appeals, Leo writes with uncharacteristic acerbity to the bishops of Vienne, 'Just how gentle of heart Hilary is becomes obvious from the fact that he considered his brother's tardiness in dying as an impediment to his presumptuous plans.'[1] Hilary's main offence had been to deny the primacy of the see of Peter, an attitude characteristic of Gallicanism, and something Leo was keen to stamp out. The arrogance of the rogue bishop is condemned in the strongest possible terms: 'Anyone who thinks that the primacy should be denied to Peter cannot in any way lessen the Apostle's dignity: inflated with the wind of his own pride, he buries himself in hell.'[2] Hilary was not deposed – even Leo was not going to try to pull that one off! – but his powers of ordination were stripped and given to the bishop of Vienne. An imperial intervention settled the matter beyond dispute. Valentinian's constitution of June/July 445 forbade bishops of Gaul to act against the bishop of Rome.[3] After Hilary's death in 449, the bishops of the province of Arles asked that metropolitan rights be restored to the new bishop of Arles, Ravennius (*ep.* 65). Leo refused, on advice from the bishop of Vienne, who was allowed to maintain power over four cities apart from Vienne: those of Valence, Tarentaise, Geneva and Grenoble (*ep.* 66). Leo's demotion of the bishop of Arles was only temporary. Some of the see's former powers of jurisdiction were restored to the bishop of Arles under Leo's successor, Hilary.

The reception of Leo's letters into canon law

Leo's seventeen decretals on disciplinary matters made an important contribution to canon law. The decretals deal with matters relating to marriage, penance, baptism, ordination, ecclesiastical hierarchy, church property, heresy and usury, among other things (Jasper 2001: 42–3). They include Leo's answers to queries from bishops in Spain (*ep.* 15 to Turibius of Astorga on the treatment of Priscillianists), Gaul (*ep.* 167 to Rusticus of Narbonne), and Italy (*epp.* 18 and 159 to bishops of Aquileia, *ep.* 166 to the bishop of Ravenna, and *ep.* 168 to the bishops of Campania, Picenum and Etruria).

Another three addressed reports of illegal practices. The ordination of slaves was condemned in *Letter* 4, which also gave a 'pre-warning' against clerical or lay usury, on which see above. *Letter* 16 reproved the bishops of Sicily for performing baptisms on the Feast of

Epiphany. In *Letter* 19 to Dorus, bishop of Benevento, the ordination of an ambitious unnamed cleric above his rank was denounced in no uncertain terms: even those priests of higher rank who had allowed him to be preferred to them were criticised. Three more decretals delivered decisions in response to appeals made to the Roman see: *Letter* 10 to the bishops of the province of Vienne (discussed above), *Letter* 17 and *Letter* 14.

Letter 17 to the bishops of Sicily answered the complaints of clerics of Taormina and Panorma regarding the sale of church property by their respective bishops. Leo forbade the sale of church property except where it would bring profit to the church, and then only with the consent of all the clergy (*ep.* 17, PL 54: 705A). Any cleric who contravened this decree was to be deprived of his rank and excluded from communion (*ep.* 17, PL 54: 706B). Leo's decretal on the alienation of church property was to have far-reaching consequences for the papacy. In the first year of his pontificate Pope Symmachus (498–514) sought to gain centralised control over the endowments of parish churches (*tituli*), which until then had been privately controlled. The resistance of local clergy to such centralisation contributed to the friction of the next few years (Davis 2000: 140), which culminated in schism between supporters of Symmachus and his rival Lawrence. Ensuing riots in the streets of Rome left many Christians dead, including priests and consecrated virgins.

Letter 14 to Anastasius, bishop of Thessalonica and papal vicar, dealt with the appeal of Atticus. An excerpt of this decretal was preserved for posterity in the *False Decretals* of the ninth century, though the forger reproduced it under another name. In his letter to Anastasius, Leo reproaches the bishop of Thessalonica for abuse of his powers as papal vicar. As bishop of the capital of the prefecture of Eastern Illyricum and the civil diocese of Macedonia, the bishop of Thessalonica had enjoyed special privileges as representative of the bishop of Rome since the end of the fourth century (Dunn 2007b). Leo had taken a special interest in the ecclesiastical province of Macedonia because its jurisdiction had, in recent times, been contested, during the pontificate of Boniface or Celestine. The occasion for the letter was Anastasius's reported ill treatment of Atticus, the aged and infirm metropolitan bishop of Old Epirus. Atticus had been summoned to Thessalonica to sign a pledge of obedience, and having delayed due to ill-health, was dragged from the doors of his church by secular officials of the prefect of Eastern Illyricum, even though he had not been accused of any crime. He was then forced to travel on foot to Thessalonica in the midst of winter blizzards, over a rough and dangerous road (*ep.* 14. 1).

Leo's letter had a specific purpose: to limit Anastasius's exercise of powers in the pope's name. To this end, Leo made the famous statement in *Letter* 14.1: 'For we entrusted your Charity with our office so that you were called to share in our pastoral concern, not in the fullness of our powers' (PL 54: 671B).

In the mid ninth century, a forger under the name of Isidore Mercator adapted this statement in his compilation of papal letters on questions of canon law, and attributed it to Pope Vigilius: 'For the church which is the first (i.e. the Church of Rome) entrusted the remaining churches with its offices, to be distributed so that they were called to a share in its pastoral concern, not to the fullness of its powers.'[4] This was tantamount to a denial of the ordinary power of the bishop, and quite at odds with the meaning of Leo's original pronouncement. The *Pseudo-Isidorean Decretals*, as they are now known, included many genuine letters from popes up to the eighth century, interspersed with forged letters, and were to have a great influence in the later Middle Ages. As late as 1580, the official promulgation of Catholic canon law upheld the *Pseudo-Isidorean Decretals* as genuine, even though their authenticity had been in question since the previous century.

Although many of Leo's decretals were addressed to specific bishops concerning individual cases, Leo intended them to have universal application. This is evident from the promulgation of collections of Leo's letters in his own time. In 449, he sent the bishops of Spain and Gaul a dossier of all the letters relating to the Eutychian controversy. The same dossier was sent to the bishops of Italy, who were summoned to a synod in Rome in October of the same year to discuss the case. The dossier formed the basis of the ninth-century collection of canon law documents, the *Collection of Novara* (Studer 1986: 757).

Except for *Letter* 2, which entered the *False Decretals* in the late eleventh century, and *Letter* 7 on Manicheism, Leo's seventeen decretals were popular inclusions in other, genuine papal letter collections (Jasper 2001: 57). Along with excerpts from sixteen of his dogmatic letters on the Eutychian controversy, they formed the basis of the *Quesnellian Collection*, which dates to the late fifth century and is of Italian origin. In the sixth century, in an effort to defend the Council of Chalcedon, whose canons had been called into question by the Three Chapters controversy, excerpts of Leo's dogmatic letters were included in the *Regensburg Collection*. The bishops of North Italy sought to clear Leo's name, which had been tainted by anti-Chalcedonian accusations of a link between Chalcedon and Nestorianism. The Three Chapters controversy culminated with the condemnation of three Syrian theologians linked with Nestorius – Theodore of Mopsuestia, Theodoret of Cyrrhus and Ibas of Edessa – and their writings at the Fifth Ecumenical Council, held in Constantinople in 553. The North Italian bishops were probably responsible for the production and distribution of the largest collection of Leo's letters, the *Grimani Collection*, which has been linked to the library of Verona (Jasper 2001: 43).

Other letters of Leo were included in three collections aimed at defending the rights of ecclesiastical jurisdictions, all compiled in the sixth century (Studer 1986: 757): the *Thessalonica Collection*, intended to establish the papacy's unbroken jurisdiction over East Illyricum from the end of the fourth century; the *Avellana Collection*, which is the sole source of Leo's last five letters (*epp.* 169–73), from 17 and 18 August 460; and the *Book of Authorities of the Church of Arles*.[5] After this, papal letters were no longer collected as general sources on church discipline or teachings. With the exception of Gelasius's *General Decretal* in 494, '[t]he great age of the pontificates of Siricius, Celestine, Innocent I, and Leo I, which produced influential decretals and instructional letters with wide circulation, was over' (Jasper 2001: 59).

Conclusion

Leo died on 11 October 461 and was laid to rest in the portico of St Peter's on 10 November, as recorded in the martyrology of Jerome.[6] Leo's personal sense of affinity with the prince of apostles is revealed by his wish to be buried as close as possible to Peter's tomb, a tradition that was followed by several popes after him.[7] Thus, even in death Leo aligned himself with the apostle and first bishop of the city.

Hilary acceded to the papal throne one week later and ruled for six years, endorsing Leo's *Tome* and the synods of Nicaea I, Ephesus and Chalcedon. In 688 Pope Sergius I decided to move Leo's body inside the basilica of St Peter. On the occasion of Leo's reburial, Sergius penned an inscription to mark the place of the original tomb of the 'great shepherd' (*pastor magnus*).[8]

> Leo, the great shepherd, long guarded this citadel,
> protecting the fold and the flock of Christ's followers.
> He sounds a warning from his tomb as he did in life,
> to stop the waiting wolf laying waste the flock of God.
> The books he sent testify to the true doctrine: books
> honoured by righteous hearts and feared by the godless
> crowd.

The epithet 'the Great' seems to have been attached to Leo's name at least from the ninth century, when Pope Nicholas I (858–67) used it in the famous letter of 865 to the Emperor Michael III. In the words of Nicholas, Leo 'the Great' was an imitator of '*the Lion of the tribe of Judah*' (Rev. 5: 5), who, 'on opening his mouth, shook the whole world and the emperors themselves' (*ep.* 88, Perels 1978: 473.17–18). Leo was just the kind of pope whom Nicholas was likely to appreciate, given his own ambitious claims to primacy over the universal church. Even Nicholas's great rival Photius, patriarch of Constantinople, in his famous letter of dogmatic instruction to Prince Michael of Bulgaria, acknowledged Leo as having great glory and a great zeal for piety (*ep.* 1, Laourdas and Westerink 1983–88 (1983): 9). That the leaders of both the eastern and western churches, on the eve of schism, could make such pronouncements is some indication of the measure of the man. Leo's most famous letter, the *Tome to Flavian of Constantinople*, did more than anything else to earn Leo his grand epithet. And yet, when we look beyond his contribution to the Council of Chalcedon, we find other characteristics of a great leader: deep pastoral concern for the spiritual welfare of his congregation in Rome and with unity and order within all the churches of the Christian East and West, matched by a practical concern for the material needs of the civic community and its protection from invaders. Added to his considerable administrative talents was a rhetorical flair that was deeply grounded in scripture and in the interpretative traditions of the West. In the following selection of his texts the reader will encounter all of these different facets of Leo, the man and the bishop.

Part II

TEXTS

6

GENERAL INTRODUCTION TO THE TRANSLATIONS

The eighteen texts within have been translated from the best available critical editions. The edition of Chavasse (CCSL 138 and 138a) was consulted for the homilies. While Biblioteca Patristica (vols 30, 31, 33, 38) offers a more recent edition of some of the homilies that is intended to improve upon Chavasse, the proposed series of six volumes is not yet complete and only two of our homilies have so far been edited there (*serm.* 27 and 69). For the sake of consistency I preferred to use the CCSL edition. The editions of Schwartz (ACO 2.2.1 and ACO 2.4) and Silva-Tarouca (1932–7) were used for the letters, with four exceptions. My translation of *ep.* 15 is based on Schipper and van Oort (CFML 1: 50–76). The translations of *ep.* 2 and *ep.* 167 rely on the PL edition, which is somewhat inferior by modern standards. The translation of *ep.* 170 is based on the excellent edition of Günther (1895). Whole texts, even if they are brief, have been preferred to excerpts, in line with the purpose of The Early Church Fathers series. Letters 2, 137 and 170 have not previously been translated into English. Those translations published before 1973, which include the first editions made by Dolle (1949–73), did not have the benefit of Chavasse's edition, in which the different recensions (A, B and sometimes C) are plainly laid out in different columns. Fortunately, only one of the homilies translated below (*Homily* 82) exists in more than one version.

Parentheses are used to indicate material that I have added for the sake of clarifying the sense. They are also used to indicate asides by Leo, as in normal English syntax. Where I have furnished an explanation it is preceded by 'sc.' (*scilicet*). Scriptural citations refer to the Vulgate, according to the translation of the *New Revised Standard Version*, Catholic Edition. Psalms are numbered according to the Hebrew version: exceptions, where Leo cites (in Latin) the Septuagint version, have been noted. Paragraph divisions are generally my own. Chavasse (1973) in particular makes very few paragraph divisions, and

I have introduced extra breaks to make it easier for the reader while retaining the CCSL division of the text into sections. I have endeavoured to avoid too great a literalism, without betraying *ipsissima verba*. This is always a difficult balance to strike and I apologise if the reader finds my version rather stilted at times. When translating the dogmatic letters (*ep.* 28 and *ep.* 124), in particular, I felt compelled not to take any liberties with the text. The more familiar tone of the homilies (Mueller 1943: 242) is reflected in my use of verbal contractions (e.g. *doesn't, it's*).

Leo uses a number of Latin terms that express a variety of meanings according to context and cannot be translated via a one-to-one lexical correspondence, e.g. *caritas* can mean the theological virtue of love, love for one's neighbour, love of enemies, and charity in the sense of good works. I have tried to be sensitive to the context when translating such terms.

7

PASTORAL CAREGIVER

Homily 87 on the September Fast

Introduction

Delivered in 442, this was the second in a series of eight homilies that marked the observance of the September fast, or fast of the seventh month.[1] These were *Homilies* 86 to 94. The fast of the seventh month was one of four Solemn Fasts celebrated in Rome in this period (see 'Importance of the Christian calendar' in Chapter 2). The celebration of this fast in autumn was a deliberate break with traditional Greco-Roman religious festivals associated with the grape and grain harvests in this season of plenty. It also coincided with the Jewish festival of Yom Kippur, to which Leo seems to have had first-hand exposure (cf. *serm.* 89). *Homily* 87 introduces many of the enduring themes of Leo's pastorate: the power of the devil to tempt humankind, the remedy of the sacrament provided by God the King, the ongoing dialogic struggle between fleshly desires and spiritual longing, and the need to be stewards of divine gifts. Here we find Leo emphasising the nexus between fasting, prayer and almsgiving. What one denies oneself during a fast can be given for the benefit of the needy. The 'chastening of the flesh' through fasting is a kind of penance, and works to strengthen the soul (*serm.* 87.1). This act of self-control prepares the Christian for struggles against the devil, who is always lurking ready to ensnare those held captive to original sin. The power of collective fasting is greater than the sum of individual fasts (*serm.* 87.2). For Leo, the Christian life was an ongoing war against the devil, but victory was assured if one joined the ranks of the church, rather than engaging in the spiritual struggle alone.[2]

Leo was not so rigorist that he could not make a pastoral accommodation for those who were too weak or too sick to fast: such persons could make up their shortfall by giving extra alms (*sermones* 87.4

and 88.5). One can well imagine the wealthy availing themselves of the opportunity afforded by such a loophole. With a certain realism he acknowledges the tenacity of the human desire for wealth among his congregation, while advising that almsgiving purifies from sin, and whatever is given to the poor is treasure laid up in heaven (*serm.* 87.3–4). The doctrine of redemptive almsgiving, as this is known, was very common in both eastern and western preaching on almsgiving in the fourth and fifth centuries (Ramsey 1982; Neil 2007: 149–51). Similarly, in *Homily* 88.3, Leo describes the September fast as a time to desist from worldly occupations and concerns, and turn one's attention to the things that profit one's eternal well-being.[3]

Translated from CCSL 138a: 542–5.

Text

1. God, the creator and redeemer of the human race, who wants us to proceed to the promises of eternal life along *the paths of righteousness* (Ps. 23: 3), instructed us in many methods of defence, dearly beloved, so that we might avoid *the devil's snares* (2 Tim. 2: 26) because there will be no lack of temptations thrown up for us upon the path of virtue by stealthy attacks. Among these he provided this defence for the safety of his servants, that they might arm themselves against all tricks of the enemy with the strength of self-control and with good works. For he who originally inspired a desire for forbidden fruit in the first human beings (cf. Gen. 3: 5–6), and wickedly infected the credulous with the disease of all lustful desires through the lure of tasting, does not cease to renew the same deceptions. And he (sc. the devil) seeks out in human nature, which he knows has been contaminated by its own seed,[4] the offshoot of its own sowing, so that he fans the desire for pleasure in order to put out the zeal for virtue.

But his punishment is the advancement of Christianity, nor can he harm in any way the souls of those who know how to govern their flesh, with the Lord's help. Therefore, rebellious lusts are to be ruled by reasonable moderation and a holy purpose, so that lustful desires of the flesh are not allowed to struggle against pure and spiritual longings.[5] For the inner person should recognise that he is the governor of his outer self, and the mind governed by divine lordship should compel earthly matter to obey good will. The most merciful King does not fail to help us preserve this balance, for it is he who shaped us by the measure of a discipline most apt for our salvation, prescribing for us through the yearly cycle certain days of fasting for strengthening the soul's virtue by chastening the flesh (cf. Zec. 8: 19).

2. The benefit of this remedy, dearly beloved, has been arranged for this month, the seventh, which it is fitting for us to take up with readiness and haste; so that apart from that abstinence, which each person exercises individually and privately in accordance with his own limitations, we might celebrate what is ordained for everyone together with greater heart. For in every trial of the Christian struggle, self-control is useful and beneficial, so that even the most savage demonic spirits, which no exorcist's commands can put to flight from the bodies they have possessed, are driven out by the virtues of fasting and prayer alone, as the Lord said: *This kind of demon cannot be expelled except through fasting and prayer.*[6] The prayer of one who fasts is therefore welcome to God and terrifying to the devil, nor is it a secret how much it obtains for one's own salvation, which offers so much to another.[7]

3. Of course, dearly beloved, although it befits us all to be devout in this observance with one mind, if there are any who, though willing, are prevented by some sickness, they may fulfil the work which exceeds their physical strength by paying money. For there are many good works which make the very necessity of eating more deserving, if they obtain by their zeal for generosity the purification achieved by those who fast.[8] For those who omit nothing from the humiliation of fasting exhaust themselves with fruitless fatigue, unless they sanctify themselves by the payment of alms, as far as they can. So it's right that generosity towards feeding the poor should be more abundant in those who have less strength for abstinence. Therefore, what someone doesn't deny himself in his weakness, he should offer gladly to another in need, and should make his own necessity common with that of the needy. For the sick person who dispenses with fasting is not blamed if the hungry poor receive food from him; nor is he defiled by taking food, who is cleansed by distributing alms, as the Lord said: *Give alms, and behold, all things are made clean for you* (Luke 11: 41).

4. In this work, dearly beloved, even those who restrict themselves from the delights of feasting ought to buy the fruit of mercy for themselves, so that what they have sowed very liberally, they might reap in greater abundance[9] (cf. 2 Cor. 9: 6). For the seed never lies to the farmer, nor is the outcome uncertain when a good work is planted (cf. 1 Cor. 9: 10).[10] Whatever the hand of the sower scatters thus is not burnt by the sun, nor carried away by floods, nor destroyed by hail (cf. Matt. 7: 25). All the costs of righteousness are always safe from harm; they not only stay safe but they even increase in number and change in quality. Heavenly things spring from earthly ones, great things are produced from little ones, and earthly gifts are transformed into

eternal reward. Therefore whoever of you loves riches, whoever longs to multiply what you have, be excited over this profit, sigh for this increase in your wealth, which no thief steals, no moth destroys, and no rust corrodes (cf. Matt. 6: 20). Don't despair of the interest; don't distrust the one who receives from you.[11] *What you did for one of these, you did for me* (Matt. 25: 40). Understand who it is that speaks; and recognise with certainty, using the perceptive eyes of faith, the one in whom you invest your wealth. The person to whom Christ owes a debt should have no doubt about its repayment. Let your generosity be free from anxiety, and don't let your fasting be gloomy, *for God loves a cheerful giver* (2 Cor. 9: 7). He is faithful in his words (cf. Ps. 145: 13), and pays back with abundance what is given away, which he graciously gave to be given away.

Homily 85 on the Feast of St Lawrence

Introduction

This homily belongs to the second series, composed in the period from 446 to 461. The feast of St Lawrence, a local Roman saint, was celebrated on 10 August. Lawrence was made an archdeacon of the Roman church during the brief pontificate of Sixtus II (257–8), who was beheaded for refusing Valerian's instruction to sacrifice to demons (*LP* 1: 155). According to legend, Lawrence was executed three days later, along with a subdeacon, a priest, a reader and a doorkeeper (*LP* 1: 155). Lawrence was buried in a crypt in the cemetery of Cyriaces in the Veranus Field, on the Tibur Way, where two *basilicae* were later founded in his honour (*LP* 1: 246 n.8).

Ambrose of Milan did much to stimulate the cult of St Lawrence in Italy with his versions of the martyrdom in prose and poetry, which celebrate Lawrence's triumph as that of a military hero.[12] Evidence for the popularity of Lawrence's cult in Rome in the fourth century is provided by the number of churches and shrines dedicated to the saint in this period: St Lawrence Outside the Walls, a foundation of Constantine, was 'one of the main suburban pilgrimage centres' (Davis 2000: 134), and St Lawrence *in Damaso*, dedicated by Pope Damasus near the Theatre of Pompey, was an important foundation within the city walls. Leo's successor, Hilary, added a monastery to St Lawrence Outside the Walls, as well as decorating the basilica with silver and bronze chandeliers and silver services for baptism and penance (*LP* 1: 244–5). Sixtus III founded St Lawrence *in Lucina*, a church on the *Via Lata*, and built and decorated a confession for Lawrence with a massive silver statue of the saint at the Constantinian foundation (*LP* 1: 233–4). The confession, an area in front of an altar above a martyr's tomb that was excavated to allow a glimpse of the tomb below (Davis 2000: 121), was an important archaeological innovation of Sixtus's pontificate. Confessions at the tombs of St Peter and St Paul also did much to improve public access to these cultic figures. The fresco decoration depicting Lawrence's incipient martyrdom in the mausoleum of Galla Placidia in Ravenna demonstrates the saint's importance to the western imperial family. Popes Sixtus III and Hilary both chose to be buried in the crypt of St Lawrence's.

Thus, by the mid fifth century, when this homily was produced, Lawrence had already become established as a powerful spiritual patron of Rome. Although this is Leo's only surviving homily on a martyr's feast, apart from *Homilies* 82 and 83 on the feast of St Peter and St Paul,[13] martyr cults became increasingly important to Leo during the period of crisis from 452 to 455, when the Hun invasion was narrowly avoided and the Vandal attack was imminent (cf. *serm.* 69 below). At that time Rome needed its local spiritual heroes more than ever before. As Leo remarks, actions speak louder than words, and 'no model is more useful for educating the people of God than that of the martyrs' (*serm.* 85.1). Just as Jerusalem had won spiritual renown by the death of the first Christian martyr, Stephen, in that city, so Rome had Lawrence.[14] Leo appeals to Lawrence's powers of intercession to protect and strengthen the faithful in times of persecution (*serm.* 85.4), a theme also found in *Homily* 69. We can see an implicit parallel between the pagan prefect's desire for gold and the barbarian lust for Rome's riches. Much of the city's portable wealth was stolen in the Vandal raids, including the gold and silver services of all the titular churches, as *Liber Pontificalis* relates. Even though the Vandal invaders were technically Christians, having accepted an Arian version of Christianity, Leo makes no such subtle distinctions. All heretics were enemies of the church and persecutors of the true religion, in Leo's view. In this homily Leo takes the opportunity to reinforce his message about almsgiving: riches that are given away to the poor are made safer, and earn more for the giver, than if they were kept.

Translated from CCSL 138a: 534–7.

Text

On the Anniversary of St Lawrence the Martyr.[15]

1. Dearly beloved, since the sum of all virtues and the fullness of all justice are born from the love of God and neighbour,[16] surely in no

one does this love rise higher or shine forth more clearly than in the most blessed martyrs. It is they who are closest to our Lord Jesus Christ, who died for all people, as much through their imitation of his love as through the similarity of their suffering. For although no human act of kindness could equal that love by which the Lord redeemed us (cf. Eph. 5: 2) – for it is one thing for a person who was mortal anyway to die on behalf of a just man, and another thing for one who is a stranger to the debt of death to die on behalf of the unrighteous[17] – nevertheless the martyrs have brought much benefit to all people. The Lord, who imparted their courage, used it (to show) that he wished the penalty of death and the cruelty of the cross to be a source of terror for no one,[18] but made it a goal for the imitation of many. If, therefore, no good person is good for himself alone, nor is wisdom a friend of any wise person for himself alone; and if this is the nature of true virtue, that the one who shines with its light leads many from the shadows of error: no model is more useful for educating the people of God than that of the martyrs. Though eloquence is adept at winning over by entreaty, and reason is effective for persuasion, nevertheless examples speak louder than words, and it is better to teach by deed than by word.

2. In this most excellent kind of teaching, how effective was the glorious dignity of the blessed martyr Lawrence, whose passion shines light on this day! Even his persecutors could sense it when his admirable spiritual courage, conceived above all from his love for Christ, not only would not yield itself, but even served to strengthen others by the example of its endurance. For when the rage of the gentile powers[19] was vented on the most chosen members of (the body) of Christ, and attacked especially those of priestly orders, the wicked persecutor raged against the deacon Lawrence, who was outstanding not only in the ministry of the sacraments, but even in the distribution of ecclesiastical property.[20] The persecutor promised himself a double reward for the arrest of one man, since if he could compel him to hand over the sacred possessions he would also make him an outcast from the true religion. And so this man,[21] desiring money and hating the truth, armed himself with twin firebrands: with avarice for snatching the gold, and with impiety for stealing Christ. He demanded that the faultless guardian of the sanctuary[22] bring him the wealth of the church, for which he was longing most eagerly. The most chaste deacon showed him where he had kept these things hidden, bringing forward a great crowd of saintly poor. By feeding and clothing them he had stored up inalienable treasure:[23] the outlays were all the more secure, the holier they proved (to be).[24]

3. The plunderer[25] roared with frustration, and burning with hatred for the religion which had treated riches thus, he attempted the theft of a more powerful treasure. Since he had been unable to recover from him any riches in coin, he would take away that deposit (of faith), the source of his more sacred wealth. He ordered Lawrence to renounce Christ, and he prepared to persuade that most unshakeable strength of the deacon's mind with dire punishments. When the first of these achieved nothing, more stringent ones followed. He ordered his limbs, mangled and carved up with many blows and cuts, to be roasted over a fire so that, by the occasional rotation of his revolving limbs through an iron grill which could already burn him at a constant heat, the torture would be more extreme and the punishment more prolonged.[26]

4. You achieve nothing, savage cruelty, you accomplish nothing! Mortal matter withdraws itself from your inventions, and when Lawrence departs to heaven you are finished. The flame of love for Christ could not be surpassed by your flames, and the fire which burned on the outside was weaker than that which was kindled within. You served the martyr when you savaged him, persecutor; you increased his prize while you added to his pain. For what did your cunning not procure for the glory of the victor, when even the instruments of torture were transformed into the honour of triumph?

Let us rejoice, therefore, dearly beloved, with spiritual joy, and in the most happy end of an outstanding man let us exult in the Lord (cf. 1 Cor. 1: 31), who *is wondrous among his saints*:[27] they are both our protection and our example. And he made clear his glory throughout the whole world in such a way that, *from the rising of the sun to its setting* (Ps. 49: 1), by the shimmering splendour of its deacons' lights, Rome became as glorious because of Lawrence as Jerusalem was made famous by Stephen.[28] We trust that we are helped always by his prayers and his patronage so that, since *everyone who wants to live righteously in Christ endures persecution* (2 Tim. 3: 12), as the apostle says, we are fortified with the spirit of love, and strengthened to resist all temptations by the perseverance of constant faith. Through our Lord Jesus Christ, who lives and reigns with the Father and the Holy Spirit for ever and ever. Amen.

Homily 27 on the Feast of the Nativity

Introduction

Homily 27, delivered on Christmas Day in 451, is Leo's seventh surviving nativity homily out of ten that span the period from his first year as pope up to 454. Leo's Christmas homilies demonstrate his concern to boost the importance of the Christian feast of the nativity, which had until then been a relatively minor occasion in the liturgical year. It was timed to coincide with the pagan feast of the Unconquered Sun (*sol invictus*) or Saturnalia. Constantine the Great had been an enthusiastic adherent of the cult of the Unconquered Sun, and does not seem to have relinquished it with his conversion to Christianity, to judge by his representations on coins, as well as contemporary iconography of Christ as the Sun God (*Helios*), riding in a chariot drawn by fiery horses.

The first two sections concern the Christological controversy that had been debated at the Council of Chalcedon in the same year. Leo gives yet another impassioned defence of the two natures in Christ, a theme that arises naturally from the liturgical context, the celebration of the virgin birth. He then targets three groups for criticism: 1) practitioners of the magic arts (*serm.* 27.3); 2) astrologers (*serm.* 27.3); and 3) adherents of cosmic religion (*serm.* 27.4–5), especially sun-worshippers. Forbidden practices include magical cures for illness, foretelling the future, charms to placate demons and spells to repel ghosts. The survival of curse tablets, amulets and charms from this period is sufficient proof that such practices were alive and well in the fifth century. Leo regarded these practices as legitimate ways for the devil to trap human beings: the Christian convert must guard against falling captive to sin once more.

In his preaching against astrology Leo echoes Old Testament condemnations of the Chaldean religion of Abram before his covenant with the God of Israel, e.g. Deut. 4: 19 in the Septuagint version, and Deut. 17: 3. Astrologers were also sometimes referred to as mathematicians, due to their skill in computing birth charts with reference to the constellations. Leo's arguments against assigning one's fate to the movements of the stars bear great similarity to those of Philo of Alexandria, the first-century Jewish philosopher. As an Alexandrian Jew, Philo was open to influence from Hellenistic religion, but he strongly condemned the casting of fortunes according to birth dates and the belief that movements of the stars were responsible for good or bad fortune in human lives.[29] Similarly, in his treatise *On the creation of the world*, Philo emphasised the limits of the powers assigned to the heavenly bodies by God (*De opificio mundi* 46, Cohn and Wendland 1962: 1, 14–15). Philo taught that God's *logos* was responsible for God's actions in the world, including the movement of the stars. In Leo's *Homily* 27.5 we find elements of Philo's doctrine of relative admiration for the created world (*De confusione linguarum*

173), that only the Creator and source were worthy of worship, not the created order, such as the sun and stars. The same creation argument is found in Leo's *Homily* 22.6. Philo's works had a significant influence on the Greek Christian teachers Clement, Origen and Didymus the Blind. Ambrose, a keen devotee of neo-Platonism, adapted five Philonic treatises on the allegorical interpretation of the Pentateuch into Latin (Runia 1993: 292). In the two years before his conversion, Augustine read Ambrose's treatises and some unnamed neo-Platonist works in the Latin translation of Marius Victorinus. Their profound influence can be found throughout Augustine's works, from the early exegetical treatises on Genesis to the *City of God*. Leo could have picked up Philonic teachings from any of these western sources.

In dealing with sun worship, Leo faced a pastoral problem that had been created by architecture. The original basilica of St Peter was built with the entry facing east, as in the seventeenth-century building that stands today. The devotees of Hellenistic religion in Rome were intellectuals, not uneducated pagans. Leo laments that even some Christians maintain the practice of bowing towards the rising sun, partly out of ignorance, and partly in the spirit of paganism (*serm.* 27.4). However, Leo concedes that any gesture of reverence towards the sun is ambiguous. Those who appear to worship the light itself may in fact be offering worship to the Creator of that light, but (like Caesar's wife) they must be seen to be doing the right thing and refrain altogether from this practice, lest they give the wrong impression to new converts (*serm.* 27.4). When read next to *Homily* 22, especially the second version of that homily preached in 449, *Homily* 27 seems to offer a more sensitive pastoral approach to an ingrained cultural practice.

Translated from CCSL 138: 132–8.

Text

Sermon VII on the nativity of the Lord.[30]

1. Today's feast, dearly beloved, is truly venerated and duly celebrated by any person who confesses nothing false concerning the Lord's incarnation, and nothing that is unworthy of his deity.[31] For either to deny him the truth of our human nature, or to deny him equal glory with the Father, are sins of equal danger.[32] Therefore when we attempt to understand the sacrament of Christ's nativity – his birth to a virgin mother – the shroud of earthly reasoning should be far removed, and the smoke of worldly wisdom should retreat from eyes illuminated by faith (cf. Eph. 1: 18). For it is divine authority that we trust and divine teaching that we follow. Whether our inner

hearing is moved by the testament of law, or the oracles of prophets, or the gospel trumpet, that remains true which was intoned by blessed John, full of the Holy Spirit: *In the beginning was the Word, and the Word was with God and the Word was God. For he was with God in the beginning. Through him all things were made, and without him, nothing was made* (John 1: 1–3). And likewise what the same preacher added is true: *The Word was made flesh and dwelt amongst us; and we saw his glory, the glory that he has as the only-begotten son of the Father* (John 1: 14). Therefore it is the same Son of God in each nature, taking up our (nature) and not losing his own, renewing humanity as a human being, and remaining unchangeable in himself. For the Godhead, which is shared by him and the Father, suffered no decrease in almighty power, nor did *the form of a slave* dishonour *the form of God* (cf. Phil. 2: 6–7), because the most perfect and imperishable essence, which lowered itself for the salvation of the human race, transformed us into its glory, but it did not cease to be what it was.[33] For this reason when the only-begotten son of God declares himself less than the Father (cf. John 14: 28) to whom he calls himself 'equal' (cf. John 10: 30), he proves the truth of each form in himself: so that his inequality proves him human and his equality reveals him as divine.

2. His birth in the flesh took nothing away from the majesty of the Son of God, nor did it add anything, because the unalterable essence could not be lessened or increased. For '*the Word was made flesh*' (John. 1: 14) doesn't mean that the nature of God was changed into flesh, but that the Word took up the flesh into the unity of his person.[34] In his name the whole human being is assuredly assumed, with whom the Son of God – conceived by the Holy Spirit in the womb of the virgin whose virginity remained forever intact – was united so inseparably that he who was begotten from the essence of the Father outside time was born from the womb of a virgin within time. For we could not be released otherwise from the chains of eternal death if he was not made lowly in our (condition), he who remained almighty in his own (condition). And so the Lord Jesus Christ was born truly human, yet never ceased to be truly God. He began a *new creation* (2 Cor. 5: 17) in himself, and in the manner of his birth he gave a spiritual beginning to the human race, so that the origin of those needing rebirth would be freed from the seed of sin in order to wipe out the contagion of being conceived in the flesh. It is said of them: *They were born not of blood, or by the will of man, or by the will of the flesh, but from God* (John 1: 13). What mind can understand this sacrament, what tongue can tell of this grace? Sinfulness returned to innocence, the old to the new; strangers came to be

adopted, and the disenfranchised came into their inheritance (cf. Rom. 8: 15, 17). The wicked began to be just, the greedy became kind, the unrestrained chaste, those on earth became people of heaven (cf. 1 Cor. 15: 49). But what caused *that change*, if not *the right hand of the Most High*? (Ps. 77: 10). *The Son of God* came *to destroy the works of the devil* (1 John 3: 8), and he implanted himself in us in such a way, and us in him, that the descent of God to humanity became humanity's advancement to the divine.[35]

3. But by this mercy of God, dearly beloved, whose magnitude towards us we cannot explain, Christians should be on their guard and exercise great caution not to fall back into the devil's traps, and get involved again in the same wrongs that they renounced (cf. 2 Pet. 2: 20). For that ancient enemy doesn't stop throwing out his nooses of deceit in all directions, by transfiguring himself into an angel of light (cf. 2 Cor. 11: 14), and (doesn't stop) working hard at corrupting the faith of believers by every possible means. He knows to whom he should apply the heat of lust, to whom he should introduce the allurements of gluttony, whom to ply with the enticements of luxury, and whom he should infect with the poison of envy. He knows whom he should disturb with sorrow, whom he can deceive with joy, whom he can oppress with fear, whom he can seduce with admiration. He examines the habits of everyone, he inflames their concerns, he investigates their affections: and he seeks opportunities for harm there, where he sees each to be occupied most busily. For among those whom he has bound by the most intimate ties, he has many who are skilled in his devices, whose minds and tongues he may use for deceiving others. By their agency remedies for illness are guaranteed, as well as predictions for the future, placations for demons, and the removal of ghosts. Added to these are those who pretend that the whole condition of human life depends on the effects of the stars, and they call the inevitability of fate that which is either the will of the divine, or our own. However, they promise – in order to do greater damage – that fate can be changed by praying to the unfavourable stars. By this means their wicked invention is destroyed by its own reasoning, because if the predictions were not permanent, then fate need not be feared; but if they are permanent, then the stars need not be revered.

4. From such foundations this impiety also arises, that certain very foolish people worship the rising sun at the first light of day from higher places.[36] Even some Christians think that this is a pious action, so much so that before they reach the basilica of the blessed apostle Peter, which is dedicated to the one true and living God, after they've climbed the steps and ascended to the platform of the raised area, they

turn around to face the rising sun and bow with heads low, in honour of the radiant disk.[37] This action, performed partly out of the vice of ignorance, and partly in the spirit of paganism, causes us much grief and sorrow: because even if some people do perhaps worship the Creator of the beautiful light, rather than the light itself which is created, they should in fact refrain from the very appearance of this practice. Otherwise, when one who has abandoned the cult of the gods discovers it among us, surely he will hold fast to this aspect of his former beliefs, thinking it appropriate, since he sees it is common to both Christians and the wicked?[38]

5. Therefore let that abominable perversity be thrown out from the practice of the faithful, and don't let the honour due to the one God be mixed with the rituals of those who serve creation. For divine Scripture says: *You will worship the Lord your God and you will serve him alone* (Matt. 4: 10). And the blessed Job, *a man without complaint,*[39] as the Lord said, *and guarding himself from every evil* (Job 1: 8), said: *I never saw the sun when it shone, and the moon in its bright progress, and rejoiced in secret in my heart, and kissed my hand: that is the greatest sin, and a denial of the supreme God* (Job 31: 26–8). For what are the sun and the moon if not elements of the visible creation and physical light? One is the source of greater brightness, the other is a lesser light. For as there are different times assigned to day and night, so the Creator instilled different qualities in the lights, and even before he made them, there were already days without the help of the sun and nights without the aid of the moon. But they were created to be useful for making human beings, so that the rational creature wouldn't make mistakes in distinguishing the months or the yearly cycles, or in calculating the seasons (cf. Gen. 1: 14). (This was) because the sun would mark the end of each year, and the moon would mark the new months over the irregular intervals of unequal hours, and the different rising times would be clear signs. For on the fourth day, God said, as we read: *Let there be lights in the vault of heaven, to shine upon earth,*[40] *and let them divide day from night, and let them be for signs and for seasons, for days and years, and let them be lights in the vault of heaven to shine upon the earth* (Gen. 1: 14–15).

6. Wake up, people, and recognise the dignity of your nature. Remember that you're made *in the image of God* (Gen. 1: 26), which, though it was corrupted in Adam, was nevertheless renewed in Christ (cf. Col. 3: 10).[41] Use visible creation as it should be used, as you use the earth, sea, sky, air, springs and rivers. Whatever is beautiful and marvellous among them, attribute to the praise and glory of the Creator. Don't be dedicated to that light which delights birds and

reptiles, wild beasts and cattle (cf. Ps. 148: 10), flies and worms. Feel the physical light with the bodily senses, and embrace with all the mind's enthusiasm that *true light, which illuminates everyone coming into this world* (John 1: 9), and concerning which the Prophet said: *Approach him and be illuminated and your face will not blush in shame* (Ps. 34: 5). For if we're the *temple of God, and the Spirit of God dwells in* us (1 Cor. 3: 16), what each of the faithful holds in his heart is greater than what he admires in the heavens. And so we don't recommend or urge you, dearly beloved, to despise God's works, or to judge anything contrary to your faith among those things which the Good created good,[42] but to use every beauty of creation and all the array of this world (cf. Gen. 2: 1) with reason and measure: *For what is visible*, as the apostle says, *is temporary; but what is invisible is eternal* (2 Cor. 4: 18). So, since we were born into the present, but reborn for the future, let's not be dedicated to temporary rewards but be intent upon eternal ones. And so that we can reflect upon our source of hope more closely, let's consider what divine grace bestowed upon our nature in the very mystery of the Lord's birth. Let us hear the apostle saying: *For you have died, and your life is hidden with Christ in God. But when Christ your life is revealed, then you too will be revealed with him in glory* (Col. 3: 3–4), who lives and reigns with the Father and with the Holy Spirit for ever and ever. Amen.[43]

Homily 69 on Holy Saturday

Introduction

Homily 69 was delivered on Holy Saturday, on 4 April 454. While little is known of the exact nature of the three-day Easter liturgical celebration of the passion and resurrection of Christ in Rome in this period, this homily was probably delivered during the Vigil on Saturday night, followed by a Eucharist at dawn on Easter Sunday (Cavalcanti and Montanari 2001: 457). All of Leo's twenty-one Easter homilies concern the passion of Christ, although they were delivered on various days of the week, from Wednesday to Sunday. While there are baptismal overtones in the second half of the homily (*serm.* 69.4–5) that could suggest another context for its delivery – the rendition of the Creed by catechumens on the morning of Holy Saturday – the reference to the gospel reading of the passion (*serm.* 69.2) makes the Vigil seem more likely.

Leo used the opportunity of a full house to preach his doctrine of salvation history. Leo's understanding of salvation history is very close to Irenaeus's doctrine of the recapitulation of Adam in Christ,[44] as his reference to the original sin in the Garden of Eden shows: the descendants of Adam are 'captives of the enslaved seed' (*serm.* 69.3). The idea that God gave the devil the right to enslave human beings as a consequence of original sin is familiar from Gregory of Nyssa.[45] Leo's understanding of how the saints of the old covenant of Israel were saved through their belief in the new covenant, even before it happened, is fairly original (cf. *serm.* 54.1, CCSL 138a: 317, lines 1–10). As Armitage asserts: 'Leo regards the crucifixion as the fulfilment and consummation of all that happened and that was foretold in the Old Testament' (Armitage 2005: 57). Leo's negative attitude to the rest of the Jews, on the other hand, is entirely typical of preachers of the Late Roman period. His enlightened doctrine of universal salvation did not apply to heretics or to Jews, apart from a few chosen patriarchs and prophets of Israel.

Leo's admonition to 'flee from arguments about worldly teaching and avoid venomous conversation with heretics' (*serm.* 69.5) probably alludes to the disputes that had ensued in the three years since Chalcedon, in which he had been constantly embroiled. This homily has nothing of the triumphant optimism of Leo's first decade (cf. *serm.* 84), but rather reads like the words of a bishop under siege from all sides, not just in a theological sense but literally, with the Arian king Geiseric and his forces waiting in the wings for the chance to attack Rome, as happened in the following year. This may explain the reference at the close of the homily to the 'terrible deaths and savage torments' endured by the martyrs (*serm.* 69.5). The righteous should expect persecution for the sake of the name of the Lord.

Translated from CCSL 138a: 419–25.

Text

On the Lord's Passion.[46]

1. The greatness of the mystery which is beyond words, dearly beloved, indeed so far surpasses the height of human understanding and the capacity of all speech, that the victory of the Lord's passion is loftier even than the most outstanding mind and the most eloquent tongue. But we should rejoice rather than be ashamed that we are conquered by the dignity of so great a subject, since no one has less understanding of it than he who imagined that what he spoke about it was sufficient. Thus it is not superfluous to preach what we have preached before. Nor should the distaste of human ears be feared by one speaking of divine things, as though they would be an object of

contempt, because they are familiar from frequent repetition.[47] This (repetition) in fact contributes all the more to the steadfastness of the Christian faith, that we all profess the same thing in accordance with apostolic teaching, and we have been *perfected in the same under-standing and the same knowledge* (1 Cor. 1: 10). Of course disbelief, the mother of all errors, is divided into many opinions, which it con-siders necessary to disguise by skill in rhetoric. But a witness to the truth never forsakes its light, and if what glitters less for some glitters more for others, it's not due to a fluctuation of the light but to the weakness of sight. With the help of heavenly illumination, even my speech can serve (the truth), so that – since *you are God's farm, God's building* (1 Cor. 3: 9) – God himself grants enough to the giver and to the receiver, since he knows how to exact a just profit from his gifts.[48]

2. Thus, dearly beloved, in the exposition of the text of the gospel reading on the glory of Christ's cross,[49] which you have received with attentive ears, perceive all the mysteries of the divine words laid open for you. And whatever was veiled under the shadow of the Old Testament in the testimonies of the prophets, rejoice that it has been made clear in the mystery of the Lord's passion. It was for this reason that the various sacrifices and different purification rites were abandoned, and the command of circumcision, the separation of foods, the Sabbath rest, and the killing of the paschal lamb (all) came to an end: that *the law was given through Moses, but grace and truth have come through Jesus Christ* (John 1: 17). The figures came first so that the outcome could follow, and when the prophecies were fulfilled the work of the prophets was finished. The reconciliation of the human race was duly arranged so that no age lacked salvation in Christ by the same act of justification. The (divine) plan[50] of postponements gained this: that what had been believed for a long time before it happened was honoured without any delays. For since the virtue of faith is founded on those matters which are not subject to sight (cf. Heb. 11: 1), heavenly teaching has been more indulgent with us, who have been deferred to this time in history, so that we rely on both prophets and witnesses much more now than previously, in order to help us understand.[51]

3. Therefore you should accept without any shadow of a doubt the information of the holy gospels *written by God's hand*[52] about the passion of the Lord Jesus Christ, and consider the order of events as clear as if you came into contact with it all by physical sight and touch. We believe that in Christ was true divinity and true humanity. That very flesh was (also) the Word, and he was of one substance with the Father, as he was of one nature with the mother.[53] He was not double in person, nor was his essence confused.[54] He was unable to

suffer because of his power, while being mortal in his weakness, but he used both (his power and his weakness) in such a way that his power could glorify his weakness, and his weakness couldn't obscure his power. He who holds the world allowed himself to be seized by his persecutors, and he was bound by the hands of those whose hearts did not embrace him. Justice doesn't resist the unjust, and truth yields to the witness of falsehood, so that, while remaining *in the form of God*, he also fulfils *the form of a slave* (Phil. 2: 6–7), and the cruelty suffered in the flesh confirms the truth of his birth in the flesh. However, it wasn't a necessary condition that the only-born son of God submit to this and endure it, but part of the merciful plan,[55] so that sin was condemned by sin (cf. Rom. 8: 3) and *the work of the devil was undone* by the work of the devil (cf. 1 John 3: 8). Indeed, that enemy of human kind implanted a deadly wound in the very beginning to bring death to all, nor could the descendants, captives of the enslaved seed, avoid his iron law. When he (sc. the devil) saw, after so many generations had been subjected to him under the law of death, that a single one among the children of men whose virtue he was amazed (to find) surpassed that of all the saints of every age, he believed himself to be safe concerning the continuation of his law, if no merits of justice had been able to overcome the power of death.[56]

And so he spurred on his servants and his mercenaries more urgently, and raged against the judgement already made against him, and while he thought that one able to be killed would owe something to him, he didn't notice the freedom of (Christ's) unique innocence, since he was persecuting a likeness to (human) nature. He wasn't wrong about the human race, but he was mistaken about (Christ's) guilt. For the first Adam and the second were equal in flesh but not in deed, and in the first (Adam) *all die*, but in the second all will be brought to life (cf. 1 Cor. 15: 22).[57] The first made a path to misery through proud desire, the second paved the way to glory through the strength of his humility. So he himself says: *I am the way, the truth, and the life* (John 14: 6). (He is) the way, of course, as our model of just behaviour; he is the truth, in our expectation of a sure reality; he is the life, in our receiving of eternal happiness.

4. In regard to this mystery of great piety, dearly beloved, the blasphemous Jews and the devil in his pride were equally ignorant. *For if they had recognised it, they would never have crucified the Lord of glory* (1 Cor. 2: 8). But because the plan of the merciful God was hidden from the enemy of the human race, and the veil of the flesh disguised *God who was reconciling the world to himself through Christ* (2 Cor. 5: 19), he (sc. the devil) continued to rage against him, in

whom he could find nothing that belonged to him. For this could have profited his wicked purpose more, if he had spared (Christ) and restrained himself from pouring out his blood, by means of which the captivity of all was to be undone and the liberty of all restored. But *the darkness could not comprehend* the light (John 1: 5), nor could deceitful blindness perceive the wisdom of truth. And so clemency held on to suffering according to the plan, and by restraining the power of the angelic hosts who served him, he drained the cup of sorrow and death, and transformed all his punishment into triumph. Sins were conquered, the powers were subdued (cf. 1 Pet. 3: 22), the world received a new beginning, so that the condemned generation would not stand in the way of salvation by the aid of rebirth. *The old has passed away and all things are made new* (2 Cor. 5: 17). For all those who believe in Christ and are reborn in the Holy Spirit, there is one common passion and one eternal resurrection, through him and with him, as the apostle says: *For you have died, and your life has been hidden with Christ in God. When Christ your life is revealed, then you too will be revealed with him in glory* (Col. 3: 3–4).

5. In this hope, dearly beloved, you have been established. Beware of all the subtleties of the devil, who not only lays snares through desires of the flesh and enticements of the body, but also, by scattering tares of falsehood among the very seeds of faith, strives to spoil the truth as it grows (cf. Matt. 13: 24–5), so that he may subvert by wicked error those whom he could not corrupt by evil actions. Therefore flee from arguments about worldly teaching and avoid venomous conversation with heretics (cf. 2 Tim. 2: 23). May you have nothing in common with such people who, opposing the catholic faith, are Christians in name alone. For they are not the temple of the Spirit of God (cf. 1 Cor. 6: 19), nor are they *members of Christ* (1 Cor. 6: 15) but, entangled in wrong thinking, they give so many faces to the devil as there are representations of falsehood. Freed from those evils through the Lord Jesus Christ, who is *the way and the truth and the life* (John 14: 6), let us endure all temptations and battles of this life with the joy of faith. For if we suffer with him*, we will also reign with him* (2 Tim. 2: 12).

This reward has not only been prepared for those who have been slain by the violence of the wicked for the sake of the Lord's name, since all those who serve God and live with God, just as they have been crucified with Christ, are also to be crowned with Christ. Indeed (they are crowned) alongside those who excel in every glory, who overcame terrible deaths and savage torments by enduring to their last breath, but (they are crowned) also alongside those who came after-wards, who, by denying their flesh, have conquered the longings of greed, the self-exaltation of pride, and the desire for luxury. So the apostle rightly said that *all who wish to live righteously in Christ, suffer persecution* (2 Tim. 3: 12). He who is no stranger to righteousness does not escape it (sc. persecution). The person who acts *not in the leavening of old wickedness but in the unleavened bread of sincerity* (1 Cor. 5: 8) celebrates the Easter feast properly; the one who lives no longer in the first Adam but in the second Adam. He is truly made a member of the body of Christ, who, *although he was in the form of God*, deigned to become *the form of a slave* (Phil. 2: 6–7), so that in the *one mediator between God and humankind, the man Jesus Christ* (1 Tim. 2: 5), there would be both the fullness of divine majesty, and the truth of human nature. And if the Godhead of the Word had not received this (nature) into the unity of his person, there would be no rebirth in the waters of baptism, nor any redemption in the blood of the passion. But because we receive nothing false in the mystery of Christ's incarnation, and nothing figurative,[58] not in vain do we believe that we die with his death and rise again with his resurrection. He abides in us *who works all things in all* (1 Cor. 12: 6), who lives and reigns with the Father and the Holy Spirit for ever and ever. Amen.

8

THEOLOGIAN AND OPPONENT
OF HERESY

Homily 16 on the December Fast

Introduction

Homily 16 was delivered on 12 December 443, during the December fast. This places it in the middle of Leo's campaign against the Manichees in Rome, which lasted for eighteen months, from 443 to 444. The Manichees posed a particular threat to the Christian community in Rome because they challenged it from within, by claiming to be Christians and participating in mainstream worship. Their ascetic regime was a variant on normal Christian practices: instead of fasting only on Wednesdays and Fridays, as Leo recommends (*serm.* 16.5), they fasted also on Sundays and Mondays (*serm.* 42.5; CCSL 138a: 247). They abstained from meat and wine at all times and even refused to accept the cup in Eucharist. Most significantly, perhaps, they proscribed procreation. In a climate of social instability the violent suppression of dissenters or heretics served the important social functions of group delineation and reinforcement of the leader's authority, helping 'to reaffirm and reinforce the commitment of group members to the ideals of the community' (Maier 1996: 447–8). Rome in the 440s was certainly in a state of social flux, with external threats to urban stability pressing on all sides. The North African settlement of the Vandals was uncomfortably close, allowing Geiseric to continue his attacks on Sicily, and it was only a matter of time before Attila turned his attention from the Balkans westwards.

Using state laws that had been instituted to deal with the threat in 425 during the pontificate of Celestine,[1] Leo convoked a commission, over which he presided in the presence of bishops, members of the Senate and other aristocracy, to bring to trial several members of the highest echelon in the sect, the 'Elect' or 'Chosen Ones' (*serm.* 16.4).

On the basis of the findings of these trials, he presents a horrifying picture of the Manichees as insidious perverts, preying on the innocent and unwary, with his allusion to the confession of several of the Elect concerning a religious ritual of sexual intercourse with a 10-year-old girl who had been raised for this sole purpose (*serm.* 16.4). Given that such 'confessions' may well have been extracted under torture, as they were later, in the reign of Hormisdas (514–23) (*LP Hormisdas* ch. 9, *LP* 1: 270), it is impossible to assess the truth of this allegation. It should be noted, however, that such an act would contradict the Manichees' alleged distaste for the body and the act of procreation. Allegations of immoral sexual acts are also made against Manichees in North Africa, where a similar trial was staged under the tribune Ursus between 421 and 428 (Lieu 1992: 199), although Augustine was forced to admit that he witnessed no such thing as a Hearer of the sect (*Contra Fortunatum* 1.3, Zycha 1891: 84–5). Leo also claims that Manichees had infiltrated the private houses of unsuspecting Christian women with their fanciful stories (*serm.*16.5). This was not the only occasion when he sought to influence household religious practices (Maier 1995: 53, 58), as we see in relation to Leo's condemnation of Pelagianists in northern Italy and Priscillianists in Spain.[2]

In Valentinian's *Novella* 18, Manicheism was declared a public crime. Its adherents were to be exiled and their books burned. Lay people and clergy were encouraged to accuse Manichees without the normal risks associated with denunciation (*delatio*), meaning that no contrary lawsuit could be brought against the accusers, with stiff penalties if their accusation was found to be false (*Val. Nov.* 18, CFML 1: 50).[3] This suspension of the normal procedures of criminal trials is witness to the seriousness of the situation. Leo, too, encouraged the laity and clergy in Rome and all of Italy to search out and denounce Manichees (*serm.* 16.5; *ep.* 7 to the bishops of Italy, 30 January 444). Christians were instructed to inform the authorities of places where Manichees held private meetings, and to avoid all contact with them. Some opportunities were given for penance (*serm.* 16.6), but the emphasis is on punishment rather than reconciliation. Prosper claims that Leo's investigation in Rome had salutary effects for the whole world, since the Manichees named in their confessions the members of other urban networks of teachers, bishops and priests. Prosper also states that many eastern clerics imitated Leo's zeal,[4] among them probably Theodoret of Cyrrhus, who wrote to Leo to congratulate him on his efforts in Rome (*ep.* 113, SC 111: 58) (Lieu 1992: 205–6).

Translated from CCSL 138: 61–7.

Text

Fifth Homily on the December Fast.[5]

1. The fullness of the grace of God, dearly beloved, is at work daily in the hearts of Christians, so that our every desire is redirected from earthly things to heavenly things.[6] But even the present life is lived through the provision of the Creator, and is sustained by his providence, because he who generously bestows temporal blessings is the same one who promises eternal ones. Thus, just as we ought to give thanks to God for the hope for future happiness to which we hasten through faith, because we are raised up to the harvest of that which is prepared for us – so also should we honour and praise God for those benefits which we accrue through every year's turn. For from the beginning he gave the earth's bounty in such a way, and so ordained the laws of fruit bearing and which plants and seeds (should bear), that he never deserted what he'd planted but the kindly rule of the Creator remained in the things he'd created.[7] Thus, whatever the plants, the vine and the olive produced for human use, all this flowed forth from the generosity of divine goodness. This generosity kindly aided the dubious efforts of the farmers when the quality of the elements fluctuated, so that wind and rain, cold and heat, and day and night served our ends. For human reason wouldn't suffice by itself for the outcome of its efforts, if the Lord didn't grant growth to our usual planting and watering (cf. 1 Cor. 3: 6–7). So, it's the fulfilment of piety and justice that we also should help others from what the heavenly Father out of his mercy has bestowed upon us. For there are very many who have no share in the fields, no share in the vines, and none in the olives, whose poverty is to be comforted from the abundance that the Lord gave, so that they too may join us in blessing God for the fertility of the earth. And they may rejoice in what has been given to those who hold possession, which has also been shared with the poor and the stranger. Blessed is that granary and most worthy of the increase of all its produce, from which the hunger of the poor and weak is satisfied, the needs of the stranger are met, and the wants of the sick are relieved. The justice of God has permitted them to suffer from various troubles, so that he may crown both the wretched for their patience, and the merciful for their generosity.

2. Although all seasons are suitable for this work, dearly beloved, it is especially appropriate and fitting now, when our holy fathers sanctioned by divine inspiration the fast of December, so that after the harvest of all the crops has been completed, reasonable abstinence would be dedicated to God, and each would remember to use his

bounty in such a way that he would be more abstinent towards himself, and more generous towards the poor. For repentance of sins is more effective when joined with almsgiving and fasting, and the prayer lifted up by such recommendations speeds its way to divine ears. Since, as it is written, *the merciful man does good to his own soul* (Prov. 11: 17),[8] nothing is so much one's own as that which one spends on a neighbour. For that portion of material wealth which is handed out to the needy is transformed into eternal wealth. From such generosity those riches are created which are not lessened by use, and no corruption can destroy. For *blessed are the merciful, since God shall have mercy on them* (Matt. 5: 7), and he will be the sum of their reward, who is the model of the commandment.

3. In the course of these works of piety, which commend us to God more and more, dearly beloved, there's no doubt that our enemy, greedy to cause harm and skilled at doing so, is spurred on by sharper goads of envy, so that those whom he is not allowed to attack by open and bloody persecutions, he may corrupt under the false profession of the Christian name. In this office he has heretics who serve him, deviants from the catholic faith whom he has subjected to himself and forced to fight in his camp under various kinds of error. And just as he employed the service of a serpent to deceive the first human beings (cf. Gen. 3: 1), so he has armed their tongues for seducing righteous souls with the venom of his falsehoods. But out of pastoral concern, dearly beloved, we are countering these traps, in so far as the Lord helps us. And, delivering prior warning lest any of the holy flock should perish, we warn you with fatherly advice to turn away from *evil lips and deceitful tongues*, from which the prophet seeks his soul to be delivered (Ps. 120: 2): since *their conversation*, as the blessed apostle says, *spreads like a cancer* (2 Tim. 2: 17). They creep up humbly, they lay hold charmingly, they bind fast softly, and they kill secretly. *For they come*, as the Saviour predicted, *dressed as sheep, but inside they are ravenous wolves* (Matt. 7: 15), who could not deceive true and simple sheep unless they disguised their bestial madness with the name of Christ. But in all of them operates the one who *transforms himself into an angel of light* (2 Cor. 11: 14), although he is an enemy of true illumination. Basilides was practised in his skill, Marcion was versed in his talents, Sabellius was driven along by his leadership, Photinus was pushed headlong by his direction, Arius waited upon his power, Eunomius was servant to his spirit; in short, the whole herd of such wild beasts departed from the unity of the church under his leadership, and deviated from the truth under his authority.[9]

4. But although he maintains a diverse supremacy in all these per-
versions, he built for himself a stronghold on the madness of the
Manichees, and found a very broad church among them, on which he
could pride himself more triumphantly. Here he could possess the
cloak of not just one irregularity but an admixture of all errors and
blasphemies in general. For whatever was profane among the pagans,
whatever was hidden among the carnal Jews, whatever was forbidden
in the secret arts of magic, last of all whatever was sacrilegious and
blasphemous among all the heresies, this flowed together into those
(sc. Manichees) as if into a sewer where all filth congeals. The list of
all their impieties and vile practices is too long to tell, for the number
of their crimes exceeds the capacity of words. A few words suffice to
demonstrate, so that you will be able to figure out from what you've
heard even what we omit for the sake of modesty. However, we do not
remain silent on what the Lord wished to make known to our inquiry
concerning their rites, which are as obscene as they are wicked, lest
anyone think we have trusted dubious rumour or vague opinion on
this matter. So, with the bishops and priests presiding with me, and
some Christian men of noble rank in the same assembly, we ordered
their Elect,[10] male and female, to be presented. When they had disclosed many details about the perversion of their teaching, and the
customs of their festivals, they made known that crime also, of which
it is shameful to speak. It was investigated with such diligence that
nothing remains unclear to the less believing or the detractors. For
there were present all the people who had perpetrated the unspeakable
offence, namely a girl about ten years old, and two women who had
brought her up and had groomed her for this crime. There was even
present a youth, the violator of the girl, and a bishop, the organiser of
their revolting criminal act. All these people offered one and the same
confession, and the desecration was brought to light, which our ears
could hardly bear (to hear). But lest we offend chaste ears by speaking
of this too openly, the records of the trial suffice, from which we learn
most fully that in this sect no modesty, no decency, and no moral
purity at all can be found. In this sect lying is the law, the devil is their
religion, and dishonour their sacrifice.

5. And so, dearly beloved, you must entirely deny friendship to
these utterly abominable and destructive people, whom the upheavals
in other parts have brought to us in great numbers. And you women
especially must withdraw from their acquaintance and fellowship lest
you fall into the devil's snares while lending a careless ear to the
delight of fabulous stories. The devil knows that man was first seduced
by the mouth of a woman, and that he threw everyone out of the

happiness of paradise through female gullibility; now he lies in wait for your sex with more certain cunning, so that he may strip of their faith and their honour those whom he can lure to himself through the servants of his deception. I offer this advice to you too, dearly beloved, begging you that if any of you know where they live, where they teach, the places where they gather, and in whose company they find protection, make it known out of faithfulness to our concern. It is of little profit to anyone who is not captured by them, being himself protected by the Holy Spirit, if he is not moved when he finds out that others have been captured. Everyone ought to have a single vigilance against our common enemies for the common safety, and the wound of one member should not be allowed to infect other members. Let those who think such people are not to be brought forward be found guilty of silence in the judgement of Christ, even if they are not stained by assent.

6. Assume therefore a proper zeal out of religious duty, and let all the faithful rise up in concern against these most brutal enemies of our souls. For merciful God made known to us a certain number of these dangerous people for this reason: that, once the danger was revealed, a cautious diligence would be aroused. May what has been achieved not suffice, but let the same inquiry continue. With the Lord's help, it will achieve this: that not only those who are righteous will continue unharmed, but even many of those who have been deceived by the devil's enticement will be recalled from their error. But your prayers and alms and fasting will be offered with more holiness to merciful God through this very devotion, when this work of faith is also added to all the duties of devotion. Therefore let us fast on Wednesday and Friday.[11] But on the Sabbath let us celebrate the vigil in the presence of most blessed apostle Peter, who – as we know from experience and believe – extends unfailing pastoral protection to all the sheep entrusted to him by the Lord. He will obtain by his own intercessions that the church of God, which was founded by his preaching, may be free from every error. Through Christ our Lord.

Homily 73 on the Ascension

Introduction

This is Leo's first surviving homily on the feast of the ascension, celebrated forty days after the Easter Vigil, and falling on 1 June in 444. The other is *Homily* 74, from 17 May of the following year. In *Homily* 73 Leo is concerned to address a theological problem that was raised by the Nestorian controversy and also by Manicheism: what was the nature of the physical resurrection of Christ?[12] An analogous question, whether the body of Christ remained in the grave between the time of burial and his resurrection three days later, was one of the problems Leo dealt with in his letter to Turibius (*ep.* 15.17, translated within). The desire to salvage human physicality as part of God's salvation plan prefigures Leo's involvement in the Christological dispute over the relationship between the divine and human natures of Christ. These concerns find full articulation in *Letters* 28 and 124 below.

Leo explains the disciples' weakness, which led them to doubt the reality of the resurrected Christ, as part of God's plan to strengthen the faith of Christians down the line. Just like Peter's betrayal of Christ (cf. *serm.* 4.3 below), the disciples' doubt was meant to help later Christians in 'our troubles and our dangers' (*serm.* 73.1). The apostle Peter rates a special mention as the disciple entrusted 'above the rest' with the care of the church after the handing over of the keys of the kingdom to the disciples (*serm.* 73.2).

The concept of liturgical time is introduced here in the second section. In the forty days between Easter and the ascension, the great mysteries of the sacraments are confirmed and made clear. Jesus appeared to the disciples so that they would know that the same nature was raised as had lain lifeless in the tomb (*serm.* 73.3). Leo's concern to define the risen nature of Christ reflects an anxiety to refute the Manichean teaching that Christ's nature was not like ours, in that he did not have a human body but merely the appearance of one. When the disciples touched the wounds in Jesus's side and his hands, they confirmed for posterity that the risen Christ had been crucified in the flesh. That every human nature has the potential to be raised to share the same dignity as the risen Christ is known as the doctrine of deification (Greek *theosis*). The ascension of Christ represents our own advancement, a true cause for thanksgiving and celebration (*serm.* 73.4). As liturgical events mirror heavenly events, each time the ascension is celebrated we are again advanced to heaven. In a divine recapitulation of the original sin and expulsion from the garden of Eden, Adam and Eve are now seated in paradise beside Christ, joined to him in body.

Translated from CCSL 138a: 450–4.

Text

First Sermon on the Ascension of the Lord.

1. Today the number of holy days was made complete, dearly beloved,[13] forty days after the blessed and glorious resurrection of our Lord Jesus Christ, in which the true temple of God that had been

destroyed by Jewish impiety was raised up in three days by divine power (cf. John 2: 19–20). It was ordained by most sacred arrangement, and measured out for the purpose of teaching us, so that while the Lord lingered as a physical presence in this stretch of time, faith in the resurrection would be strengthened by necessary proofs (cf. Acts 1: 3). For Christ's death greatly troubled the hearts of the disciples, and a certain lethargy of distrust had crept into their minds, weighed down by sadness over the humiliation of the cross, (Jesus's) last breath, and the burial of his lifeless body. For when the holy women announced the stone rolled away from the tomb, as the gospel story reveals, (and) the grave empty of a body, and the angels bearing witness that the Lord lived, their words seemed to the apostles and the other disciples like nonsense (cf. Luke 24: 11). In fact the Spirit of truth would in no way have allowed such wavering hesitation, born of human weakness, to dwell in the hearts of its preachers, unless that fearful anxiety and curious doubt had laid the foundations of our faith. Therefore there was regard for our troubles and our dangers in the apostles. By means of those men we were instructed against the insults of the wicked, and against the arguments of earthly wisdom. Their sight has taught us, their hearing has informed us, their touch has been a confirmation for us (cf. Luke 24: 39). We give thanks for the divine economy[14] and the necessary slowness of the holy Fathers. They doubted so that we would have no doubt.

2. Therefore these days which elapsed between the resurrection of the Lord and his ascension did not pass in leisurely course, dearly beloved, but great sacraments were confirmed in them and great mysteries revealed. In these (days) the fear of dreaded death is dismissed, and not only the immortality of the soul but even that of the flesh is made clear. In these (days) the Holy Spirit is poured out on all the apostles, breathed into them by the Lord (cf. John 20: 22), and care for the Lord's flock is entrusted to the blessed apostle Peter above the rest, after the keys of the kingdom (cf. John 21: 15–17). In these days, the Lord joins two disciples as a third companion on the road, and rebukes them for their slowness, though they are afraid and trembling, so as to wipe away all the darkness of our hesitation.[15] Their illuminated hearts grasp hold of the flame of faith, and when the Scriptures are laid open by the Lord, those that were lukewarm start to burn. In the breaking of the bread too, their sight becomes clear as they eat with him (cf. Luke 24: 30–1). When their eyes were opened to reveal the glorification of their nature, they were much happier than those ancestors of our race, when the confusion of their prevarication[16] was presented to them.

3. But in the midst of these and other miracles, when the disciples were in a frenzy of fearful thoughts, the Lord appeared among them and said: *Peace be with you.* So that those opinions which they were turning over in their hearts would not remain – for *they thought they were seeing a ghost* (Luke 24: 36–7), not the flesh – he refuted those thoughts that were contrary to the truth. He showed those who doubted the enduring marks left by the cross on his hands and feet, and he invited them to examine him more carefully, because the traces of the nails and the spear had been preserved to heal the wounds of their unbelieving hearts (cf. Luke 24: 38–40). This was so that they would know with a most steady knowledge, rather than hesitant faith, that it was the same nature that would sit on the throne of God the Father, which had lain in the tomb.

4. Therefore, dearly beloved, through all this time between the resurrection of the Lord and his ascension, the providence of God looked after this, taught this, introduced this to the eyes and hearts of his people, so the Lord Jesus Christ would be recognised as actually resurrected, who truly was born and suffered and died.[17] The most blessed apostles and all the disciples who had been terrified by his death on the cross and dubious about believing in the resurrection were thus strengthened by the transparent truth, so that when the Lord entered the heights of heaven, not only were they affected by no sadness but they were even filled *with great joy* (cf. Luke 24: 51–2). And the cause of their rejoicing was truly great and beyond description, since in the sight of the holy hosts the nature of the human race was raised above the honour of every heavenly creature to surpass the ranks of the angels, and to be elevated above the heights of the archangels.[18] There would be no limit on its advancement to any height, except when it reached its place sitting beside the eternal Father, to share his glory on the throne, being joined to his nature in the Son. The ascension of Christ is thus our own advancement, and where the glory of the head leads, there too is called the body's hope. So, dearly beloved, let us rejoice with fitting joy, and let us be glad with proper thanksgiving. For today we are not only confirmed as those who possess paradise, but in Christ we have even gained entrance to the heavens above. We have obtained greater things through Christ's ineffable grace than we had lost through *the devil's envy.*[19] For those whom the poisonous enemy drove out from the happiness of their first dwelling are seated at the right hand of the Father with the Son of God, joined in body to him, who lives and reigns with God the almighty Father and the Holy Spirit for ever and ever. Amen.

Letter 15 to Turibius, Bishop of Astorga

Introduction

In 447 Bishop Turibius of Astorga sent a number of documents to Pope Leo, describing and condemning Priscillianism. Turibius's dossier included an account of the heresy's major deviations in sixteen points, a tract and a personal letter. The documents were delivered to Leo by Turibius's deacon for endorsement. Turibius's urgent communication with the pontiff was occasioned by the resurgence in Spain of the sect founded by Bishop Priscillian of Avila, who had been put to death for sorcery *c.* 386. The circumstances of Priscillian's trial and execution together with several of his followers were exceptional (see 'The struggle against heresy' in Chapter 3). Priscillian's followers continued to flourish, especially in Galicia in the 390s, until the condemnation of their practices at the Synod of Toledo in 400 (Chadwick 1976: 157). However, they seem to have survived underground until the 440s, when they appear again in their former stronghold of Galicia, having been allowed to flourish free from imperial persecution, due to the Suevi and Vandal domination of the region. The remote and mountainous province of Galicia had fallen under the control of the Suevi after the Vandals and Alans had passed through Spain on their way to settlement in North Africa (Moorhead 2001: 61).[20]

Leo's response to Turibius, dated 21 July 447, is a commentary upon the sixteen points of Priscillianist error raised in Turibius's tract. The Priscillianists' Trinitarian beliefs, their Christology, their fasting regime, their anthropology, i.e. their beliefs about the relationship between the human soul and the material order and God, all come in for criticism. Their belief in the devil having substance is rejected. Like the Manichees in *Homily* 16.5, Priscillianists are accused of sexual deviancy and at the same time of dissolving the marriage bond by rejecting procreation (*ep.* 15.7). In the context of the recent criminal persecution of another religious group in Rome, the Manichees, Leo's severe response is not surprising. Priscillianism had been proscribed by imperial rescript under Honorius in 407 (Chadwick 1976: 188), just as Manicheism was in 445. Indeed, Leo likened the Priscillianists to Manichees on several occasions in this letter. His portrait of their theological and sacramental commonalities stretches the facts: however, Leo was not concerned here with giving an accurate précis of their beliefs but with putting an end to their existence as a group. That group, like the Manichees, challenged the Christian religion from within by using its name while manifesting some extreme and occasionally bizarre ascetic behaviours. As in *Homily*

16, Leo uses the language of disease and contagion to describe the heresy and how it spreads to others in the Christian community. Priscillianism is likened to a 'plague', a 'deadly disease', 'filthy dregs' (*ep.* 15, Preface), and a 'poison' (*ep.* 15.15). Lest this language seem excessive, we note that Turibius comments that those infected by 'the pestilence of depraved doctrines' are expelled by the church 'as if they were either the fruit of a miscarriage or illegitimate bastards' (*S. Turibii Asturicensis ep.* 1, CFML 1: 78–9). Like Manicheism, its belief system is said to be derived from all the heresies that go before it, including those of Arius, Paul of Samosata, Photinus, Cerdo and Marcion, but it is also influenced by the pagan art of astrology. Another feature it shares with Manicheism is its 'corruption' of catholic priests. Like Mani, Priscillian is described as a servant of the devil (*ep.* 15, Preface).

Followers of Priscillian are said to operate in secret, just like the Manichees, seducing the gullible through 'the enticements of fables' and 'miraculous tales' (*ep.* 15.15). Women are not singled out for special mention here, as they were in *Homily* 16. Leo recommends the same remedy of vigilance by the priesthood as he does for the laity in *Homily* 16. He hoped that the delineation of clear boundaries by denunciation and excommunication would serve to reinforce papal authority over the church of Spain and North Africa, and he requests Turibius to see to it in his final exhortation: 'It will be a matter for Your Beloved's concern that the authority of our rank should be recommended ... ' (*ep.* 15.17). Leo's proscription of Priscillianism and other heresies also gave people a sense of comfort in 'an ambiguous social situation', as Maier points out in relation to the Manichean investigation in Rome (Maier 1996: 460). Clergy under barbarian rule in a region as remote from Rome as Galicia could feel safe in the knowledge that the shepherd was keeping the wolf of heresy from their door. The turning to Roman authority by this Spanish bishop was not new – Innocent I had been called upon to uphold the decision of the Council of Toledo to readmit bishops who had renounced Priscillianism.[21]

Translated from CFML 1: 50–74, an emended version of Vollmann (1965), taking into account some suggestions of Campos (1962).

Text

Bishop Leo greets his most beloved brother Turibius, bishop of Astorga.

Preface

The documents from Your Brotherhood, handed to us by your deacon,[22] make plain how commendably you are stirred on behalf of the true catholic faith and how anxiously you turn your attention to your pastoral responsibility for the Lord's flock.[23] In these (documents) you have made an effort to bring to our attention how much the disease of error has flared up in your region from the remnants of an ancient plague. For the message of the letter and the points of your memorandum and the text of your tract speak of the filthy dregs of the Priscillianists heating up again among you. For there is no sordid element from the thinking of any godless persons that has not flowed into this teaching, since they have made for themselves a complex mixture of dregs from all the mud of earthly speculation, so that they alone might drink whole what others sipped in part. And then if all the heresies which had arisen before the time of Priscillian were retraced more carefully, almost no error would be found, from which this very impiety did not contract infection. Not content to accept the lies of those who have strayed from Christ's gospel under the guise of Christ's name, it immersed itself even in the shadows of paganism, so that it might place religious faith and the basis for moral conduct under the power of demons and the influence of the stars, by means of the profane secrets of magic arts and the empty falsehoods of the astrologers.[24]

But if the belief and teaching (of Priscillian) is allowed, there will be no due reward for virtue or due punishment for vice; and every decree – not only human laws but even divine constitutions – will be dissolved, because there can be no judgement of good or bad actions if in both cases the necessity of fate controls the mind's activity, and people's actions are not determined by people but by the stars. Added to this craziness is that unnatural division of every human body according to the twelve signs of the sky,[25] so that different powers preside over different parts, and the creature which God made in his image is in thrall to the stars as much as it is to the connections of its limbs.

In the times when this wicked heresy spread through the whole world our fathers rightly strove hard to drive out this godless madness from the whole church, since even the princes of the world hated this blasphemous madness so much that they proscribed its author along with several of his disciples by the sword of public laws.[26] For they saw that every concern for decency could be abolished, and every marriage bond of couples dissolved, and the divine and human law overturned at the same time, if people with such beliefs were allowed to live in any place. That strictness[27] benefited the church's leniency for a long time. Although (the church) is content with the judgements of priests and avoids bloody vengeance, it is helped nevertheless by the strict regulations of Christian emperors, since those who fear corporal punishment sometimes have recourse to spiritual cures.[28] But since the enemy invasion occupied many provinces and the tempests of war interrupted the implementation of laws; and since travel has begun to be difficult for God's priests and councils rare, the hidden perfidy has found freedom due to the disturbance of public life and it has been incited to the subversion of many minds by those evils which ought to have corrected it.[29]

But which people and how many are untouched by that plague, where, as Your Affection reveals, even the hearts of some priests have been corrupted by the deadly disease? And the very people who were entrusted with suppressing falsehood and defending the truth are the ones subjecting Christ's gospel to Priscillian's teaching, so that, after the holiness of the sacred volumes has been depraved by profane interpretations, they preach not what the Holy Spirit taught under the names of the prophets and apostles, but what the servant of the devil has introduced.[30] Therefore, because Your Affection has understood by faithful diligence – as far as you could – those opinions previously condemned in sixteen chapters, we will also examine all of them briefly, lest any of these blasphemies seem either tolerable or in doubt.

1. In the first chapter it is shown how impiously they believe in a divine Trinity which they claim to be one and the same person of the Father, Son and Holy Spirit, as though the same God is now named 'Father', now 'Son', now 'Holy Spirit'. And (they assert) that there is not one who begot and another who is begotten, and another who proceeded from both, and that a singular unity should be accepted in the three names but not in three persons.

They have adopted this sort of blasphemy from the belief of Sabellius, whose disciples are rightly called the Patripassians,[31] since if the Son is the same as the Father, the cross of the Son is the passion of the Father, and whatever the Son underwent in the form of a slave, out of obedience to the Father, the Father suffered it all in himself. That is clearly contrary to the catholic faith, which confesses the Trinity of the Godhead as 'consubstantial'[32] in the sense that there is an undivided Father, Son and Holy Spirit, without mingling, everlasting without time, equal without difference,[33] because unity is not constituted in the Trinity by one person but by the same essence.

2. In the second chapter is revealed an inept and foolish invention concerning the procession of certain virtues from God, which arose in him and which were preceded by his essence. In this they favour also the error of the Arians, who say that the Father is prior to the Son, because he was once without the Son and then he began to be the Father when he begot the Son.[34]

Just as the catholic church detests them (sc. the Arians), so also (it detests) those who think that God ever lacked what is of the same essence as God. It is as wicked to speak of him as changeable as it is to speak of him progressing. For just as what is decreased undergoes change, so what is increased also changes.

3. But the discourse of the third chapter indicates that these same godless persons claim that the Son of God is called 'Only Begotten' for the reason that he alone was born of a virgin. They would not dare to claim this if they had not drunk the poison of Paul of Samosata[35] and Photinus, who asserted that our Lord Jesus Christ did not exist before he was born of the virgin Mary.[36]

But if they want their meaning to be understood otherwise, and do not attribute Christ's origin to his mother, it is necessary for them to assert that there is not one Son of God, but also others begotten of the highest Father, of whom he is the (only) one born of a woman and on this account should be called 'only begotten', because no other son of God undertook this condition of birth. In whichever direction they turn, therefore, they head for a precipice of great godlessness, if they either want Christ the Lord to take his origin from his mother, or they deny that he is the only begotten of God the Father, since he who was God the Word was born of a mother, and no one was begotten of the Father except the Word.

4. The fourth chapter contains the fact that they do not truly honour the birthday of Christ, which the catholic church venerates as (the day) he took up the real human being, because *the Word was made flesh and dwelt amongst us* (John 1: 14), but they pretend to honour it by fasting on the same day, as (they do) also on the Lord's day which is the day of Christ's resurrection.[37]

In fact they do this because they do not believe that Christ the Lord was born with a true human nature but rather, they want a simulation of reality to appear to be revealed by some sort of illusion, following the teachings of Cerdo[38] and Marcion and in total agreement with their relations, the Manichees.[39] For they (sc. Manichees), as was discovered and proved in our investigation, spend Sunday in gloomy fasting, (the day) which the resurrection of our Saviour made holy for us. They devote this constant reverence to the sun, as is known, so that they are in total disagreement with the unity of our faith, and the day which is a source of joy for us is passed by them in affliction.[40] So it is right that the enemies of the cross and resurrection of Christ should receive such a sentence as their choice of doctrine (deserves).

5. The fifth chapter relates their claim that the human soul is made of divine substance and that the nature of our (human) condition is no different from the nature of its creator.

The catholic church condemns this impiety which originates from the opinion of certain philosophers and the Manichees, since it knows that no creation is so sublime and special that it has for its nature God himself. In fact, what comes from him is him and is none other than the Son and Holy Spirit. Apart from this unique, consubstantial, everlasting and unchangeable godhead of the highest Trinity, there is no other creature that was not originally created out of nothing. Nothing that stands out among creation is God, and if there is any-thing great and wonderful, this is not he *who alone does great wonders* (Ps. 136: 4). There is no human being who is truth, no one who is wisdom, no one who is justice, but there are many who participate in truth and wisdom and justice. But only God does not need any parti-cipation. If anything is perceived of him worthily in any way, it is not a quality but an essence.[41] For nothing can be added to the unchangeable, and nothing taken away, because God's existence is always eternal, is always his own.[42] For this reason, he creates all things while remaining in himself, and receives nothing except what he himself gave. Therefore they are too arrogant and too blind when they say the human soul is of a divine substance, and do not understand that they say only that God is changeable and that God himself suffers whatever can be suffered by his nature.[43]

6. The sixth remark indicates that they say that the devil was never good nor is his nature created by God, but that he emerged out of chaos and darkness, because he of course has no creator, but is himself the beginning and the substance of all evil.

However the true faith, that is the catholic faith, confesses that the substance of all creation, whether spiritual or corporeal, is good, and there is no nature of evil, because God, who is the creator of the uni-verse, made nothing that was not good. So also the devil would be good, if he had remained in the state in which he was made, but because he made bad use of his natural excellence and *did not stand in the truth* (John 8: 44), he did not pass over into the opposite sub-stance, but separated himself from the highest good to which he ought to have clung. So those who claim such things rush from the truth into falsehood and they blame nature for their voluntary deficiencies, and they are condemned for being perverse by choice. This will assuredly bring evil to them; and this very evil will not be a substance but the punishment for a substance.

7. In seventh place it follows that they condemn marriages and abhor the begetting of children. In this – as in practically everything – they agree with the profanity of the Manichees, as their behaviour proves, in rejecting conjugal bonds for the reason that there is no freedom for indecency where the decency of marriage and children is maintained.

8. Their eighth (teaching) is to say that the fashioning of human bodies is the creation of the devil and that the seeds of conception are shaped in women's wombs by the work of demons. For this reason the resurrection of the flesh should not be believed (they say), because the body's materiality does not befit the soul's dignity.

This falsehood is without doubt the devil's work, and such extravagant imaginings are the creations of demons, who do not fashion human beings in women's wombs, but fabricate such errors in the hearts of heretics. The catholic faith previously discovered and condemned this most foul poison arising especially from the spring of Manichean impiety.

9. The ninth remark reveals that they say children of the promise[44] are indeed born of women but are conceived of the Holy Spirit, lest that offspring which is born from the seed of flesh seem to belong to the condition of God.[45]

This is repugnant and contrary to the catholic faith, which confesses that every human being is shaped in the substance of body and soul by the creator of the universe and receives life in the mother's womb. While there remains that contagion of sin and mortality which was transferred from the first parent to his offspring, the sacrament of rebirth comes to its aid by which the children of the promise are reborn through the Holy Spirit, not in the womb of flesh but by virtue of their baptism. So also David, who was indeed a son of the promise, said to God: *Your hands made me and shaped me* (Ps. 118: 73), and the Lord said to Jeremiah: *Before I formed you in the womb, I knew you; and in your mother's womb I sanctified you* (Jer. 1: 5).

10. In the tenth chapter they are reported to claim that the souls which are put in human bodies were incorporeal and sinned in the heavenly dwelling place, and for this reason they fell from the heights to the depths, and they fell upon principalities of different qualities. Through the powers of the air and stars they have been shut in bodies, some (souls) more dense and others softer, with diverse fates, and in dissimilar states, so that the variable and unfair events of this life seem to occur because of prior causes.[46]

They have woven this godless fable for themselves from the mistakes of many, but the catholic church has cut off all of them from the unity of its body,[47] by constantly and truthfully preaching that human souls did not exist before they are breathed into their bodies, nor are they put into bodies by anyone other than God their creator, who makes both the souls and their bodies.[48] And because the whole generation of the human race has been spoiled by the transgression of the first human being, no one can be liberated from the condition of the man of old (sc. Adam) except through the sacrament of Christ's baptism, in which there is no distinction among the reborn, as the apostle said: *Whoever of you has been baptized in Christ, you have put on Christ. There is neither Jew nor Greek, neither slave nor free, neither male nor female. For you are all one in Christ Jesus* (Gal. 3: 28).

What therefore do the movements of the stars have to do with this, or the imaginings of fates, or the changing condition and restless diversity of earthly things? Behold, God's grace makes equal so many who were unequal. They cannot be miserable if they remain faithful among all the labours of this life, repeating in every temptation the apostle's words: *Who will separate us from the love of God? Will tribulation or distress or persecution or hunger or nakedness or danger or the sword? As it is written:* For your sake we are afflicted by death all day long, we are regarded as sheep for the slaughter. *But in all these things we overcome through him who loved us* (Rom. 8: 35–7). And so the church, which is the body of Christ, fears nothing from the injustices of the world, because it desires nothing from temporal goods nor does it fear being overwhelmed by the empty din of fate; for it has learned to grow by bearing tribulations with patience.

11. Their eleventh blasphemy is that they think that both human souls and bodies are restricted by the fatal influence of the stars. This madness forces them, being tied up in all the errors of paganism, to strive to worship those stars that favour them (as they believe) and to mollify those that are adverse.[49] But there is no place in the catholic church for those who pursue such things. He who has given himself over to such persuasions has totally separated himself from the body of Christ.

12. The twelfth of these (points) is that they ascribe to some powers the parts of the soul, and to others the members of the body, and they determine the qualities of inner 'presidents' under the names of the patriarchs. They oppose to them on the other hand the star signs, to whose power bodies are subject.

And in all these things they entangle themselves in inextricable error, not listening to the apostle who says: *Beware lest anyone deceive you through the empty fallacies of philosophy following human tradition, according to the rudiments of the world and not according to Christ; because in Him lives all the fullness of divinity in a body, and you are complete in him who is the head of every principality and power* (Col. 2: 8–10). And again: *Let no one seduce you by insisting on humility and the worship of angels, setting foot upon that which he has not seen, puffed up without cause by the mind of his flesh, not holding fast to the head from which the whole body, governed and held together*

by joints and sinews, grows to the honour of God (Col. 2: 18–19). What
need is there, therefore, to allow into the heart what the law did not
teach, what prophecy did not foretell, what the truth of the gospel did
not preach, and what apostolic teaching did not hand down? But these
things befit the minds of those of whom the apostle says: *For the time
will come when they will not endure sound teaching but will pile up
teachers for themselves for their own desires, their ears itching, and they
will indeed turn away from hearing the truth and will turn towards
fables* (2 Tim. 4: 3–4). And so those who dare to teach or believe such
things have nothing in common with us. They strive to assert by any
means whatsoever that the substance of the flesh is foreign to the hope
of resurrection, and so they let go the whole sacrament of the incarnation, because it was unworthy for the whole human being to be
undertaken (by Christ) if the whole was not worthy of liberation.

13. In thirteenth place it is stated that they say that the entire body
of canonical scriptures should be accepted under the names of the
patriarchs, because those twelve virtues which reform the inner person
are indicated by their names. Without this knowledge no soul can
attain reformation in that substance from which it issued.

But Christian wisdom, which knows that the nature of true divinity
is inviolable and unchangeable, holds this godless vanity in contempt.
And the soul undergoes many passions, whether it lives in the body or
separate from the body; but if it were from the divine essence, then of
course nothing adverse could happen to it. And for this reason the
creator is one thing and the creature is another, by an ineffable mystery. For the creator is always the same and cannot be changed by any
variation; but the creature is subject to change even when it has not
been changed, because it can (only) be unchangeable as a gift, not as a
characteristic.

14. In the fourteenth chapter they are said to believe that the condition of the body is under the power of the stars and the star signs
because of its earthly quality. And for this reason many things are
found in the holy Scriptures concerning the outer person, so that in
the holy Scriptures there is a kind of struggle between a divine nature
and an opposing earthly nature, with the presidents of the soul
claiming one for themselves, and the creators of the body claiming the
other.

They disseminate these fables so that they may affirm that the soul
belongs to a divine substance while the flesh is believed to be of an
evil nature, since they claim that even the world itself with its elements
is not the work of a good God but the invention of an evil creator.
And so as to gloss these sacrilegious lies of theirs with fair labels, they

have violated almost all the divine utterances with the introduction of accursed opinions.

15. The discourse of the fifteenth chapter complains of this issue and rightly rejects (their) devilish presumption. We too have discovered this from the accounts of truthful witnesses, and we have found many of their books to be most corrupt, although they are labelled as canonical. For how could they deceive the simple minded, except by smearing poisoned cups with honey, lest any altogether disagreeable elements which are meant to be lethal be noticed?

Therefore one must watch out and priests must be especially diligent lest the falsified books that are foreign to the genuine truth are used in any reading (of the scriptures). But the apocryphal scriptures, which are named after the apostles, contain the seed-bed of many falsehoods, and should not only be forbidden but even absolutely removed and consigned to the fire. Although there are certain elements in them which seem pious, however they are never empty of poison and they operate in secret by the enticements of fables to entangle those seduced by miraculous tales in snares of all kinds of error. So if any bishop either does not forbid the apocryphal books to be kept in homes or allows these books which have been corrupted by Priscillian's fake 'corrections' to be read in church under the name of the canon, let him know that he should be judged a heretic, because he who does not recall others from error reveals himself to have gone astray.

16. In the final chapter there is just complaint that the treatises of Dictinius, which he composed according to the teachings of Priscillian, are being read with reverence by many. If they think anything should be attributed to Dictinius's memory, they ought to admire his repentance, not his lapse.[50] And so it is not Dictinius that they are reading but Priscillian, and they are approving what he taught in error, not what he chose after being corrected. But let no one presume to do this without punishment, and let no one be counted as catholic who consults these writings that have been condemned not only by the catholic church but even by their own author.

The perverse should not be permitted to pass off their inventions as true, nor to reject imperial decrees under pretext of the Christian name. For they come to the catholic church with such division in their hearts in order both to convert whomever they can, and to escape from the severity of the law, while pretending that they belong to us. The Priscillianists do this, the Manichees do it, whose hearts are so tied up with them that they are found to be united in their sacrileges, different in name alone. Because even if the Manichees reject the Old Testament, which the Priscillianists pretend to accept, the intention of both is directed towards a single end, since what they (sc. Manichees) impugn by refusal, the others corrupt by accepting.

There is certainly (just) one crime, a single depravity and a similar disgrace in their accursed mysteries, which are more carefully concealed the more unclean they are. Although we blush to speak of that (disgrace), which was however found out in our most careful investigation and uncovered by the confession of Manichees under arrest, we acted to bring it to public attention lest it could seem in any way dubious. It was related in our trial – in which not only the most numerous presence of priests but also the ranks of illustrious men and a certain portion of the Senate and people took part – in the words of those who perpetrated the whole offence, as those acts (of the trial) which we have now sent to Your Affection now prove. But what was once discovered about the vilest crime of the Manichees, has also been discovered and made quite public concerning the most incestuous practices of the Priscillianists, and those who are completely equal in the impiety of their beliefs cannot be dissimilar in their sacred rites.

Therefore, since I believe we have run through in sufficient detail every point that the booklet contains – without digressing from the form of the memorandum – we have shown what we think about those matters which you related to us, brother, and how it is not to be tolerated if any priests agree in their hearts with such profane errors or, to put it more gently, do not resist them. With what conscience do they claim for themselves the honour of overseers who do not strive on behalf of the souls entrusted to them? Beasts attack and they do not close the sheepfolds. Thieves lie in wait and they do not post guards. Diseases flourish and they apply no remedies. But when they add to this that they decline to agree with those who act more diligently, and they neglect to anathematize with their signatures the impieties already condemned by the whole world, what do they want to be understood about themselves except that they do not number among the brothers but are on the side of the enemy?

17. But on that point which you raised in the very last part of your personal letter, I wonder that the intelligence of any catholic could be so exercised as though it were uncertain whether Christ's flesh remained in the tomb when he descended into hell. As it is true that the flesh was both dead and buried, so it is true that it was raised on the third day. For the Lord himself proclaimed this when he said to the Jews: '*Tear down this temple and in three days I will rebuild it*' (John 2: 19), to which the gospel writer adds: *But he was speaking about the temple of his body* (John 2: 21). The prophet David had also foretold the truth of this matter, when he said, speaking in the person

of the Lord (and) Saviour, *Furthermore, my flesh will rest in hope, since you will not abandon my soul to the underworld nor will you allow your holy one to see corruption* (Ps. 15: 9–10). From these words it is indeed clear that the flesh of Christ both truly rested in the grave and did not undergo corruption, because it quickly rose again, restored to life by the return of the soul. To disbelieve this is quite godless and doubtless pertains to the teaching of Mani and Priscillian, who pretend with sacrilegious intention to confess Christ in such a way that they even rob the truth of his incarnation and death and resurrection.

Therefore let an episcopal council be held amongst you, and let the priests of neighbouring provinces gather at a place which is convenient for everyone so that, in accordance with these responses we have made to your enquiries, it may be discovered by the fullest investigation whether there are any bishops who are polluted by the infection of this heresy. They should be removed from communion without hesitation, if they refuse to condemn that most wicked sect because of the depravities of all its opinions. For on no account should one who takes up the office of preaching the faith be allowed to dare argue against the gospel of Christ, against apostolic teaching, or against the confession of the whole church.

What kind of disciples will they be in the place where such masters teach? What piety will there be for the people in that place? What deliverance will there be for people where the holiness of modesty is removed against (the laws of) human society, the bond of marriage is abolished, the generation of children is prevented, the nature of the flesh is condemned; where in opposition to the true worship of the true God, the Trinity of the Godhead is confused by denying the (individual) properties of the persons;[51] where a divine essence is attributed to human souls and the same (essence) is shut up in the flesh at the devil's will; where the Son of God is preached as 'only begotten' due to the fact that he took his origin from a virgin, not because he was born of the Father; and where the same one is said to be neither the true child of God nor the real offspring of the virgin, so that, by means of a feigned crucifixion and a fake death, even the resurrection of the flesh exhumed from the grave is regarded as a hoax? In vain do they employ the catholic name if they do not resist these blasphemies. They are capable of believing these things if they can listen to them with tolerance.

We have sent letters to our brothers and fellow bishops of Tarragona, New Carthage, Lusitania and Galicia[52] and we have suggested to them a meeting of the general synod. It will be a matter for Your Beloved's concern that the authority of our rank should be recommended[53] to the bishops of the aforementioned provinces. But if anything (God forbid!) stands in the way of the celebration of a general council, at least let the priests of Galicia gather as one. Our brothers Hydatius[54] and Ceponius will strive eagerly for such a gathering, with your insistence being added to theirs, so that a swifter cure can be applied to such great wounds by means of a provincial council.[55]

Dated 21 July in the consulship of Calepius and Ardaburis.[56]

Letter 28 to Flavian, Bishop of Constantinople

Introduction

The version of the *Tome to Flavian* presented here is that preserved in the *Acts of the Council of Chalcedon* (451). The original *Tome* was redacted on 13 June 449, in answer to Flavian's complaint about Eutyches and his heretical activities in Constantinople since 448 (see 'Eutychianism' in Chapter 3). The letter was intended to be read out at the Council of Ephesus in 449, but the Eutychian party under the leadership of Dioscorus of Alexandria ensured that it did not get a hearing. It is uncertain whether Flavian ever actually read it: he died shortly after the Council of Ephesus, as a result of the brutality inflicted upon him there. In the course of the 'Robber Synod', as Ephesus was dubbed by Leo, Flavian was deposed as patriarch of Constantinople and Dioscorus's supporter Anatolius was appointed in his stead.

The main achievement of the *Tome* was its succinct formulation of the unique relationship of unity between the two natures of Christ, while avoiding use of the word 'one'.[57] Christ had a human form (by which we understand 'nature') and a divine form in such a way that 'each form performs what is proper to it in communion with the other, with the Word accomplishing what is proper to the Word and the flesh fulfilling what is proper to the flesh' (*ep.* 28.4). This formula trod the middle ground between the two extremes of 'one nature' Christology, where the humanity of Christ was dissolved in the hypostatic union (Eutychianism), and the teaching of two distinct persons in Christ, the human and the divine, each with their own nature (Nestorianism).[58] It also seemed to be close enough to Cyril of Alexandria's formula 'one incarnate nature of God the Word' to satisfy all but the most extreme Cyrillians, the followers of Eutyches in Egypt and Palestine, who were labelled 'monophysites' (from the Greek *mono* 'one' + *physis* 'nature') by their detractors. According to Leo's formulation, the natures were joined without confusion or mingling on the one hand (Eutychianism), and on the other hand, without division and separation

(Nestorianism). The *Tome* was to take on a life of its own through its inclusion in the *Acts of the Council of Chalcedon*, convened in 451 to overturn the findings of the Robber Synod of 449. It remained a standard for western and eastern theologians in the Christological controversies of the next two centuries, and contributed more than anything else to Leo's being assigned the epithet 'the Great'. However, it was not immune from criticism in the decade following Chalcedon, and Leo found himself having to fine-tune his ideas in a second Christological statement (*Letter 124 to the monks of Palestine*, translated below).

The *Tome* did not spring fully formed from Leo's head. In its composition the pope drew on seven sermons from his first collection of homilies.[59] Several major western patristic authors exercised an influence, including Augustine, Ambrose and Hilary of Poitiers. Echoes of Gaudentius of Brescia's anti-Arian tract *Homily* 19 can be found in the *Tome*, as in *serm.* 40a (Green 2008: 219). The reader should bear in mind that originality was not considered a virtue in a dogmatic statement such as this. Rather, Leo was concerned to show that his exposition of the relationship between the two natures in the one person of Christ was grounded firmly in tradition, both biblical and patristic. This was the only point from which he could safely condemn Eutyches and Nestorius as heretics. Thus, he appended to *Letter* 165 a long list of excerpts from various authors to demonstrate that what he was saying had already been said before, in both Latin and Greek.

Leo's authorship of *Letter* 28 has been questioned since the late seventeenth century, with some scholars claiming that the *Tome* was primarily the work of Prosper of Aquitaine in his role as secretary to Leo, a position he is assumed to have held for at least a decade, from *c.* 440 (Gaidioz 1949; James 1993).[60] This claim relies primarily on the statement of the late fifth-century biographer Gennadius (*On illustrious men* 85) that Prosper was said to have drafted certain letters of Leo against Eutyches (Herding 1924: 106). It is noteworthy that Gennadius does not claim that this was the case, but that it was reported to be so. The linchpin of Gaidioz's argument for Prosper's redaction of the *Tome* was that the word 'substance' (*substantia*), Leo's typical term in documents prior to 449, was avoided in the *Tome* in favour of 'nature' (*natura*).[61] The preference for 'nature' terminology in the letters of 449 was interpreted as evidence of the presumed superiority of Prosper's theological acumen.

Gaidioz's case is damaged by the fact that the term *substantia* is used in *ep.* 31 to Pulcheria, a letter redacted on the same day as the *Tome*. There Leo wrote that Nestorius had erred 'in believing that the substance (*substantia*) which issued from the same virgin was not ours ... ' (*ep.* 31, ACO 2.4: 13). In the previous sentence of this letter both terms, 'nature' and 'substance', appear (*ep.* 31, ACO 2.4: 12–13). Similarly, in *Letter* 30, redacted on the same day as *Letter* 31 and sent to the same person, Pulcheria, the term 'substance' is replaced with 'nature'. So one cannot make a sound argument for authorship based on the appearance of one term or the other. In spite of this, James concluded on very slight evidence that Prosper was the author of the *Tome*, and quite possibly of *Letter* 124 and *Letter* 165 (James 1993: 557–63), as well as the first five accession sermons attributed to Leo (1993: 569–70). More convincing is his argument that the choice of 'substance' or 'nature' terminology was determined by audience: *substantia* is preferred in *Letter* 124 *to the monks of Palestine* as appearing less Nestorian, but in the reworking of this text in *Letter* 165 *to the Emperor Leo*, all the instances of *substantia* are changed back to *natura* in order to distance Leo from Eutychianism (James 1993: 557–8). Green, after a judicious assessment of the evidence, concludes that claims for Prosper's authorship and Leo's inferior theological capability are largely unsubstantiated (Green 2008: 195–201). However, it does seem likely that Prosper prepared the materials that were used in the compilation of the *Tome* and that he may have been involved in editing the text (CCSL 138: cliii). The theological content nevertheless pertains to Leo.[62]

Translated from ACO 2.2.1: 24–33.

Text

Here begins the letter of Pope Leo to Flavian, bishop of Constantinople, concerning Eutyches.[63]

1. On reading your Charity's letter (whose late arrival amazed us),[64] and after reviewing the acts of the episcopal council,[65] we have finally found out about the scandal that arose among you against the integrity of the faith. What at first seemed obscure has now been revealed and disclosed to us. Eutyches, who seemed worthy of respect from his priestly title, has been exposed to us as very unwise and extremely ignorant, so that the prophet could have even been speaking about him: *He refused to understand so as to do well; he plotted mischief even in his bed* (Ps. 36: 3–4). What is more wicked than to be learned in blasphemies and not to yield to greater wisdom and learning? But into this foolishness fall those who do not turn to the words of the prophets when some obscurity hinders their understanding of the truth, or to the letters of the apostles, or to the authority of the gospels, but

to themselves. This is why they are masters of error: because they have not been disciples of the truth. For what learning has he gained from the sacred pages of the New and Old Testaments if he does not even understand the beginning of the creed itself, and if the profession of faith made by everyone seeking rebirth throughout the whole world[66] is not yet held in that old man's heart?

2. So, since he did not know what he should believe about the incarnation of the Word of God – nor did he want to make the effort to gain the light of understanding from the breadth of the holy scriptures – by listening carefully he could have understood at least that common and uniform confession of faith, by which all the faithful proclaim their belief *in God the Father almighty and in Jesus Christ his only son, our Lord, who was born of the Holy Spirit and the virgin Mary.*[67] These three statements destroy the schemes of almost every heretic. For when God is believed to be the almighty Father, the Son is proven coeternal with him, in no way different from the Father, because he was born *God from God,*[68] almighty from the almighty, coeternal from the eternal, not subsequent in time nor inferior in power, no different in glory, undivided in essence. And the same only-begotten eternal Son of the eternal Father was born of the Holy Spirit and the virgin Mary, and his birth in time diminished his divine and eternal birth in no way, and added nothing to it. Rather, he expended himself[69] completely for restoring humanity, who had been deceived, so that by his virtue he both conquered death and destroyed the devil, who used to have power over death. For we could not overcome the originator of sin and death, if he (sc. Christ) had not assumed our nature and made it his own, he whom sin could not stain nor death detain.[70]

He was conceived in fact by the Holy Spirit in the womb of a virgin mother, who bore him with her virginity intact, in the same way as she had conceived him with her virginity intact. But if he (sc. Eutyches) could not draw a sound understanding from this most pure source of the Christian faith, because he was darkening the splendour of clear truth by his own blindness, he should have submitted himself to gospel teaching. And since Matthew says, *the book of the genealogy of Jesus Christ, the son of David, the son of Abraham* (Matt. 1: 1), he should have sought out also the instruction of apostolic preaching. And when he read in the letter to the Romans: *Paul, a servant of Christ Jesus, called to be an apostle, set apart for the gospel of God which he had promised long ago through his prophets in the holy scriptures concerning his Son, who descended from the seed of David according to the flesh* (Rom. 1: 1–3), he should have paid just attention to the prophetic pages. And when he discovered God's promise to Abraham, saying: *In your descendant all peoples will be blessed* (Gen. 22: 18), lest he doubt the characteristics of this descendant, he should have followed the apostle who said: *The promises were made to Abraham and his descendant. It does not say: 'the descendants', as if there were many, but [speaks] of one, 'and in your descendant', that is Christ* (Gal. 3: 16). He should have listened with his inner ear to the preaching of Isaiah too, who said: *Behold, a virgin will conceive in the womb and will bear a son and they will call him Emmanuel, which means 'God with us'* (Is. 7: 14). And he should have faithfully read the words of the same prophet: *A child has been born to us, a son has been given to us, and dominion will be upon his shoulder and they will call him messenger of great counsel, mighty God, prince of peace, father of the age to come* (Is. 9: 6), and he would not say – speaking so as to hinder – that the Word was made flesh in such a way that Christ, born of the virgin's womb, had the form of a human being and yet did not have the true imprint of his mother's body.

Or perhaps he thought that the Lord Jesus Christ did not share our nature because the angel sent to blessed Mary said: *The Holy Spirit will come upon you and the power of the Most High will overshadow you. So the holy one to be born from you will be called the Son of God* (Luke 1: 35), so that because he was conceived of a virgin by a divine act, the flesh of the one conceived was not (derived) from the nature of the one who conceived him? But his birth, a unique wonder and wonderfully unique, is not to be understood such that through the novelty of his creation the 'characteristic' of the (human) race is removed. The Holy Spirit made the virgin fertile, but the reality of his body was taken up from (her) body, and with wisdom building for herself a house (cf. Prov. 9: 1), *the Word became flesh and dwelt among us* (John 1: 14), that is in that flesh which he took up from humankind and which he animated with the spirit of rational life.

3. Therefore with the characteristic of each nature maintained and joined in one person, majesty took up humility, power took up weakness, eternity assumed mortality, and in order to pay off the debt of our condition the inviolable nature was joined to a passible nature,[71] so that, as was fitting for our healing, *one* and the same *mediator of God and humankind, the man Jesus Christ* (1 Tim. 2: 5), was both mortal in respect to one and immortal in respect to the other.[72] Therefore in the perfect and complete nature of true man he was born true God, wholly in his own (nature), wholly in ours. And we call 'ours' what the creator established in us in the beginning and what he took up in order to restore; for what the deceiver offered and the deceived accepted left no trace in the Saviour. Nor did he share in our

sins because he undertook to share in human weakness. He assumed the form of a slave without the stain of sin, adding to humanity but not diminishing divinity, because that emptying by which the invisible made itself visible and the creator and Lord of all things wanted to become mortal was an inclination of mercy, not a failure of strength. Accordingly, the one who created humankind while abiding in the form of God was made man in the form of a slave. For each nature keeps its own characteristics without loss, and just as the form of God does not consume the form of a slave, so the form of a slave does not diminish the form of God. Because the devil was boasting that humankind, deceived by his trickery, was deprived of divine gifts;[73] and that after man was stripped of the gift of immortality he endured the harsh sentence of death; and that man found some solace in his wickedness from the collusion of a partner in crime; and that God, following the demands of the logic of justice, had also changed his mind towards humankind, whom he had established with such great honour: (for these reasons) a secret plan needed to be arranged, so that the unchangeable God, whose will cannot be robbed of its kindness, could fulfil the original arrangement of his paternal care[74] towards us by a very secret mystery, and humankind, having been driven into guilt by the devil's wicked cunning, would not be lost contrary to God's purpose.

4. And so the Son of God approached these depths of the world, descending from his heavenly throne but not withdrawing from the Father's glory in the new order; born by a new kind of birth 'in the new order' (as I said) because he was made visible in our (nature) while invisible in his own (nature). The incomprehensible wished to be comprehended;[75] he – who was there before time began – took a beginning in time; the Lord of the universe took up the form of a slave with the grandeur of his majesty overshadowed; the impassible God did not disdain to become a passible human, and the immortal (did not disdain) to submit to the laws of death. But he was born 'by a new kind of birth', because the inviolate virgin did not know lust, (yet) furnished the material of the flesh. From his mother the Lord took up his nature but no guilt, and the nature in the Lord Jesus Christ, born of a virgin's womb, was not unlike ours just because his birth was a miracle. For the one who is true God is also true man. There is no falsity in this union, whereby the lowliness of humanity and the loftiness of divinity are mutually united. For just as God is not changed by mercy, so his humanity is not swallowed up by his majesty. For each form performs what is proper to it in communion with the other, with the Word accomplishing what is proper to the Word and the flesh

fulfilling what is proper to the flesh. One of these shines forth in miracles, the other succumbs to injuries.[76] And as the Word does not retreat from glory equal to the Father's, so the flesh does not give up the nature of our race.

For it should be repeated often that the Son of God is truly the son of man, one and the same. He is God because *in the beginning was the Word and the Word was with God and the Word was God* (John 1: 1), (but) man because *the Word was made flesh and dwelt among us* (John 1: 14). He is God in that *all things were made through him and without him nothing was made* (John 1: 3), (but) man in that *he was born of a woman, born under law* (Gal. 4: 4). His birth in the flesh is the revelation of his human nature; the virgin birth is the sign of divine power. The infancy of a little child is revealed in the lowly cradle; the grandeur of the Most High is declared by the voices of angels. He whom Herod wickedly strives to murder is like the most helpless infant, but he whom the wise men rejoice to worship as suppliants is the Lord of all. Now, when he came for baptism by his forerunner John, lest he remain hidden by the veil of the flesh that was cloaking his divinity, the Father's voice sounded from heaven, saying: *This is my beloved son, in whom I am well pleased* (Matt. 3: 17). And in the same way as the devil's cunning tempts him as a man, so the help of angels ministers to the same one as God.[77] To hunger, to thirst, to grow weary and to sleep is clearly human, but to satisfy five thousand with five loaves, and to bestow living water on the Samaritan woman, a draught which promised the one who drank it that she would thirst no more (cf. John 4: 7–15) (is divine); to walk on the sea's crest without sinking (cf. Matt. 14: 25) and to level the high waves by rebuking the storm (cf. Luke 8: 24) is without doubt divine.[78]

Therefore, passing over many things, just as it is not characteristic of the same nature to weep for a friend who has died, being moved by compassion, and to raise to life the same person by the command of his voice, after rolling back the tombstone from a burial four days old (cf. John 11: 38–44); or to hang on a tree and make all the elements tremble with day turned to night (cf. Matt. 27: 45); or to be nailed up and to open the gates of paradise to a faithful thief (cf. Luke 23: 40–3); so it is not characteristic of the same nature to say: *I and the Father are one* (John 10: 30) and to say: *The Father is greater than I* (John 14: 28). For although there is one person of God and man in the Lord Jesus Christ, the humiliation shared by both belongs to one, and the glory shared by both belongs to the other. For his humanity that is less than the Father comes from us, while his divinity that is equal to the Father comes from the Father.[79]

5. Therefore on account of this unity of person, which is to be understood of both natures, we read that the Son of man descended from heaven, when the Son of God assumed flesh from that virgin from whom he was born. And again the Son of God is said to have been crucified and buried. He suffered these things in the weakness of human nature, not in the divinity which makes him the only-begotten, coeternal and consubstantial with the Father. So we all confess in the creed the only-born son of God, crucified and buried,[80] according to that (statement) of the apostle: *For if they had understood, they would never have crucified the Lord of glory* (1 Cor. 2: 8).[81] But when our Lord and Saviour was instructing his disciples in the faith by questioning them, he asked: *Who do people say that the Son of Man is?* (Matt. 16: 13); and when they repeated various opinions of other people, he said: *'But who do you say I am?'* (Matt. 16: 15). That is, I, who am the Son of Man and whom you see in the form of a slave and in the reality of the flesh: *Who do you say I am?* When blessed Peter said by divine inspiration (thereby bringing profit to all peoples by his confession): *You are the Christ, the Son of the living God* (Matt. 16: 16), the Lord pronounced him blessed, and he deserved it. And from the first rock[82] Peter drew steadfastness both in power and in name, who through the revelation of the Father confessed the same one as Son of God and Christ,[83] because one of these received without the other was no use for salvation; and it was equally dangerous to believe that the Lord Jesus Christ was either only God without man, or only man without God.

But after the Lord's resurrection, which was indeed the resurrection of the true body – because he who was resurrected was none other than he who had been crucified and killed – why else did he tarry for forty days (cf. Acts 1: 3) except so that the integrity of our faith should be cleared of all obscurity? For this reason he spoke with his disciples and stayed with them (cf. Acts 1: 4) and ate with them, and allowed himself to be examined by the thorough and curious touch of those gripped by doubt. He appeared through closed doors to his disciples and gave the Holy Spirit by breathing on them, and he opened the hidden parts of the holy Scripture by giving them the light of understanding. And again he showed the same wound in his side, the holes of the nails and all the signs of his most recent suffering, saying: *See my hands and feet; it is I myself! Touch and see; a ghost does not have flesh and bones, as you see I have* (Luke 24: 39): so that we would recognise that in him the characteristics of the divine and human natures remained undivided[84] and so we would know this Word was not the flesh,[85] and so might confess one Son of God, both Word and flesh. In this mystery of faith Eutyches should be considered empty headed: he did not acknowledge our nature in the only-born Son of God either through the lowliness of his mortal condition or through the glory of the resurrection. Nor did Eutyches fear the opinion of the blessed apostle and evangelist John, who said: *Every spirit who confesses that Jesus Christ came in the flesh is from God and every spirit who does away with Jesus is not from God: it is the Antichrist* (1 John 4: 2–3). But what does it mean 'to do away with Jesus' if not to separate his human nature from him and to render void by insolent fictions the sacrament, which is our only means of salvation? But if he is blind about the nature of Christ's body, he (sc. Eutyches) must be void of understanding regarding the passion, due to the same blindness. For if he does not regard the Lord's cross as false and does not doubt that it was a true punishment undertaken for the salvation of the world, let him also acknowledge the flesh of the one whose death he believes in. Let him not deny our flesh to the man whom he acknowledges as capable of suffering, since the denial of the true flesh is also a denial of bodily suffering. If, therefore, he subscribes to the Christian faith and does not avoid hearing the preaching of the gospel, let him see which nature, pierced by nails, hung on the wooden cross; let him understand whence the blood and water flowed when the side of the one crucified was opened by the soldier's spear, so that the church of God might be watered both by the baptismal font and by the cup. May he hear the blessed apostle Peter when he preaches that sanctification by the Spirit happens through the sprinkling of Christ's blood (cf. 1 Pet. 1: 2), and let him read in no careless fashion the words of the same apostle saying: *Knowing that you have been redeemed from your empty way of life handed down by your fathers, not by perishable silver and gold but by the precious blood of Jesus Christ like a pure and spotless lamb* (1 Pet. 1: 18–19). Let him also not resist the witness of the blessed apostle John saying: *And the blood of Jesus the Son of God cleanses us from every sin* (1 John 1: 7); and again, *This is the victory that conquers the world, our faith. For who is it who conquers the world except the one who believes that Jesus is the Son of God? This is the one who came with water and blood, Jesus Christ, not with water only but with water and blood, and the Spirit is the one who testifies, for the Spirit is the truth. Because there are three that testify, the Spirit and the water and the blood, and these three are one* (1 John 5: 4–8), namely the spirit of sanctification and the blood of redemption and the water of baptism. These three are one and remain undivided and none of them is severed from its connection (with the others), because the catholic church lives by this faith and advances by it, believing that (Christ's) humanity does not exist without true divinity, nor his divinity without true humanity.

6. But when Eutyches responded to your cross-examination by saying: 'I confess our Lord was of two natures before the union, but after the union I confess one nature',[86] I am amazed that such an absurd and perverse confession was constrained by no rebuke from the judges and that such an extremely foolish statement was passed over as if nothing offensive had been heard, since the impiety of saying that the only-begotten Son of God was of two natures before the incarnation is as wicked as his assertion of a single nature in him after the Word was made flesh. But lest Eutyches think this pronouncement was either right or tolerable because it was refuted by no judgement of yours, we advise Your Beloved's diligence, dearest brother, that if the case is brought to a satisfactory conclusion through the inspiration of God's mercy, the imprudence of an ignorant man should be also purged of the plague of this opinion. Indeed, as the order of the proceedings makes plain, he made a good beginning in retreating from his persuasion, when he professed what he had not said before, under the influence of your judgement, and agreed to that faith to which he was formerly a stranger.[87] However, when he refused to consent to anathematize the wicked teaching, Your Fraternity understood that he persisted in his falsehood and that he deserved to receive a judgement of condemnation. If he repents of it faithfully and with profit, and recognises even tardily how rightly episcopal authority was provoked, or if he condemns everything which he wrongly believed with a loud voice and his own signature, in full satisfaction (of the requirements), any degree of mercy shown the penitent will not be criticised. For our Lord, the true and *good shepherd*, who laid down *his life for his sheep* (John 10: 11), and who came to save the souls of humankind, not to lose them, wants us to imitate his pity,[88] so that justice indeed might compel sinners, but mercy might not turn away those who have repented. For then, at last, is the true faith defended most profitably, when a false opinion is condemned even by its adherents.[89]

I have sent our brothers Julius the bishop and Renatus the priest of the titular church of Clement, and also my son Hilary the deacon[90] in my stead to pursue every case correctly and faithfully. We have sent to accompany them our notary Dulcitius, whose faith has been proved to us, trusting that divine help will be at hand so that he who had strayed will be saved when the wickedness of his opinion is condemned. God keep you safe, dearest brother. Dated 13 June in the consulship of Asturius and Protogenes.[91]

Letter 124 to the monks of Palestine

Introduction

Letter 124 to the monks of Palestine is Leo's second major statement on the Christological debate that had opened in 448. While the *Tome* had satisfied some parties, especially the imperial family, who were looking for a basis for unity between the opposing factions, many were not satisfied with it, including the so-called 'monophysite' monks in Palestine and Egypt. These opponents of the Council of Chalcedon regarded the resolution reached there as a betrayal of both Cyril and Eutyches. Much of their energetic opposition was focused on discrediting the *Tome*.

In Palestine, and later in Alexandria, the monastic reaction to the *Definition of Faith* and the canons approved at Chalcedon was violent. Rioting broke out in 453, and Leo felt compelled to address a long epistle to those who were causing the disturbance. This was *Letter* 124, composed *c.* 15 June 453 on the basis of *Homilies* 64 and 65, delivered in April of that year.[92] In his preface Leo adopts a gentle approach, seeking to excuse the monks' scandalous behaviour by attributing it to a misunderstanding caused by a poor translation of the *Tome* into Greek. Leo himself seems to have had limited knowledge of Greek, and the erroneous versions of the *Tome* that were circulating in the East caused him much concern. We see an unaccustomed touch of real humility when Leo confesses that he is not surprised by the shortcomings of the Greek translations since he, as one of the disputants, could hardly explain such theological subtleties in Latin, his mother tongue (*ep.* 124.1).

As in *Letter* 28, Leo insists that his Christological statement was in line with 'ancient teaching', and that what the Palestinian monks abhor, that is, the Nestorian heresy, he also absolutely rejects. His condemnation of Nestorius is explicit in this letter, unlike in *Letter* 28. In a significant departure from the *Tome* he reverts to his original, pre-449, terminology of 'substances' in Christ rather than 'natures', since talk of two natures in Christ seemed to have Nestorian resonances for the Palestinian monks, being read as implying two persons in Christ (Barclift 1997: 227 n.219). *Letter* 124 was later reworked as *Letter* 165 to Emperor Leo, usually known as the '*Second Tome*', in which the 'nature' terminology was reinstated (James 1993: 557–8).[93] Two other developments in Leo's thinking and terminology since the composition of the *Tome* are worth mentioning in relation to *Letter* 124: first, his adoption of the Antiochene formula of 'the human being having been taken up' (*homo assumptus*), and second, his distinction between the terms 'human being' (*homo*) for the specific reality of Jesus as a concrete human being, and the adjective 'human' (*humanus*) for the abstract concept of humanity or human nature (Barclift 1997: 230–9). This was a distinction that Leo did not observe prior to 452, and reflects a new emphasis on the humanity of Christ as a corrective to the 'high' Alexandrian Christology exemplified by Eutyches. As Green puts it in a succinct formulation that underlines the significance of this letter, 'The Christ whom Leo preached as the source of his message of civic Christianity, the Mediator bringing humanity and divinity together in his person, creating a community of love for all people, was the Christ whose identity reached fullest expression in his letter to the Palestinian monks of 453' (Green 2008: 252).[94]

The conciliatory tone of *Letter* 124 is markedly different from that of Leo's letter of the preceding November to Juvenal of Cos, where Leo denounces the same 'false monks' for the riots that spread from Jerusalem to the whole of Palestine after the monk Theodosius returned from Chalcedon supporting one-nature Christology. These Palestinian monks had killed Severian, bishop of Scythopolis, and threatened to do the same to Juvenal, bishop of Jerusalem, who wisely fled into exile. Leo roundly condemned their violence and ignorance, likening them to soldiers of the Antichrist: 'But these insolent disturbers (of the peace), who boast of their insults and injuries to priests, are to be considered not servants of Christ, but soldiers of the Antichrist, and must be chiefly brought low through their leaders, who incite the ignorant mob to defend their insubordination' (*ep.* 109.2, ACO 2.4: 137). It is in the context of monastic unrest in the aftermath of Chalcedon that we can understand several other letters sent by Leo to Syrian bishops of Antioch and Cyrrhus. Writing to Maximus, bishop of Antioch, on 11 June 453 – around the same time as the composition of *Letter* 124 – Leo forbids preaching by monks and laymen, reserving this activity to priests and bishops (*ep.* 119.6). His letter to Theodoret of Cyrrhus, written on the same day, reiterates the injunction sent to Maximus (*ep.* 120.6). *Letter* 118 to Julian of Cos also forbids monks to preach.

Unfortunately these letters did not prevent violence breaking out in Egypt over the Alexandrian patriarch Proterius's adherence to the *Tome*. Proterius had been ordained in place of Dioscorus in 452, after the latter's deposition at Chalcedon. In a letter of 454, Leo advised Proterius to clear himself of all charges of Nestorianism by reading out selections from certain fathers and finally from Leo's *Tome*.[95] This must have infuriated those who felt that Proterius had betrayed the memory of his predecessor, Dioscorus, by omitting his name from the diptychs, the list of persons of holy memory that was recited in the course of each liturgy. The anti-Chalcedonians had to bide their time until the death of Emperor Marcian in early 457, whereupon, under the leadership of Timothy Aelurus and his associate Peter Mongus, they besieged the patriarch in church. Proterius was put to the sword in a baptistery on Easter Day and his corpse was dragged around the city streets on a rope before being dismembered and burned.[96] Timothy Aelurus was then illegitimately installed as patriarch. When Leo found out about it some months afterwards, he was furious and appalled, as *Letters* 149 and 150 indicate: 'For the entire Christian religion – and this must often be repeated – is disturbed if any of the decisions made at Chalcedon is done away with' (*ep.* 149, ACO 2.4: 98; FOTC 34: 238). This dreadful affair was the catalyst for Leo's definitive Christological statement, *Letter* 165 to Emperor Leo in 458.

Translated from ACO 2.4: 159–63 [*ep.* 113], edited from the late fifth-century *Quesnel Collection*.

Text

Likewise begins the letter of the same Pope Leo to the Palestinians.[97]

1. It has been brought to my attention, which I owe to the whole church and to all its children, by the word of many people, that some offence was committed against your beloveds' souls, because certain translators, whether out of ignorance as seems likely, or out of malice,[98] gave you to understand something other than what I preached.[99] They were not able to render the Latin into Greek speech with fitting accuracy since each disputant can hardly manage to explain in his own tongue such subtle and difficult matters. But this case has brought me one advantage: that your condemnation of what the catholic faith rejects makes me realise that you are greater friends to the truth than to falsehood and that you rightly reject what I myself abhor, following the institution of ancient teaching. For although my letter sent to Bishop Flavian of holy memory should suffice for the revelation of itself, and needs no exoneration or exposition, some other writings of mine are also in harmony with it, in which the meaning of my preaching is similarly clear.[100] For since I deemed it necessary to argue against the heretics who had disturbed many of Christ's people, I revealed to the most merciful princes and the holy synodal council and the church of Constantinople what we ought to know and believe about the incarnation of the Word according to the teaching of the gospel and the apostles. And I have never wavered

from the creed of our holy Fathers, because there is only one true catholic faith, to which nothing can be added and nothing taken away. For first Nestorius and now Eutyches has tried to attack it, making opposite claims but with similar impiety, and attempting to introduce two contradictory heresies into the church of God, so that they were both justly condemned by the disciples of truth, because what they each believed, though false in different ways, was quite senseless and blasphemous.

2. Therefore Nestorius should be condemned because he believed that the blessed virgin Mary was the mother of the man alone, so that he made the flesh (of Christ) one person, and the deity another. He did not believe in one Christ in the Word of God and in the flesh, but preached one son of God and another (son) of man, distinct and separate; when (in fact), with the essence of the Word remaining unchangeable – that timeless and coeternal essence he shares with the Father and the Holy Spirit – the Word was made flesh in the virgin's womb in such a way that by one conception and one birth, the same virgin was both the handmaiden of the Lord and his mother according to the union of each substance.[101] Elizabeth realised this too, as the gospel writer Luke declares, and she said: *Why has this happened to me, that the mother of my Lord comes to me?* (Luke 1: 43). Eutyches also should be struck down by the same anathema, because he, after due consideration of the godless errors of ancient heretics, picked out the third teaching of Apollinaris.[102] And so he denies the reality of the human flesh and soul, and asserts that our Lord Jesus Christ is wholly of one nature, as though the deity of the Word had converted itself into flesh and soul; and as though it belonged only to his essence – which does nothing by itself without the reality of the flesh – to be conceived and born, to be nourished and grow, to be crucified and die, to be buried and rise again, to ascend to heaven and sit *on the right hand of the Father, whence he will come to judge the living and the dead.*[103] For the nature of the only-begotten is the nature of the Father and the nature of the Holy Spirit, and the undivided unity and consubstantial equality of the eternal Trinity is impassible and unchangeable at the same time.

If that heretic withdraws from the perversity of Apollinaris, lest he be convicted of believing in a deity that is capable of suffering and death, and he nevertheless dares to pronounce one nature of the incarnate Word, that is of the Word and the flesh, no doubt he passes over into the madness of the Manichee and of Marcion;[104] and he believes that the *mediator between God and humankind, the man Jesus Christ* (1 Tim. 2: 5), did everything by simulation, and he did not have a human body, but that a phantom semblance of a body appeared to the sight of those who observed it.[105]

3. Since the catholic faith of old abhorred these impious lies, and the blasphemies of such people were condemned throughout the whole world by the unanimous judgement of the blessed Fathers,[106] whoever these are who are so blinded and foreign to the light of truth that they deny the presence of a human nature – that, is our nature – in the Word of God from the time of the incarnation, let them show on what grounds they have assumed the name of Christian for themselves, and in what way they agree with the gospel of truth if either the flesh without the deity, or the deity without the flesh, has its origin in the birth from the blessed virgin. For just as it cannot be denied that *the Word was made flesh and dwelt among us* (John 1: 14), so it cannot be denied that *God was in Christ, reconciling the world to himself* (2 Cor. 5: 19). For what reconciliation can there be, through which the human race might propitiate God, except that the mediator between God and humankind undertook the case of all (cf. 1 Tim. 2: 5–6)? By what means could anyone fulfil the true role of mediator, except if one who was equal to the Father in the form of God would share with us the form of a slave, so that the renovation of the old occurred through one new human being, and the chains of death, contracted by the collusion of a single man, were broken by the death of a single man who alone owed nothing to death? For the outpouring of his just blood for the unjust was so mighty a privilege, so rich a prize, that, if all those held captive would believe in their redeemer, no bonds of tyranny would hold them, since, as the apostle says: *Where sin increased, grace abounded all the more* (Rom. 5: 20). And since those born under the sentence of sin have accepted the power of rebirth for justification, the gift of liberty was made stronger than the debt of servitude.

4. As a result, what hope do those who deny the reality of the human substance in the body of our Saviour leave for themselves in the refuge of this sacrament? Let them say what sacrifice reconciles them, and what blood has redeemed them. Who is he, *who has handed himself over for us as a fragrant offering and sacrifice to God* (Eph. 5: 2)? Or what sacrifice was ever more holy than that which the true high priest laid on the altar of the cross through the immolation of his flesh? Although the death of many saints was precious in the sight of the Lord (cf. Ps. 116: 15), nevertheless the world's redemption was not achieved by the killing of those innocents. The just have received their crowns, not given them, and from the courage of the faithful examples of patience were produced, not gifts of justification. In fact those individuals were affected by individual deaths, and none of them paid

off another's debt with their own lives. For among the sons of men only one, our Lord Jesus Christ, stood out in whom all were crucified, all died, all were buried, and all were raised. Of them he himself said: *When I have been exalted, I will draw all things to myself* (John 12: 32). For true faith, which justifies the impious and makes them just, is drawn to him as one who shares in its humanity, and gains salvation in him, in whom alone humankind finds itself without guilt. Through God's grace it is free to boast of the power of the one who, having met the arrogant foe in the humiliation of our flesh, shared his victory with those in whose flesh he had triumphed.[107]

5. Therefore although there is one person of the Word and the flesh in our one Lord Jesus Christ, the true son of God and man, and each essence has a share in every action,[108] yet the qualities of those works must be understood, and one should discern with the contemplation of genuine faith, in which actions his humble weakness is lifted up, and in which his sublime virtue is lowered; what it is that the flesh does not do without the Word, and what the Word does not perform without the flesh. Without the power of the Word the virgin would not have conceived or given birth; and without the reality of the flesh the infant would not have lain wrapped in swaddling cloths. Without the power of the Word the wise men would not have adored the child revealed by a new star; and without the reality of the flesh there would have been no command to take the boy into Egypt and remove him from Herod's persecution. Without the power of the Word the voice of the Father sent from heaven would not have said: *This is my beloved son in whom I am well pleased* (Matt. 3: 17); and without the reality of the flesh John would not have borne witness: *Behold the Lamb of God, behold him who takes away the sins of the world* (John 1: 29). Without the power of the Word there would have been no healing of the sick or raising of the dead; and without the reality of the flesh he would not have needed either to eat when he was hungry or sleep when he was tired. Finally, without the power of the Word the Lord would not have professed himself equal to the Father; and without the reality of the flesh the same one would not have said that the Father was greater than he, since the catholic faith upholds and defends both statements. It believes in one son of God, both man and Word,[109] according to the properties of the divine and human substances.[110]

6. Therefore, although from the very beginning when *the Word was made flesh* (John 1: 14) in the virgin's womb, there was never any means of division between the divine and human substances, and throughout his entire physical growth his acts were always the work of a single person, nevertheless we do not confuse with any mixing those

acts which were done inseparably, but we know from the quality of the deeds what pertains to which nature. The divinity did not prejudice the humanity, nor did the humanity prejudice the divinity, since in that very man both met in such a way that neither property was subsumed in the other nor was the (single) person duplicated.

Let those imaginary Christians explain then which substance of the Saviour was nailed to the cross? Which flesh lay in the tomb and rose on the third day after the tombstone was rolled away? And which body did Jesus present to the disciples' eyes when he appeared among them although the doors were closed and, in order to remove the doubts of those looking on, he demanded that they see with their own eyes and trace with their own fingers the still obvious holes made by the nails and the fresh wound of his punctured side (cf. John 20: 26–7)?[111] But if heretical obstinacy does not give up its shadows in so great a light of truth, let them show how they claim the hope of eternal life for themselves[112] since one cannot attain that except through *the mediator between God and humankind, the man Jesus Christ* (1 Tim. 2: 5). *For there is no other name given to human beings under heaven by which we must be saved* (Acts 4: 12). There is no redemption of human captivity except in his blood, *who gave himself as a ransom for all* (1 Tim. 2: 6), who, as the blessed apostle preaches, *while in the form of God, did not regard equality with God as something to be exploited, but emptied himself, taking the form of a slave, being made in human like-ness. And being found in human form, he humbled himself and became obedient to the point of death – even death on a cross. Therefore God also exalted him and gave him the name that is above every name, that at the name of Jesus every knee should bow, in heaven and on earth and under the earth, and every tongue should confess that Jesus Christ is Lord, in the glory of God the Father* (Phil. 2: 6–11).

7. Therefore, although there is one Lord Jesus Christ and the person of the true Godhead and the true humanity really is one and the same in him, nor can the solidity of this union be separated by any division, nevertheless we understand the exaltation – by which *God exalted him and gave him the name which is above every name* – to pertain to that form which had to be enriched by being so greatly increased in glory. Of course 'in the form of God' the Son was equal to the Father and between the Father and the only-begotten there was no distinction of essence, no difference in majesty, nor did the Word lack anything through the mystery of the incarnation that should be restored to him as a gift of the Father. 'The form of a slave', through which the impassible deity fulfilled a pledge of great pity,[113] is human lowliness and it was lifted up to the glory of divine power. The divinity and the

humanity were joined together in such unity from the virgin's very conception that divine actions were not performed without the human being, nor were human actions performed without God. For this reason, as the Lord of majesty is said to have been crucified, so he who is forever equal with God is called exalted. Nor does it matter by what substance Christ is called, since – with the unity of person remaining inseparable – he is at once both wholly Son of man because of his flesh, and wholly Son of God because of his divinity that is one with the Father. Whatever Christ received in time, he received as a man, and what he did not have is added to him. For according to the power of the Word everything that belongs to the Father belongs to the Son without distinction, and what he received from the Father in the form of a slave, those same things he himself gave in the form of the Father. And the very same one was both rich and poor, rich because *in the beginning was the Word and the Word was with God and the Word was God. He was in the beginning with God. All things were made through him and without him nothing was made* (John 1: 1–3), and poor because *the Word was made flesh and dwelt among us* (John 1: 14). But what is his emptying or his poverty except receiving the form of a slave, through which the dispensation of human redemption was fulfilled, with the Word's majesty veiled? For since the original bonds of our captivity could not be broken if there did not exist a person of our species and our nature, whom the terms of the ancient debt could not hold, and who could blot out the decree of death by his immaculate blood, as was divinely ordained from the beginning, so it happened in the fullness of the appointed time that the promise signified in many ways would come into effect after a long wait, and what had often been announced by frequent testimonies could not be doubted. (Up to here to Emperor Leo.)[114]

8. And so I am amazed that Your Charity[115] struggles to discern the light of truth, after the demolishing of so many heresies, which were cut out from the body of catholic unity through the presiding fathers' holy zeal, and which have deservedly been banished from Christ because they made *a stumbling block* for themselves *and a rock of scandal* (1 Pet. 2: 8) from the incarnation of the Word, which is rightly the only path to salvation for believers. And since many proofs have demonstrated how justly the Christian faith condemned both Nestorius and Eutyches with Dioscorus, and that no one can be called a Christian who agrees with the blasphemy of one or the other, I grieve that you recoil from the teaching of the gospels and the apostles, as I hear. You stir up strife in the cities, you disrupt churches, you inflict not only injuries but even slaughter on priests and bishops, so that you

forget your purpose and your profession in the face of outrage and fury.[116] Where is your rule of meekness and quietness? Where is your long-suffering patience? Where is your peaceful serenity? Where is the foundation of love and the strength of forbearance? What persuasion has snatched you up, what persecution has led you away from the gospel of Christ? Or what great treachery of the deceiver has turned up so that you would give yourselves up to the devil's deceits, forgetting the prophets and apostles, forgetting the saving creed and the confession that you pronounced before many witnesses when you took the oath of baptism? What would the claws do to you,[117] or savage torments, if the empty utterances of heretics alone were able to expunge the integrity of your faith? You believe that you act on behalf of the faith and yet you go against the faith. You take up arms in the name of the church and yet you strive against the church. Is this what you have learnt from the prophets, from the gospels, from the apostles, that by denying the true flesh of Christ and subjecting the very essence of the Word to passion and death you make our nature foreign to its restorer, and you believe that everything which the cross punished, which the lance wounded, which the tomb received and gave back was only the work of divine power, not also of human lowliness? In regard to this lowliness the apostle says: [*For*] *I am not ashamed of the gospel* (Rom. 1: 16), since he knew what slurs were cast at Christians by their enemies, and for that reason also the Lord pronounced these words: *He who confesses me before men, I will confess him before my father* (Matt. 10: 32). For those who now find the flesh of Christ a source of shame will not be worthy to confess the Son and the Father. And those who have accepted to bear the sign of the cross on their brows but blush to utter it with their lips will prove themselves to have assumed no virtue from that sign.

9. Desist, my children, desist from these persuasions of the devil: nothing injures the truth of God, but the truth does not save us except in our flesh. Indeed, as the prophet says, *Truth sprang out of the earth* (Ps. 85: 11), and the virgin Mary conceived the Word in such a way that she would provide that flesh from her substance to be united with him, but not with the addition of a person or the disappearance of her nature. For he who was in the form of God received the form of a slave in such a manner that Christ would be one and the same in each form. God lowered himself to the depths of a man and the man was lifted up to the heights of divinity, as the apostle says: *to them* (sc. the Israelites) *belong the patriarchs, and from them, according to the flesh, comes the Christ who is over all, God blessed forever. Amen* (Rom. 9: 5).

9

HEIR OF ST PETER

Homily 82B on the Feast of the Apostles

Introduction

Homily 82, celebrating the feast of Saints Peter and Paul, apostolic founders of the Christian city of Rome, was delivered in three versions (recensions A, B, and C). The first recension was delivered on 29 June 441. The second recension also pertains to Leo's first sermon collection (440–5). While the third recension is merely a slight variation of the second, recensions A and B differ quite significantly. Recension B has been chosen as the basis for my translation below, as it provides an extended version of some of the homily's more important themes. The double vigil of Peter and Paul, a feast native to Rome, was celebrated in the octave preceding the pagan feast of the *Ludi Apollinares*. The feast of Saints Peter and Paul was the occasion of a collection of alms throughout the city. Leo delivered *Homily* 83 on another celebration of this feast, in 443 at the latest (CCSL 138: clxxxi): most of its content can be found in *Homily* 4, translated in this chapter.

Delivered in the second year of Leo's pontificate, this homily reveals his attempt to build up an alternative source of civic splendour: the spiritual adornment of martyr-saints, and in particular the two leading apostles, Peter and Paul. The saints crown the city like a diadem of precious stones (*serm.* 82B.6). The power of Christian Rome over the world is spiritual rather than temporal: it commands more widely, by virtue of divine religion, than by earthly domination (*serm.* 82B.1). Rome, he claims, has gained more subjects under the Christian peace than it ever did through warfare. As was noted in the Introduction, Leo, unlike Augustine, does not dismiss pagan Rome; rather, he considers the pre-Christian period of Rome's history as part of the divine plan to bring Christianity to the world. God was 'the author of its progress' (*serm.* 82B.2). The role of the bishop of Rome and heir of St Peter is obviously reinforced by such a reading of history. The teaching authority of the prince of the apostles is transmitted through possession of the chair (*cathedra*) of St Peter, which gives the see of Rome its status as 'head of the world'. The fall of pagan Rome in 410 thus was not, for Leo, the great catastrophe for civilisation that Jerome believed it to be, but rather a point of transition where the old was left behind and Christian Rome took a new and triumphant beginning at the forefront of God's plan for the conversion of all nations.

In Recension B Leo calls pagan Rome 'the teacher of error' and Christian Rome 'the disciple of truth'. The second recension tones down the military imagery of the original somewhat (e.g. Leo refers to 'people' rather than 'ranks' surrounding the city), but makes more of pagan Rome as a crucible of vice: the opinions of philosophers, the vanity of worldly wisdom, the cult of demons, religious cults of every kind (*serm.* 82B.2) were all gathered in one place where they could be destroyed simultaneously. He draws a striking picture of Christ and the devil competing for power over Rome: as strongly as the devil held the city in his grip, so much more miraculous is its liberation by Christ (*serm.* 82B.2). We can compare *Homily* 84.1, where a similar contrast is made between apostles and demons as protectors of the city. In Recension B Leo also alludes to the more ignominious aspects of Rome's origin myth, the story of Romulus and Remus, twin sons of Mars, god of war, and the priestess Rhea Silvia, a Vestal Virgin. According to the tradition passed down in Livy's *History of Rome* 1.4–6, the infants were left for dead on the mudflats of the river Tiber but were found and suckled by a she-wolf. They were then taken to safety by a shepherd named Faustulus, and brought up by him and his wife. As adults they were rivals for rule over the new foundation of Rome, and Romulus killed his brother Remus in 753 BCE. Romulus, after whom the city was named, lived up to his father's reputation in his aggressive expansion of Roman territory. Romulus's first act as king was to consolidate the city walls on the Palatine Hill. Perhaps the most significant variation in the third recension is the allusion to the walls founded by Romulus and Remus around Rome (*serm.* 82C.1), which find a parallel further on in the crowd of martyrs surrounding the city like a protective wall (*serm.* 82B.6).

In Leo's appropriation of this myth we can see a transformation of the city's typology taking place. Apostrophising Rome, Leo declares that Peter and Paul were 'your holy fathers and true shepherds', thus replacing Faustulus. They were Rome's true founders, 'who founded you to be included in the heavenly kingdom', so much more blessed than the temporal kingdom of Romulus. Unlike the warring twins Romulus and Remus, the two chief apostles, Peter and Paul, are equals: their election, their trials and their execution made them peers. In an echo of Tertullian, Leo praises the persecutions which increase rather than diminish the church (*serm.* 82B.6). Recension A ends with an appeal to Peter and Paul, the special patrons of the city, to pray for God's mercy (*serm.* 82A.6).

Translated from CCSL 138a: 508–18.

Text

On the feast of the Apostles.

1. The whole world partakes in all the holy feasts, dearly beloved, and the devotion of the one faith demands that any action for the salvation of all that is observed anew should be celebrated everywhere with equal joy. Nevertheless, apart from that respect which it deserves in the whole world,[1] today's feast should be venerated with special delight by our city in particular: so that in the place where the death of the foremost apostles (sc. Peter and Paul) is glorified, there is found supreme happiness on the day of their martyrdom. For they are the men through whom the gospel of Christ shone brightly on you, Rome, and you who had been the teacher of error became the disciple of truth.[2] They are your holy fathers and true shepherds, who founded you to be included in the heavenly kingdom, far better and much more happily than those men[3] of whom the one who gave you his name defiled you with fratricide.[4] They (sc. Peter and Paul) are the ones who advanced you to this point of glory,[5] so that as a holy nation, a chosen people, a priestly and royal city (cf. 1 Pet. 2: 9), you – made head of the world[6] through the sacred chair of blessed Peter – would command more widely by virtue of divine religion than by earthly domination. For although you extended the law of your power over land and sea, increased by many victories, nevertheless what the effort of warfare conquered for you is less than what the Christian peace has made subject to you.

2. Since God is truly good and just and almighty, and has never denied his mercy to the human race, and has always taught all mortals in common to understand him through his most generous kindness, he took pity on the voluntary blindness of sinners and their wickedness that was inclined to moral degeneration, by a more secret plan and deeper devotion, by sending his Word, who is equal to him and coeternal with him. The Word made flesh (cf. John 1: 14) united the divine nature to human nature in such a way that his inclination to the

115

depths became our progress to the heights. But so that the effect of his ineffable grace (cf. 2 Cor. 9: 14) would spread throughout the whole world, divine providence prepared the Roman empire, whose growth reached as far as those borders that would join it with all other peoples as neighbours on all sides. For indeed it was absolutely appropriate to the divine plan that many kingdoms would be joined under one power, and that the general message would quickly be able to pass through peoples who were held under the rule of a single state. But this state, ignoring the author of its progress,[7] since it was master over almost all races, used to serve the errors of all races, and seemed to itself to have adopted a great religion because it rejected none as false. So, as strongly as it was held bound by the devil's grip, it is so much more miraculously freed by Christ.[8]

3. For when the twelve apostles – who had received from the Holy Spirit the ability to speak in every tongue, and were assigned to the various regions of the earth – had undertaken to spread the Gospel through the world, most blessed Peter, the prince of the apostolic order, was headed for the stronghold of Roman power.[9] This happened so that the light of truth that was being revealed for the salvation of all peoples would pour forth more effectively from the very head throughout the whole body of the world.[10] But what nationality was not present in this city then? What races ever ignored what Rome had learnt? Here the philosophical opinions had to be crushed, here the vanities of worldly wisdom had to be dissolved, here the cult of demons had to be suppressed, here the impiety of every sacrilege had to be destroyed, where an inventory was held, through the most diligent superstition, of whatever had ever been invented by various errors.

4. And so you did not fear to come to this city, most blessed apostle Peter,[11] and while your companion in glory, the apostle Paul, was still occupied in organising other churches, you entered this forest of raging beasts and the stormy depths of (this) ocean more steadily than when you walked upon the sea (cf. Matt. 14: 30). Nor did you fear Rome, the mistress of the world, you who had been terrified in Caiaphas's house by the (high) priest's maid (cf. Matt. 26: 69–70). For surely the power of Claudius or the cruelty of Nero was no less than the judgement of Pilate, or the violence of the Jews? Thus the power of love conquered the object of fear; and you did not regard as a source of fear[12] those whom you had undertaken to love. But by then, in fact, you had already conceived this ardour[13] of fearless love when the profession of your love for the Lord was confirmed in the mystery of the question he asked three times (cf. John 21: 15–17). Nothing else was sought by this focusing of your mind, except that you should

serve the food on which you yourself grew fat,[14] to feed the sheep of him whom you loved.

5. So many miraculous signs were also increasing your confidence, so many gifts of the Holy Spirit, so many experiences of spiritual powers. You'd already instructed the people who had believed after circumcision (sc. the Jews).[15] Already you'd founded the church of Antioch, where the dignity of the Christian name first arose (cf. Acts 11: 26), already you'd fully provided Pontus, Galatia, Cappadocia, Asia and Bithynia with the commands of the gospel message.[16] Nor were you doubtful about the yield of (your) work, nor ignorant of the space of time allotted to you (cf. 2 Peter 1: 14). You were bringing the trophy of the cross of Christ to Roman strongholds, where both the honour of your power and the glory of your martyrdom preceded you by divine predestination.[17]

6. Your blessed fellow apostle Paul, *the chosen instrument* (Acts 9: 15), and special *teacher of the gentiles* (1 Tim. 2: 7), upon coming to Rome, was companion to you at that time, when already all innocence, all shame and every liberty were oppressed under the rule of Nero. His (sc. Nero's) fury, inflamed through his excess in every vice, tipped him into a torrent of madness, to the point where he was the first to inflict on the Christian name the atrocity of widespread persecution, as if the grace of God could be extinguished by the slaughter of his saints.[18] This was its greatest profit: that their scorn for this hour of mortal life would become the gaining of eternal happiness. Thus *the death of his holy ones is precious in the sight of the Lord* (Ps. 116: 15), and no act of cruelty can destroy the religion founded on the mystery of the cross of Christ. For the church is increased, not lessened, by persecutions. And the Lord's field is always covered with a richer crop as long as the grains which fall down singly spring up multiplied.[19] So those two outstanding sprouts of the divine sowing have increased into as many plants, as the thousands of blessed martyrs testify. Emulating the apostles' victories, they've surrounded our city with people[20] clad in purple and shining far and wide, and they've crowned it like a single[21] diadem entwined with the glory of many precious stones.

7. Dearly beloved, as we commemorate all the saints there should be universal rejoicing over this protection, which was divinely prepared for us as a model of endurance and a confirmation of our faith. But the excellence of these (two) fathers deserves prouder boasting, whom the grace of God has advanced to the highest honour among all the members of the church, by placing them[22] like the light of a pair of eyes in the body, whose head is Christ. We should see no difference and no variation in their merits and powers, which surpass all

117

powers of speech, because their election made them peers, and their trials made them alike, and their end made them equals.[23] Through our Lord Jesus Christ, who shares equal glory and power with the Father and the Holy Spirit, one Godhead for ever and ever. Amen.

Homily 84 on the anniversary of Alaric's sack of Rome

Introduction

The title of this homily comes from a Dublin codex dating from the thirteenth to fourteenth centuries (CCSL 138a: 523). The Gothic leader Alaric's third and final siege of Rome lasted three days, from 25 to 27 August 410. Alaric, being an Arian, respected the sanctity of martyr shrines and church sanctuaries, in which many Christians and not a few pagans took refuge: Augustine even claims that the enemy delivered some of their captives to the sanctuaries for their safety (*De civitate Dei* 1.1, PL 41: 14). The city itself was not destroyed, a decision which Leo attributes to the intercession of the saints (*serm.* 84.1), although the Goths departed with much booty and many hostages. The salvation of the people was the reason for thanksgiving offered on the anniversary of the siege, an annual commemoration that may have been established by Pope Innocent I, as Michele Salzman has argued (forthcoming). Innocent himself was absent from the city at the time of Alaric's final invasion, having departed for the safety of Ravenna as part of the second embassy to Emperor Honorius in 409. Innocent probably returned to Rome at some point after the final siege, but in 413 he went back to Ravenna, where his court remained for some considerable time (Dunn 2009). Several scholars have seen reference here to the two-week siege of Geiseric, who withdrew from the city on 29 June 455, and have therefore placed the sermon with others delivered in the Octave of Peter and Paul, after 29 June (SC 200: 66 n.2). Superficial evidence for a date in the mid 450s is found in Leo's reference to circus games (*serm.* 84.1), which were a feature of the *Ludi Apollinares*, held from 6 to 13 July and still going strong in the mid fifth century in Rome. However, the end of Alaric's siege in 410 also coincided with the celebration of circus games on 28 August (CCSL 138a: 523). Chavasse argued from manuscript evidence that this homily belongs to the first collection, being delivered between 440 and 445. His conclusion is confirmed by Leo's reference to the people of Rome's recent neglect of this occasion for thanksgiving (*serm.* 84.1). This suggests that the ritual had become less popular over a long period of time. This sermon therefore was mostly likely delivered, as

Chavasse maintained, on 30 August or 6 September 442, being the first Sunday after 28 August, the date of Alaric's departure from the city in 410 (CCSL 138a: 525).

Leo portrays the salvation of this city as a triumph of the saints over demons, omitting to mention that Alaric himself was a Christian of sorts. Leo attributes the sparing of citizens during the sack of Rome to the protection of the saints in whose shrines Christians and others took refuge. This is not an appeal to a new kind of Roman triumphalism – after all, Alaric's sack of Rome was an ignominious defeat for the city – but a plea to honour its new patrons, the martyr-saints who had proved more powerful than the pagan gods of traditional state religion. We find here a rare reference to the number of people present in the liturgy, which Leo considers pitifully small (*serm.* 84.1). The theme of a popular preference for empty spectacles over Christian liturgies is also found in the preaching of near-contemporaries such as John Chrysostom and Augustine. Leo's lament that more is spent on demons than on the apostles brings to mind Augustine's complaint that people would rather throw away their money putting it on lavish games than give it to the poor (*Enarrationes in Psalmos* 102.13; Dekkers and Fraipont 1956: 1463). As Salzman observes, in this homily Leo seems to assume responsibility for God's good favour towards the city of Rome in much the same way as Roman emperors, in their role as *pontifex maximus*, gave thanks to the gods on occasions of imperial victories (Salzman forthcoming). Christian emperors continued to adopt the title of *pontifex maximus* up until the rule of Gratian (367–83). Constantine I, as the first Christian emperor, simply changed the focus of thanks to the one God of the Christians, as, for instance, in his offering of thanksgiving after his 'liberation' of Rome from 'the tyrant' Maxentius in 312 (Eusebius of Caesarea, *Vita Constantini* 1.38–9, Richardson 1890: 492–3). The adoption of this civic role is one more way in which the bishop of Rome reinforced his authority, in conjunction with welfare activities on behalf of the poor and displaced, diplomatic negotiations, ransoming of prisoners, and an extensive building and repair programme within the city (Neil forthcoming).

Translated from CCSL 138a: 525–6.

Text

Commemorating the day when Alaric invaded Rome.[24]

1. Dearly beloved, the religious devotion with which the whole congregation of the faithful used to come together for thanksgiving, on account of the day of our chastening and our liberation, has lately

been neglected by almost everyone, as the rare few who are present demonstrate: and my heart has been touched by great sadness and struck by a very great fear. For it is a grave danger when people are ungrateful to God, and through forgetfulness of his goodness feel no remorse at reproof nor gladness in pardon. I fear, therefore, dearly beloved, lest the prophet's words be seen as a reproach to such people, when he says: *You beat them and they did not grieve; you chastened them, and they refused to receive discipline* (Jer. 5: 3). For what correction appears in those in whom such great aversion is found? It shames me to say it, but it's necessary to speak out: more is spent on demons than on the apostles, and the empty spectacles attract greater crowds than the blessed martyr shrines.[25] Who restored this city to safety? Who snatched it from captivity? Who defended it from slaughter? The circus games,[26] or the care of the saints by whose prayers the divine decision to punish was altered, so that we who deserved wrath were saved for pardon?

2. I beg you, dearly beloved, to let your hearts be touched by the words of the Saviour, who, when he had cleansed the ten lepers by his merciful power, said that only one returned to thank him (cf. Luke 17: 11–19), meaning, of course, that the ungrateful failed in this pious duty. Even if they had attained wholeness of body, (they were) not, however, without impiety of mind. Therefore, lest that same mark of ingratitude be ascribed to you, dearly beloved, turn back to the Lord and grasp the miracles which he saw fit to perform amongst us. Attribute our liberation, not, as the godless think, to the effects of the stars,[27] but to the ineffable mercy of the almighty God, who saw fit to soften the hearts of the raging barbarians, and devote yourselves to commemorating so great an act of mercy with all the strength of your faith. The more serious the neglect, the greater the satisfaction required. Let's benefit from the mercy of the one who spares us for our improvement: so that blessed Peter and all the saints who have been with us through many trials might see fit to support our prayers to merciful God on your behalf, through Christ our Lord.

Letter 6 to Anastasius, Metropolitan of Thessalonica

Introduction

This is Leo's first letter to Anastasius, bishop of Thessalonica. Thessalonica was the major city in Eastern Illyricum, and came under Byzantine rule at the end of the fourth century. Prior to Theodosius I, jurisdiction over the civil prefecture of Illyricum, now known as the

Balkans, had been subject to a variety of administrative arrangements. After his accession Theodosius I divided the new prefecture of Eastern Illyricum into two civil dioceses, Dacia and Macedonia. The diocese of Macedonia included Thessaly, Greece and Epirus. Western Illyricum became a diocese, Pannonia, in the prefecture of Italy. Law and order in Pannonia was maintained by a vicar of the praetorian prefect of Italy, based at Sirmium; in the East, by the praetorian prefect of Illyricum, based at Thessalonica. The location of Thessalonica on the major trade and communications route between the eastern and western parts of the Roman empire made the city strategically important. The Egnatian Road ran from Constantinople, through Thessalonica, to the port city of Dyrrachium, which afforded easy sea access to the eastern coast of Southern Italy (Moorhead 2001: 157–8). The general Stilicho's ambition to reclaim Eastern Illyricum for the western empire made the region an area of contest from 406 until his death in 408.

After Attila struck Sirmium, the capital of Western Illyricum, in 440–1, he could hold the eastern empire to ransom. During the 440s Constantinople paid out around 13,000 pounds of gold to keep the Huns in check (Moorhead 2001: 160). While much of the Balkans was devastated by the Huns, the Byzantine policy of containment worked. Thus the boundary between Eastern and Western Illyricum became an important line of defence for the security of the eastern empire.

In parallel with the secular power struggle over the civil dioceses of Illyricum, bishops of Rome and Constantinople fought for ecclesiastical control over the region. From the late fourth century, bishops of Rome had tried to maintain their influence over the eastern part by making the bishops of Thessalonica their 'vicars' or representatives.[28] In *Letter* 6 of 12 January 444, Leo responds positively to the new bishop of Thessalonica's request for the papal authority assigned to his predecessors. We can assume that Anastasius had been ordained in the previous year. Leo extends the power to act in his name with a strict caution: Anastasius is to abide strictly by the canons, especially in relation to clerical ordination. One existing abuse is already singled out in this letter: priests and deacons were being ordained on days other than Sunday, and without observing the proper period of formation. Another ongoing problem discussed here is the ordination of married bishops. Anastasius is instructed to refer to Rome any difficult matter arising at local councils. Illyrian bishops were to maintain the right of appeal against the papal vicar, a right which Anastasius was not keen to uphold, as future events revealed. In *c.* 446 Atticus, metropolitan bishop of Old Epirus, appealed to Rome. He had been summoned to

Thessalonica to sign a pledge of obedience, and when he failed to appear, on the grounds of ill-health, was forcibly removed there by officers of the praetorian prefect of Illyricum. Leo was outraged, both by the treatment of an aged and sick bishop, and by the use of secular powers to implement ecclesiastical business. As Leo pointed out in a famous dictum, he had called Anastasius 'to share in our pastoral concern, not in the fullness of our powers' (*ep.* 14.1, PL 54: 671B).[29]

On the same day as *Letter* 6 was issued, Leo notified all the metropolitan bishops in the provinces of Illyricum of Anastasius's new position as vicar of the apostolic see (*ep.* 5, ST 23: 57–9). Anastasius was given the sole right to ordain metropolitans, and also the power of veto over ordination of bishops by those metropolitans in their own provinces, if they contravened canon law. Anastasius was succeeded by Euxitheus: the consecration of his unnamed successor is announced in *Letter* 117 of March 453. The Roman vicariate lasted for almost a century, until it was lost during the Acacian Schism (484–519), the first great schism between Greece and Rome. The vicariate was eventually restored, and even after the Byzantines lost control of Eastern Illyricum in the sixth century, Rome's claim to jurisdiction over the eastern ecclesiastical province continued apparently uncontested until the mid eighth century. Pope Hadrian I (*c.* 785) unsuccessfully contested ecclesiastical jurisdiction over the churches of Eastern Illyricum, Sicily and Calabria, all by then under Byzantine control, and in the following century Pope Nicholas I (858–67) was unable to reinstate the vicariate of Thessalonica, despite his best efforts.

Translated from ST 23: 53–7.

Text

Leo to his most beloved brother Anastasius.

1. Love for our brotherly[30] colleagues makes us read over the letters of all bishops[31] with glad hearts indeed since, through spiritual grace, we embrace as if present those whom we engage in mutual conversation through the exchange of letters. But that affection seems greater to us[32] in this (letter) which, by informing us about the state of the churches, compels us out of consideration for our duty to exercise careful vigilance. Being established in watchtowers, as the Lord wished,[33] we should furnish our assent to the events which occur in accordance with our will, and we should correct those things which we see being distorted by some abuse of power. (We do so) by applying the remedies of coercion, in the hope that the seed that is sown will

yield abundant fruit for us, if we do not allow to grow those elements which have begun to sprout to the detriment of the Lord's harvest.

2. And so our son priest Nicholas informed us of your beloved's request that we offer you, too, authority throughout Illyricum in our stead, as (was done) for your predecessors, in order to maintain the canons. While we give our assent, we urge by our exhortation that there be no dissimulation or negligence concerning the government of the churches located in Illyricum, which we assign to Your Beloved in our place, following the example of Siricius of blessed memory.[34] By a fixed plan he assigned (them) then for the first time to your predecessor, Anysius of holy memory[35] – who was (considered) very worthy of the apostolic see at that time and proved so by subsequent events – so that he might assist the churches located throughout that province which he wanted to be kept under discipline. Excellent examples should be followed with haste, and we should demonstrate ourselves in every way like those whose privileges we wish to enjoy. We want you to imitate your predecessor (sc. Rufus) as much as his predecessor (sc. Anysius), who is known to have deserved this (privilege) equally and to have carried it out similarly, so that we might rejoice in the advancement of the churches that we assign to you in our place. Just as a delegated task brings honour to the one who does it well and pursues with skill whatever befits episcopal authority, so it is recognised as a burden for him who does not use the power assigned to him with due moderation.

3. And so hold most carefully the helm entrusted to you, dearest brother, and turn your mind's eye to everything which you see enjoined to your care, protecting what will bring you future reward, and resisting whatever tries to obstruct discipline according to the canons. The sanction of divine law should be respected and the decrees of the canons preserved most of all. Throughout the provinces assigned to you, consecrate such bishops to the Lord as are chosen solely for the merits of their lives and their clerical rank. Do not allow any room for personal favours, or canvassing of votes, or bribery. Make a careful assessment of those who are to be ordained and during their whole lifespan let them be imbued with church discipline. They should be accepted, however, if they meet all the conditions that were observed by the holy fathers, and they conform to what we read in the blessed apostle Paul's instructions about such men – namely, that they have only one wife (1 Tim. 3: 2), and that *she was a virgin* (Lev. 21: 13) – as the authority of the divine law dictates. And we want this to be observed so carefully that we refuse any possibility of exceptions, lest anyone believe himself capable of gaining the bishopric[36] who took a wife before he received

the grace of Christ,[37] and upon her death married another woman after his baptism, since that (first) wife cannot be denied, nor can the previous marriage be uncounted.[38] And he is just as much the father of those children whom he had by her before his baptism, as he is the father of those whom he is known to have had by the other woman after his baptism.[39] For just as only[40] sins and deeds known to be forbidden are washed away by the waters of baptism, in the same way what is allowed or permitted by the law's teaching is not annulled.

4. No one should be ordained bishop in those churches without consulting you. For in that way mature decisions will be made as to who should be elected, as long as there is fear of Your Beloved's scrutiny. But whoever is ordained among the metropolitan bishops without your notice, contrary to our instructions, should know that there will be no confirmation of his status by us, and those who have made this presumption will render an account for their usurpation of powers. But just as that power is assigned to individual metropolitans, so that they hold the right to ordain in their provinces, so we wish those metropolitans to be ordained by you, though only after mature and seasoned judgement.[41] For although it is fitting for all who are consecrated bishops to be approved and pleasing to God, nevertheless we want them to stand out, whom we know will preside over fellow bishops who belong to them. So we warn Your Beloved to tread carefully and with caution, so that you are shown to observe that apostolic injunction: *Do not lay hands on anyone hastily* (1 Tim. 5: 22).[42]

5. Let any brother who is called to a council attend, and not withdraw himself from the holy gathering, where he knows that those matters should be particularly shared, which could effect church discipline. For every fault will be better avoided if meetings of the Lord's bishops are held more frequently. A united gathering offers much scope for improvement and equally for charity. If any problems arise there, they can be dealt with as the Lord directs in such a way that no controversy remains, but the brothers are bound together by love alone. But if any major problem comes up which cannot be resolved there under Your Brotherhood's direction, you should consult us by sending your account of the trial, so that by the Lord's revelation, by whose mercy we claim to be what we are, we may write back what God himself has inspired in us. This way we may claim for our examination (cases)[43] by our inquiry, in line with the tradition founded of old and the reverence owed to the apostolic see. For, just as we wish you to exercise your authority in our place, in the same way we reserve for ourselves those matters that cannot be settled there, or anyone sending a word of appeal.

6. And you should bring these matters to the attention of all the brothers in such a way that, from now on, no one can be excused out of ignorance from observing these precepts of ours. We have sent our decretal to the metropolitans of individual provinces,[44] warning them so that they know that obedience to the apostolic judgements is required, and that they obey us when they begin to comply with Your Brotherhood who is our delegate, in accordance with our writings. We realise, of course, that we cannot pass over in silence the fact that only bishops are ordained on Sundays by certain of our brothers, but priests and deacons – concerning whom an equal (time) of consecration should (be observed)[45] – here and there receive the dignity of priestly office on any day at all. This abuse committed against the canons[46] and the tradition of the Fathers should be corrected, since the custom handed down to us concerning all holy orders ought to be preserved in every way. In that way, through the lengthy passage of time, those who are going to be ordained as priests or deacons should proceed through every rank of clerical office, so that they learn from day to day what they will eventually teach.

Sent on 12 January in the consulship of Theodosius (for the eighteenth time) and Albinus.[47]

Homily 4 on the anniversary of Leo's ordination

Introduction

Homily 4 is the fourth in a series of five homilies from the first collection, given on the fourth anniversary of Leo's ordination, 29 September 444. The main focus of this homily is the unity of the church, consisting in the proper relationship between the head and its parts. This homily was delivered in the year that Leo's dispute with Hilary of Arles came to a head (SC 200: 19–21), and we can sense here echoes of his concern to reassert the authority of Rome over the bishops of Gaul. Presumably he had in mind a wider audience for *Homily* 4 in its written form. Valentinian III's edict of June or July in the following year reinforced the bishop of Rome's authority in unambiguous terms, by insisting that all appeals had to be made directly to Rome. It also forbade the bishops of Gaul from acting against the bishop of Rome. Another significant event of this period was the investigation against Manicheans in Rome over eighteen months from 443 to 444. This was a true test of Leo's authority, but also of his duty to protect his flock from heresy. Again, Leo's judgements were given imperial backing in the edict of June 445.[48]

The main theme of the first section of *Homily* 4 is the church united under one faith and one baptism. Rather than recalling the familiar Pauline passage (1 Cor. 12: 12–26) to explain the proper relationship between the head of the church and its members, Leo turns to a less commonly exegeted text, the first letter of Peter. Leo's honour as head of the church is shared by the church as a whole. By 'the single sacrament of high priesthood' the whole body of the church is blessed and anointed as a royal people, sharing in the priestly office (cf. 1 Pet. 2: 9). Leo's emphasis in *Homily* 4.2–4 on the power and authority handed down by Peter is partly explained by the fact that this part of the text has been recycled from *Homily* 83, delivered the preceding year on the feast of Saints Peter and Paul, 29 June 443.

The foundation of Peter's power to 'reign over all' is twofold: first, his correct confession of Christ (*serm.* 4.2) and second, God's forgiveness after his betrayal and repentance (*serm.* 4.3). Just as Peter denied Christ three times, he was given the chance to repent and confess his love for the Lord three times (*serm.* 4.4). As Uhalde points out, Leo's acknowledgement of the weakness and uncertainty at the heart of the first leader of the church has often been ignored in favour of the more triumphalist aspects of Leo's anniversary homilies, especially *Homily* 5 (Uhalde forthcoming). However, Leo's concern as a bishop is to point out that his own authority as head of the church is based on the power entrusted to Peter, a fallible human being. As a pastor he wants to remind his flock that forgiveness is available to all who truly repent. Just as Jesus prayed for Peter lest he be overcome, Peter now prays for all Christians that they might remain firm in the face of temptation, but with particular concern for those Christians in the city where he was laid to eternal rest (*serm.* 4.4). Once again, the element of spiritual civic pride is being fostered here.

Just as Christ is the head of the church and all its members, Leo is appointed head of the church through his direct descent in the episcopal line established by the apostle Peter. As he declares in *Hom.* 4.2, 'Peter alone is chosen, who is put in charge of the calling of all peoples, and of all the apostles, and all the Fathers of the church.' The notion of the calling of all peoples is important to Leo, and relates to his reading of Gal. 3: 16–17. Leo's understanding of these verses is strictly Pauline:[49] through Abraham, and his direct descendant Christ, God blessed all peoples who receive the inheritance of salvation through God's gift of his son. On this reading Leo based his doctrine of universal salvation, the idea that salvation is offered to all through Jesus, even if all do not take it up. The establishment of a direct line from Abraham to Christ was critical to the early church, as indicated by the pseudo-historical genealogies included in chronicles of the history of the church, from Eusebius of Caesarea's *Chronography* onwards. Likewise, the direct episcopal line from Peter to Leo was reinforced by the forged *Letter of Clement to James the brother of the Lord*, which was translated into Latin by Rufinus at the end of the fourth century and circulated in Italy in the fifth century (Neil 2003: 25–39). This letter, a confection of the late second or early third centuries, represents Clement, fourth bishop of Rome[50] (*c.* 95 CE), as claiming anointment by the hand of the apostle Peter himself. The author of the forgery sought to clear up any confusion that might be occasioned by the somewhat obscure line of succession from Peter through Linus and Anacletus, a problem that is neatly glossed over in the *Liber Pontificalis*. The sixth-century compiler of the *Liber Pontificalis* endorses the forgery in these words: 'On St Peter's instruction he (sc. Clement) undertook the pontificate for governing the church, as the *cathedra* had been handed down and entrusted to him by the Lord Jesus Christ; you will find in the letter written to James how the church was entrusted to him by Peter' (*LP Clement* ch. 1, Davis 2000: 3). The seat (*cathedra*) from which the bishop of Rome handed down doctrine was the symbol of his Petrine authority.

In his conclusion, Leo dedicates the anniversary of his ordination to Peter. Through Peter's patronage Leo became bishop of Rome. Through Peter's prayers of intercession Leo is strengthened and nourished. Peter is the good shepherd who feeds Christ's lambs, just as Leo is acknowledged as 'the good shepherd' who keeps the wolf away from the flock.

Translated from CCSL 138: 16–21.

Text

On the anniversary of his own ordination.

1. I rejoice, dearly beloved, in the affection of your religious devotion, and I give thanks to God because I recognise in you the proper conduct of Christian unity. For as your numerous presence itself indicates,[51] you understand that the return of this day concerns the happiness of the community, and the annual feast of the shepherd celebrates the honour of the whole flock. For although the whole church of God is assigned different levels, so that the wholeness of the sacred body subsists in the different members; nevertheless, as the apostle says, we are *all one in Christ* (Gal. 3: 28); nor is anyone so separate in function from another that any humble part has no connection to the head. Therefore in unity of faith and baptism (cf. Eph.

4: 5), dearly beloved, our fellowship is undivided and my dignity is shared by all, according to the gospel of the most blessed apostle Peter, who spoke the most sacred words: *And you yourselves like living stones are built up into spiritual homes, a holy priesthood, making spiritual sacrifices acceptable to God through Jesus Christ* (1 Pet. 2: 5); and further on: *But you are a chosen people, a royal priesthood, a holy nation, a people belonging (to God)* (1 Pet. 2: 9). For all who are reborn in Christ are made kings through the sign of the cross, (and) are consecrated priests by the anointing of the Holy Spirit; so that apart from the special service of my ministry, all spiritual and rational Christians recognise themselves as belonging to a kingly race, and sharing in the priestly office. For what is so kingly as a soul that is subject to God yet rules over its own body? And what is so priestly as to dedicate to the Lord a clean conscience, and to offer pure sacrifices of devotion on the altar of the heart? Since this has been shared by all, through the grace of God, it shows your devotion and you deserve praise when you rejoice in the day of my advancement as if in your own honour (cf. 1 Cor. 12: 26); so that a single sacrament of high priesthood[52] is celebrated in the whole body of the church. When the ointment of blessing was poured out, it flowed forth indeed more abundantly on the upper limbs, but proceeded down unsparingly even on the lower limbs.

2. And so, dearly beloved, since there is great cause for common rejoicing for us in the sharing of this gift, there will, however, be a reason for us to rejoice that is more true and excellent, if you are not hindered by consideration of my humility. For it is much more useful and worthy to raise the power of the mind to contemplate the glory of most blessed Peter the apostle, and to celebrate this day chiefly in veneration of him. (For) he has been flooded with such abundant streams from the very source of all spiritual gifts that, since he alone received many (gifts), nothing has passed to anyone else without his sharing in it. The Word made flesh was already living among us (cf. John 1: 14), and Christ had devoted himself wholly to restoring the human race. Nothing was unforeseen by his wisdom, nothing was beyond his power. The elements were at his service (cf. Matt. 8: 27), the spirits attended him, the angels served him (cf. Matt. 4: 11), nor could the sacrament, which the oneness of the Godhead itself and the Trinity performed together, fail in any way. And yet, from the whole world, Peter alone is chosen, who is put in charge of the calling of all peoples, and of all the apostles, and all the Fathers of the church. And so, although there are many priests among the people of God and many shepherds, yet Peter properly reigns over all whom Christ also

rules first of all. To this man, dearly beloved, the divine dignity attributed a great and marvellous share of its power. And if it (sc. the divine dignity) wanted other leaders to have something in common with him (sc. Peter), it never gave whatever it granted to others[53] except through Peter.

The Lord asked all the apostles what people were saying about him, and their communal response went on for so long as to reveal the ambiguity of human understanding.[54] And when he demanded the opinion of the disciples, the one who is first in apostolic dignity was first to confess the Lord. When he had said: *You are Christ the Son of the living God*, Jesus answered him: *Blessed are you, Simon son of Jonas, because flesh and blood did not reveal this to you, but my Father who is in heaven* (Matt. 16: 16–17). That is to say, you are blessed for this reason: that my Father taught you this, and you were not deceived by worldly opinion, but instructed by heavenly inspiration. For neither flesh nor blood revealed me to you, but he whose only-born son I am (revealed me). *And I say to you*, he said, – that is, just as my Father showed my divinity to you, so too I make known to you your excellence – *that you are Peter* (Matt. 16: 18a). That is to say, although I am the inviolable rock, I am the cornerstone (cf. Eph. 2: 20), who makes two one (cf. Eph. 2: 14), I am *the foundation and no one can lay any other* (1 Cor. 3: 11), yet you are also a rock, because you stand strong through my power. What is mine by my power, you will share by participation in me.[55] *Upon this rock I will build my church, and the gates of hell will not prevail against it* (Matt. 16: 18b). Upon this strength, he says, I will build an everlasting temple, and the height of my church as it thrusts up to heaven will stand on the firmness of his faith.

3. The gates of hell will not hold back this confession, the ties of death will not bind it. For that word is the word of life, and just as those who confess it are raised to heaven, those who deny it sink into hell. This is why it was said to the most blessed Peter: *I will give you the keys to the kingdom of heaven: and whatever you bind on earth will be bound also in heaven, and whatever you loose on earth will be loosed also in heaven* (Matt. 16: 19).[56] The right of that power indeed also passed to the other apostles, and the institution of this decision passed on to all the leaders of the church, but not without reason does he entrust to one what is made familiar to many. For he entrusts it to Peter alone for this reason: that Peter is set before all church leaders as a model. Therefore the privilege of Peter is maintained everywhere that judgement is made in virtue of his fairness. There is not too much severity or too much concession, where there is nothing bound or loosed except what blessed Peter has either bound or loosed. Now,

when the Lord's passion, which was to shake the faithfulness of his disciples, was approaching, he said: *Simon, Simon, look, Satan has demanded you, in order to sift you like wheat. But I have prayed for you, that your faith may not fail; and when you have recovered, you must strengthen your brothers* (Luke 22: 31–2) *lest you*[57] *enter into temptation* (Luke 22: 40). There was a shared danger for all the disciples in the temptation to fear, and they were equally in need of the aid of divine protection, since the devil was longing to persecute and crush them all. Nevertheless the Lord took special care of Peter, and for Peter's faith he prayed especially, as though the condition of the others would be more secure if the soul of the leader was not overcome. In Peter therefore the strength of all is fortified,[58] and the help of divine grace is dispensed in such a way that the steadfastness which is attributed to Peter through Christ is conferred on the apostles through Peter.

4. And so, dearly beloved, since we see such protection divinely decreed for us, we rejoice with good reason in the merits and worthiness of our leader. We give thanks to the eternal King, our redeemer the Lord Jesus Christ, because he gave such great power to him whom he made the prince of the whole church, so that whatever I perform rightly and prescribe properly in my time, should be accounted to his works (and) to his governing. To Peter it was said: *And when you have recovered, you must strengthen your brothers* (Luke 22: 32), and to him the resurrected Lord said three times: *Feed my sheep* (John 21: 17), in a mystical inculcation for a threefold confession of eternal love. That is what he is doing now in fact, fulfilling the command of the Lord as a good shepherd, strengthening us by his encouragement and never ceasing to pray for us,[59] so that we are not overcome by any temptation. But if this devoted concern of his extends to all the people of God everywhere, as we ought to believe, how much more should he see fit to offer his help to us, his nurslings, among whom he rests on the sacred bed of blessed sleep, in the same body with which he governed.[60] Therefore may I dedicate this anniversary of my service and this feast to him. By his patronage I have merited to share in his see, always aided by the grace of our Lord Jesus Christ, who lives and reigns with God the Father and the Holy Spirit, for ever and ever. Amen.

10

ADMINISTRATOR OF THE WIDER CHURCH

Letter 2 to Septimus, Bishop of Altinum

Introduction

This letter on the subject of Pelagian clergy was addressed to the bishop of Altinum, a wealthy city of the province of Venice and Histria, on the Adriatic sea board. The city was destroyed in the Huns' invasion of northern Italy in 452. Aquileia suffered the same fate, being almost razed to the ground, and Milan surrendered itself to the invaders rather than face destruction. However, at the time of this letter, Aquileia, at the head of the Adriatic, was one of the most important ecclesiastical centres in northern Italy, and its archbishop functioned as metropolitan for the province to which Altinum belonged.

The letter dates to the early years of Leo's pontificate, with most commentators following the Ballerini in dating it to *c.* 442.[1] This assumption is made on the grounds of its close links with *Letter* 1, addressed to an unnamed bishop (PL 54: 594–5).[2] *Letter* 1 refers to Leo's own decretals forbidding clerics to move from one see to another against the canons (*ep.* 1.5). The earliest decretal issued by Leo on this subject seems to be *Letter* 14 to Anastasius, bishop of Thessaloniki, which was issued after 6 January 446.[3] On these grounds I would suggest a somewhat later date than 442 for both *Letters* 1 and 2.[4] The latest possible date for *Letter* 2 would seem to be 30 December 447, when *Letter* 18 was sent to Januarius, the bishop of Aquileia (PL 54: 706–9).[5]

There are strong similarities in the content of *Letters* 1 and 2, as one would expect, since Leo names Bishop Septimus, the recipient of *Letter* 2, as his source of information on the difficulties that the Aquileian see was having with Pelagianism (*ep.* 1.1). Leo's opposition to Pelagianism began long before his accession to the pontificate in 441. Pelagians had been expelled from Italy in 418 by an imperial rescript of Honorius.

However, Caelestius had returned to Italy in the early 430s, after being expelled from Constantinople in 430 along with Julian, bishop of Eclanum, and other Pelagian clergy.[6] In 431 Pelagius and his followers, among them the Italian jurist Caelestius and Julian of Eclanum, were condemned at the Council of Ephesus. As deacon under Sixtus III, Leo was instrumental in preventing Julian of Eclanum from regaining his see in 439. Julian's opposition to the anti-Pelagian arguments of Augustine, which he characterised as 'anti-marriage' and as Manichean, must have infuriated Leo, who was about to undertake his own prosecution of Manicheism in Rome. As bishop of Rome, Leo was forced to address the problem of formerly Pelagian clergy wishing to return to their churches in northern Italy. In *Letter* 2 he recommends the rehabilitation of clergy who make sincere confessions and who are prepared to condemn with anathemas the leaders of the heretical group. Leo is careful to respect the local provincial hierarchy of bishops and metropolitans, instructing Bishop Septimus to cooperate with his metropolitan bishop in Venice, to whom he had sent similar letters (*ep.* 2.1).

In this early letter we find Leo using the familiar rhetoric of wolves and sheep that characterises so many of his later letters on heresy.[7] The wolves in this case are the adherents of Pelagianism, particularly the followers of Caelestius. The bishop is called to act as a good shepherd, protecting his sheep from attack by heretics. Several other features of Leo's portraits of Manichees and Priscillianists are applied to the Pelagians: they go from house to house corrupting Christians, under cover of the Christian name (*ep.* 1.1). They are cunning and deceitful (*ep.* 1.2). In the guise of sheep, they attack simple folk (*ep.* 2.1). They refuse correction while corrupting the healthy (*ep.* 2.1).[8] In *Letter* 1.2 Leo instructs the bishop of Aquileia to convene a provincial synod, summoning all reformed Pelagian clergy to a public recantation of their error by means of a signed declaration. Whether or not such a synod was actually convened – and one suspects not from the tone of *Letter* 18 at the end of 447 – Pelagianism was to have a long history in the West, especially in Gaul, Britain and Ireland and, closer to Rome, in Dalmatia.[9]

Translated from Casula 2002: 264 (= PL 54: 597–8); not previously translated into English.

Text

Bishop Leo greets Bishop Septimus.

1. Having read your letter, brother,[10] we acknowledge the vigour of your faith, which was already known to us, and we congratulate you

on pursuing with vigilance your pastoral duty to protect Christ's flock, so that the wolves, who have crept in disguised as sheep (cf. Matt. 7: 15), do not tear apart any simple folk with the savagery of beasts. Not only do they themselves profit from no correction but they even corrupt what is healthy. But so that this deception of serpents cannot succeed, we have sent letters to the metropolitan bishop of the province of Venice,[11] that he might understand the danger it poses to his position, if anyone coming from the company of the Pelagians or following Caelestius[12] is admitted to catholic communion without making a confession or valid reparation. For it is most fruitful for salvation, and a spiritual medicine most useful, for those who want to show that they have been corrected, whether they be priests or deacons or clergy of any other order, to confess their error, and to condemn the very authors of the error without ambiguity. (They should do this) so that no opportunity for hope remains for their crooked opinions that were condemned long ago, and no member of the church can be damaged by association with such people, since its own confession is completely incompatible with theirs.

2. We order also that the constitution of canons be maintained in regard to them, lest they should be allowed to retire from those churches to which they properly belong, and by their own free will to cross over to places to which they have not been appointed. Since this is rightly not permitted to those who are not guilty, it ought to be much less permissible for those under suspicion. Therefore may your Beloved, in whose devotion we rejoice, add your concerns to our instructions, and along with the above-mentioned metropolitan, take care that those things be implemented with foresight and speed, which have been suggested in a manner worthy of praise for the safety of the whole church and ordained for its salvation.[13]

Letter 108 to Theodore, Bishop of Fréjus

Introduction

This is one of two decretals sent to individual bishops of Gaul, the other being *Letter* 167 to Rusticus of Narbonne. This letter to Bishop Theodore of the Gallic see of Fréjus on the south-eastern coast of modern France was penned on 11 June 452, in the year after Attila made his fateful attack on Gaul. Fortunately for Rome, the Hunnic forces were defeated at Châlons-en-Champagne, where they were routed in the Battle of the Catalaunian Plains (also known as the Battle of Châlons) by Aetius's combined army of Romans, Franks, Burgundians, Alans and Visigoths (Moorhead 2001: 72). The impact that such military engagements had on those responsible for the pastoral welfare of the injured and dying was enormous. The clergy had quickly to resolve the problem of administering the sacraments of penance and reconciliation to those at point of death. The problem was compounded if the sinners were also unbaptised, having deferred their baptisms until the risk of committing a mortal sin was minimal. Such serious sins as apostasy, murder and adultery demanded public penance, which was severe and could last for decades, as well as incurring significant social stigma. Public penance meant embracing celibacy, and renouncing all worldly honours and public positions for life, as well as abstaining from military service and the conduct of lawsuits. On top of these restrictions was the proscription of a second penance, so that fear of falling back into sin after public penance kept many from undertaking it in the first place. In this letter and *Letter* 167 (below) we find the bishop of Rome advising compromise in the interests of pastoral care.

At the outset of *Letter* 108 Leo reprimanded Theodore for seeking advice directly from him instead of going through the proper channels and approaching his metropolitan first. This again shows Leo's concern with hierarchical order within the ecclesiastical provinces. In pastoral matters at least, Leo did not employ a top-down management style but respected a chain of command that started at the local level.[14] However, the gulf between clergy and lay persons in sacramental matters remained absolute: only a priest could administer the rite of reconciliation and offer absolution for sins (*ep.* 108.2). Reconciliation and penitence were not to be denied to anyone, unless they were guilty of apostasy. This inclusive attitude seems consonant with the extension of penance to dissolute but baptised Christians on their deathbeds made by Pope Innocent I in 405 (see 'Penance' in Chapter 2).

The PL edition of *Letter* 108 was drawn from several canon law collections, including the *Corbie Collection* and the *Pithou Collection*, two of the earliest collections dating to the sixth century. It was also included in the late fifth-century *Quesnel Collection*, immediately following the *Tome* (Jasper 2001: 45, 50). Thus it served as an important model for Gallic bishops on questions of penitence in Late Antiquity.

Translated from PL 54: 1011–14 (cf. Hinschius 1963: 625–6).

Text

Bishop Leo to Theodore, bishop of Fréjus.[15]

1. This ought to have been the approach taken by your concern: first of all you should have conferred with your metropolitan concerning the apparent matter of complaint, and if even he himself did

not know what your Beloved wanted to know, you should have asked for both of you to be instructed equally. In cases which pertain to the general observance of all the Lord's priests, it is fitting to enquire about nothing without the involvement of the Primates. But so that the doubts on which you have consulted me might be resolved somehow, I shall not keep silent on what ecclesiastical regulations dictate concerning the status of penitents.

2. The manifold mercy of God has provided for human error in such a way that the hope of eternal life might be restored not only through the grace of baptism but also through the medicine of penitence, so that those who have violated the gifts of rebirth, condemning themselves by their own judgement, can attain the remission of sins. The protection of divine goodness was so ordained that God's forgiveness cannot be obtained except by the entreaties of priests. For *the mediator between God and humankind, the man Jesus Christ* (1 Tim. 2: 5), handed down this power to the leaders of the church, that they might give the sacrament of penitence to those who make confession, and that they might permit those same people who have been cleansed by saving reparation to enter into communion of the sacraments through the door of reconciliation.[16] The Saviour himself undertakes this work without ceasing, nor is he ever absent from those duties which he commissioned his servants to look after when he said: *Behold I am with you always, till the end of the age* (Matt. 28: 20). So if any thing is carried out through our ministry that is in good order and has an outcome deserving of praise, we should not doubt that it was given by the Holy Spirit.

3. But if any one of those for whom we pray to the Lord has cut himself off from the gift of (God's) forgiveness in this life, having been hindered by some obstacle, and has ended his worldly existence in the human condition before he could attain to the remedies set down, he cannot obtain after he has put off the flesh what he did not receive while he remained in the flesh. Nor are we required to judge the merits and actions of those who have died in this state, since our Lord God, whose judgements cannot be understood, has reserved for his justice what could not be fulfilled by the priestly ministry. He wants his power to instil fear in such a way that this terror might be present in all, and there is no need for anyone not to fear what happens to those who are lukewarm or negligent. For it is very useful and necessary[17] that the guilt of sinners should be resolved by the prayers of priests before the final day.

4. To those who beg for the protection of penitence and then of reconciliation in a time of need and in a moment of urgent danger, satisfaction should not be forbidden, nor reconciliation denied: because we cannot impose limits on the mercy of God, nor can we

define the times. In his presence true confession[18] suffers no delays of pardon, as the Spirit of God says through the prophet: *When you lament in repentance, then you will be saved* (Is. 30: 15), and elsewhere: *Tell of your sins first in order that you may be justified* (Is. 43: 26).[19] And again, *For there is mercy with the Lord, and plentiful redemption with him* (Ps. 130: 7). And so in dispensing the gifts of God we ought not to be difficult, nor neglect the tears and groans of those who accuse themselves, since we believe the very emotion of the penitent to have been inspired by God, as the Apostle says: *Unless perhaps God grants them repentance ... so that they may escape from the snares of the devil, by whom they are held captive to his will* (2 Tim. 2: 25–6).

5. So it is fitting for each Christian to pass judgement on his conscience, lest he put off being converted to God from day to day, and mark out a time for reparation at the end of his life. Human fragility and ignorance keep him unsafe in this state, that he might hold it back for the uncertainty of a few hours. And although he could earn forgiveness by means of fuller satisfaction, he chooses the narrow limits of that particular time, when there is hardly time for either the confession of the penitent or reconciliation by the priest. But as I said, one should meet the needs even of such people in such a way as not to deny the action of penitence to them, and the grace of communion, if they demand it with the indication of full understanding even when they have lost the use of their voice. And if they have worsened in any sickness in such a way that what they were demanding a little while before, they cannot indicate in the presence of a priest, those of the faithful who are standing near ought to bear witness for them, so that they achieve the simultaneous benefits of penitence and reconciliation. However, the regulations of the canons of the Fathers ought to be observed concerning people who have sinned against God by leaving the faith.[20]

6. And you should bring these responses to your Beloved's questions to the notice of your metropolitan, brother, for this reason: lest anything contrary be done with the excuse of ignorance. If there are any brothers who think there should be any doubt about these things, let them be guided by him on all the things which I have written to you.

Dated 11 June, in the consulship of the most illustrious Herculanus.[21]

Letter 137 to Emperor Marcian

Introduction

Letter 137 is one of Leo's fifteen letters to Emperor Marcian and was composed on 29 May 454.[22] Two questions pertaining to Leo's role as (self-appointed) administrator of the wider church are addressed in this letter: the date of Easter in 455, and the trial of clergy accused of embezzlement. The Easter question had already been raised with Marcian in *Letter* 121 of the previous year, and also in *Letter* 134 of April 454. *Letter* 137 reads like a postscript to *Letter* 136, which was addressed to Marcian on the same day (ACO 2.4: 90–1, ST 20: 144–6). In *Letter* 136 Leo expressed alarm at the perseverance of Eutychians in Constantinople and complained of his continuing problems with Anatolius, the anti-Chalcedonian bishop of Constantinople. *Letters* 136 and 137 were perhaps once a single letter but have been preserved in two unequal parts in the canon law collections in which they are found.

The first question, the dating of Easter, was a perennial problem for bishops in all of the five most important sees, the more so as the bishops of Alexandria were believed to have been commissioned at the Council of Nicaea in 325 to produce calculations of the correct date for Easter each year.[23] The English church historian Bede asserted that Prosper had helped Leo in disputes over the computation of Easter, an assertion supported by Gennadius's remark that Prosper of Aquitaine produced a computational paschal table of his own.[24] Leo's correspondence on this subject stretches back to an exchange of letters with Cyril of Alexandria, whom Leo consulted on the correct date for Easter celebrations in 444. A decade later, Leo applied to the emperor to clear up the correct date of Easter in 455 with Proterius of Alexandria (*ep.* 121), and asked Julian of Cos to follow the matter up with Marcian (*ep.* 122, *ep.* 127). Proterius had replied in April 454 with a lengthy letter (*ep.* 133) to the effect that Egypt and the East would observe Easter on 24 April, and Leo and the rest of western Christendom should do the same, so that 'one faith, one baptism, one most holy paschal rite would be celebrated by all Christians everywhere' (PL 54: 1093B). In *Letter* 137, Leo informs the emperor that he has reluctantly accepted Proterius's ruling. Two months later he advised bishops in Gaul and Spain to follow suit (*ep.* 138).

The second subject under discussion is all the more tantalising for its lack of detail. Leo simply repeats his previous request, which had obviously gone unanswered, that the emperor should not allow clerics to be tried in public courts in Constantinople. Such a move for the public trial of church stewards (*oeconomi*) accused of embezzlement or corruption in association with their management of church funds and property is elsewhere unattested. Church stewards had control over the financial affairs of a diocese, under the bishop's supervision. Leo was trying to prevent the discovery of any irregularities by those outside the household of faith. This is another instance of the incipient 'two powers' theory – that the temporal and spiritual powers of church and state respectively should be regarded as distinct but complementary – that was to take hold at the end of the century due to the efforts of Pope Gelasius.

Translated from Schwartz, ACO 2.4: 89–90; not previously translated into English.

Text

Leo to Emperor Marcian. I rejoice that by your Clemency's holy zeal for my request you have dispelled my concerns about the observance of Easter. With great diligence you ordered that there be an inquiry in the church of Alexandria as to whether the coming Easter feast could be celebrated on 24 April in accordance with the definition of Bishop Theophilus,[25] and against the ancient observance, since the day assigned to the Lord and Saviour's passion in all our records is 17 April.[26] But since another reckoning pleases the Egyptians, I gave my consent, lest there be any discrepancy throughout the provinces concerning the observance of such a venerable (feast),[27] so that the greatest sacrament of the Lord's resurrection should never be celebrated on another day and among the Lord's priests there should be no variance in so great a rite, but through all the churches there should be prayers to our God for your Piety's prosperity and your rule in equal measure.[28] I make it known that I have received a letter from my brother and fellow bishop Proterius, bishop of Alexandria,[29] to which I have replied giving my consent to your Piety, not because his reasoning seemed clear, but because we were persuaded by a desire for unity, which is our greatest concern.

I trust that what I sought from your Piety in an earlier letter is not unreasonably appended to this letter. May I request that you should not allow stewards of the church of Constantinople to be heard by public judges, by a new kind of trend and in a manner peculiar to the rule[30] of your Piety, and that you should remove this injury too from the holy orders, but you should command church cases to be tried in the traditional manner by the examination of bishops.[31]

Dated 29 May in the consulship of Aetius and Studius.[32]

Letter 167 to Rusticus, Bishop of Narbonne

Introduction

Letter 167 to Rusticus of Narbonne is a late letter of indeterminate date. Hunt (FOTC 34: 289) suggested a possible dating of 458 or 459. From Leo's complaint about being beset by trouble on all sides, this seems a reasonable surmise. The uprising of the Alexandrian monks and the subsequent death of the patriarch Proterius in 457 (cf. *epp.* 124 and 170), as well as the Vandal invasion of Rome in 455, were catastrophes with long-lasting ripple effects.

Narbonne, a city of south-eastern France, was founded as the Roman colony *Narbo Martius* in 118 BCE. It was in Narbonne that the Visigothic king Athaulf married his captured bride, Galla Placidia, in 414. Narbonne came under Visigothic control briefly in 413 and permanently from 462. In the intervening period it suffered frequent Visigothic attacks. At the beginning of *Letter* 167 Leo expresses regret that it is not possible for Rusticus to make the journey to Rome to discuss in person the knotty problems of church discipline he had raised in an earlier letter to Leo. This sentiment is probably to be taken at face value: questions of canon law in Gaul had caused sufficient problems for Leo in the 440s for him to be willing to make the time for personal interviews with those who sought his counsel.

Letter 167 opens with the matter of Sabinian and Leo's appeal to Rome. These two priests of the diocese of Narbonne seem to have been punished by their bishop for being overzealous in their prosecution of Christians guilty of adultery. Pope Leo finds that they have no just complaint against Rusticus, and leaves their punishment to the bishop's discretion, while urging moderation. Likewise in the matter of deciding questions of canon law, he recommends a mild approach. We find the same moderate stance on questions of penance and reconciliation in his earlier *Letter* 108 (translated within).

The bulk of the letter conveys Leo's responses to nineteen questions put to him by Rusticus. These concern clerical ordination (Question 1), marriage law (Questions 3–6, 15), penance (Questions 2, 7–14), and baptism (Questions 16–19). Similar material was covered in two other letters of the same period: *Letter* 159 to Bishop Nicetas of Aquileia, written on 21 March 458, and *Letter* 166 of 24 October 458 to Neo, bishop of Ravenna, on the baptism of returned captives. The canon law questions arising from the capture and enslavement of Christians by Vandals and pagans were not new. In particular the validity of second marriages remained a problem, especially if the first wife or husband returned from captivity and wished to be reunited with their spouse. In *Letter* 159 Leo ruled that returned husbands had a right to reclaim their wives, and that second marriages were in this case invalid, even if the wife did not wish to return to her first husband. Innocent I was the first Roman bishop to deal with similar problems in the first quarter of the fifth century, ruling against the imperial law that marriages where one party had been taken into captivity by a foreign enemy were dissolved (*ep.* 36 of Innocent to Probus). Leo here upholds Innocent's position against remarriage, but we must assume that, as was the case with Innocent's decretal (Dunn 2007a: 107), his ruling carried ecclesiastical force only and had no binding civil effect. In the sixth century, Emperor Justinian reinforced the imperial law dissolving such marriages with the *proviso* that remarriage was only permitted after a five-year waiting period had elapsed (Dunn 2007a: 112).

The rules for prescribing public penance, which was required for the serious sins of murder, adultery and apostasy – including the worship of pagan idols under duress – are laid out quite clearly here for the first time. Public penance is also required of clergy who have abandoned their vow of celibacy. Lesser sins, such as eating burned offerings at pagan banquets while in captivity, may be redressed by fasting and the laying on of hands (Question 19). It should be noted that the questions in the rubrics are not found in all manuscripts, and in some the questions are itemised differently so as to number seventeen, rather than nineteen.

Translated from PL 54: 1199–1209 (cf. Hinschius 1963: 615–18).

Text

Bishop Leo to Rusticus, bishop of Narbonne.

I was glad to receive your letter, brother, from the hands of your archdeacon Hermes. It was detailed in its coverage of various problems, but not so burdensome to the reader's patience that I skipped over any of the contents, even though I am troubled by cares on all sides. So having comprehended what you have alleged in your whole discourse, and after reviewing the acts of the investigation undertaken by the bishops and honoured men, we realised that the priests Sabinian and Leo lacked confidence in your course of action. They had no just cause for complaint, since they removed themselves of their own accord from the discussions that had begun. What sort and measure of justice you ought to direct towards them is a matter I leave to your discretion, while encouraging you at the bidding of charity to apply a spiritual remedy to the sick in need of healing. As Scripture says: *Do not be too righteous* (Eccl. 7: 16). Be gentle with those who seem to have exceeded moderation in dealing out punishment only out of their zeal for chastity, lest the devil who deceives adulterers triumph over the avengers of adultery.

I am amazed that Your Charity is so distressed by the trials of so many scandals that arise at any opportunity, that you declare you long for a break from the labours of the episcopacy, and prefer to pass your life in peace and leisure than to endure these (labours) which have been entrusted to you. But in the words of the Lord, blessed is *the one who perseveres to the end* (Matt. 10: 22): where will that blessed perseverance come from, if not from the virtue of patience? For according to the apostle's preaching, *everyone who wishes to live righteously in Christ will suffer persecution* (2 Tim. 3: 12). This is not to be interpreted as meaning only that Christian piety is subject to the sword or the flame or any other punishments, since the savagery of persecutions also includes dissimilar customs, disobedient obstinacy, and the arrows of malicious tongues. When all the members (sc. of the church) are continually struck by these afflictions, and none of the pious is free from temptation, so that not even a life of leisure is free of danger, nor a life of labour, who will guide the boat on the waves of the sea if the helmsman quits? Who will keep the sheep safe from the wolves that lie in wait, if the care of the shepherd does not keep watch (cf. John 10: 12)? Finally, who will resist robbers and thieves, if, out of love of a quiet life, the sentinel who is posted to keep surveillance is distracted from his duty of care? Therefore one should remain in the office entrusted to him and in the work he has undertaken. Justice has to be maintained constantly and mercy offered with kindness. You should hate the sin but not the sinner. Pride should be corrected and weakness tolerated, and when a sin has to be punished more severely, it should not be punished with the spirit of an avenger but of a doctor. And if a more violent trial threatens, let us not fear as if we had to resist that adversity with our own strength, since Christ is both our counsel and our strength. Without him we can do nothing (cf. John 15: 5), but through him we can do all things (cf. Phil. 4: 13). For when he commissioned the preachers of the gospel and the ministers of the sacraments, he said, *Behold, I am with you always, even to the end of the age* (Matt. 28: 20). And again he said: *I have told you these things so that in me you might have peace. You will face persecution in this world, but be of good cheer, because I have conquered the world* (John 16: 33).[33] These promises, which have been clearly revealed, we ought not to weaken by any scandal, lest we seem ungrateful for being chosen by God, whose powers are as helpful as his promises are true.

What judgements should be made concerning your problems, beloved, which your archdeacon delivered in separate documents, it would be more appropriate to consider individually in my presence, if an opportunity of seeing you arose for us. For since certain questions seem to surpass the limits of (your) diligence, I understand that they are better settled in meetings than in letters. Because just as there are certain cases which cannot be overturned by any reasoning, so there are many that ought to be moderated, either out of consideration of the times, or the necessity of the circumstances: always on the observance of this condition, that in those matters which are doubtful or unclear, we know that (a course of action) should be followed which is found to be neither contrary to the gospel teachings nor opposed to the decrees of the holy Fathers.

Question 1. Concerning a priest or deacon who has lied that he was a bishop, and concerning those who have ordained clerics.

Response. No reason permits you to admit to the rank of bishop those who were not elected by clerics, sought out by the people, and consecrated by the bishops of the province with the metropolitan's consent. Hence, since the question often arises concerning the incorrect acceptance of an honour, who can doubt that what is not shown to have been conferred, ought not to be assigned to them at all? But if any cleric has been ordained by those pseudo-bishops in those churches which used to belong to proper bishops, and their ordination has been performed with the consent and agreement of those presiding, it can be regarded as valid, on the condition that they remain in those churches. Otherwise their ordination[34] should be regarded as invalid, since it was not established for a (specific) place or supported by any authority.

Question 2. Concerning a priest or deacon who seeks penance[35] after being convicted of a crime: should the laying on of hands be given to him?

Response. It is foreign to ecclesiastical custom for those who have been consecrated as priests or deacons to receive the remedy of penance for some crime through the laying on of hands. This custom has certainly come down from apostolic tradition, according to what is written: *If a priest has sinned, who will pray for him?*[36] Hence such lapsed persons should seek out a private retreat to merit the mercy of God. There, if their satisfaction is deemed worthy, it may also bear fruit for them.

Question 3. Concerning those who serve at the altar and are married, whether there should be any contact with them?

Response. The law of chastity is the same for ministers of the altar as for bishops and priests, who as laypersons or readers were permitted to marry and have children, but when they attained the ranks I have mentioned, what was allowed (before) was no longer permissible. Hence, so that a spiritual marriage may be made from a carnal one, it befits them not to dismiss their wives, (but) to keep them as if they did not have them. The love of the marriage partners is thereby preserved while the conjugal act ceases.

Question 4. Concerning a priest or deacon who has given his virgin daughter to marry a man who already had a concubine, by whom he also had children.

Response. Not every woman who is joined to a man is that man's wife, nor is every child the heir of the father. But marriage contracts are valid between those of free birth and between equals. The Lord laid this down long before the beginning of Roman law.[37] A wife is one thing and a concubine another, just as a servant girl is one thing and a freed woman[38] another. For this reason even the Apostle pointed to the witness of Genesis, in order to show the difference between these women, where it is said to Abraham: *Get rid of your servant girl and her son: for the son of a servant girl will not be an heir along with my son Isaac.*[39] Hence, since the association of marriage was so founded from the beginning that apart from the joining of the sexes it might contain a symbol of Christ and the church (cf. Eph. 5: 32), there is no doubt that that woman does not belong in a marriage, in which the nuptial mystery was obviously not present. Therefore if a cleric in any place has given his daughter in marriage to a man who has a concubine, it is not to be accepted as if he gave her to a man already married, except if perchance it seems that the other woman has been manumitted, and given a legitimate dowry, and honoured with public wedding rites.

Question 5. Concerning girls who marry men who have concubines.

Response. Girls married to men by the decision of their fathers are free from guilt if the women whom those men had (previously) were not married to them.

Question 6. Concerning those men who leave women by whom they have children, and take wives.

Response. A wife is one thing, and a concubine another, so to reject a slave girl from the marriage bed and to receive a wife of confirmed free birth is not bigamy but a respectable procedure.

Question 7. Concerning those who receive penance while ill and refuse to carry it out when they recover.

Response. The negligence of such people is at fault, but they should not be abandoned altogether, so that, spurred on by frequent encouragement, they might faithfully fulfil what they asked for out of necessity. For no one is to be given up as hopeless while he remains in this life,[40] because sometimes what is deferred due to youthful lack of confidence is achieved with more mature counsel.

Question 8. Concerning those who receive penance while they are ailing and die before taking communion.

Response. Their case is to be reserved to God's judgement, in whose power it lay to defer their death until the remedy of communion (had been applied). But we cannot be in communion with them when they are dead if we have not been in communion with them while they were alive.

Question 9. Concerning those who asked to be given penance while under the influence of an extremely overwhelming grief, and when the priest comes to give what they requested, if the grief has abated somewhat, they excuse themselves and refuse to accept what is offered.

Response. This dissimulation can occur not out of contempt for the remedy but out of fear of sinning more seriously (later). Hence the penance that has been delayed should not be denied when it is sought with greater zeal, so that in some way the wounded soul might attain the healing of forgiveness.

Question 10. Concerning those who have professed penance, and then start pursuing a case in the law courts.

Response. It is one thing to demand the payment of a just debt, and another to scorn one's property out of love for perfection. But it befits a person seeking pardon for what is unlawful to abstain from many lawful things also, as the Apostle says: *All things are allowed to me, but not all things are beneficial* (1 Cor. 6: 12). Hence, if a penitent has a case that perhaps he ought not to neglect, it is better to seek a ruling from the church than from a court of law.[41]

Question 11. Concerning those who pursue business in the course of penance or following penance.

Response. It is the quality of the gain that either excuses or convicts the one who does business because there is both honest and disreputable profit. However, for the penitent it is more useful to suffer loss than to be tied up in the dangers of business, because it is difficult to avoid contact with sin in the trade of buying and selling.

Question 12. Concerning those who return to military service after performing penance.

Response. It is completely against ecclesiastical regulations to return to secular military service after performing penance, since the apostle says: *No one serving God should involve himself in secular affairs* (2 Tim. 2: 4).[42] Hence he who wishes to involve himself in worldly warfare is not free from the devil's snares.

Question 13. Concerning those who take wives or concubines after they have done penance.

Response. As for young men who have performed penance, urged by either fear of death or danger of captivity, and afterwards, for fear of falling into the intemperance typical of the young, have chosen the bond of marriage lest they incur the sin of fornication, they seem to have committed a pardonable sin if they know no other woman apart from their wife. On this we have not ordained a law, however, but what we deem the more tolerable. For according to true understanding nothing is more fitting for him who has performed penance than to persevere in chastity of mind and body.

Question 14. Concerning monks who either begin military service or get married.

Response. The intention of monastic life undertaken voluntarily by one's own decision cannot be deserted without sin. For he who makes a vow to God ought to keep it.[43] Hence a man who has abandoned his profession of solitude, having turned away to the army or to marriage, must be cleansed by making satisfaction through a public penance. Although armed service can be harmless, and marriage can be respectable, his sin is to have renounced the better choice.

Question 15. Concerning girls who adopted the religious life for a time but were not yet consecrated, and then marry.

Response. Girls who have not been forced by parental command, but by their own free decision have undertaken the intention of virginity and its way of life, then afterwards choose to marry, cross the boundary, even if they are not yet consecrated. Of course they would not be deprived of that gift if they persisted in that way of life.

Question 16. Concerning those who were abandoned by their Christian parents while they were young, and cannot discover whether they were baptised, or need to be baptised.

Response. If there is no evidence among family or relatives, clerics or neighbours that might prove that those in question were baptised, then they should be reborn (in baptism), lest they obviously perish, for in their case reason does not allow that an action which is not proven is seen as a repetition.

Question 17. Concerning those who were captured by enemies while they were young, and do not know if they were baptised, but know that their parents sometimes took them to church: can they be baptised, or should they be, when they come to Roman territory?[44]

Response. Those who can remember that they used to attend church with their parents can remember whether they received what was given[45] to their parents. But if even this fact is beyond their memory, it seems that what they do not know they received (sc. baptism) should be conferred on them, because there can be no rash presumption where there is pious diligence.

Question 18. Concerning those who have come from Africa or Mauritania,[46] and do not know into which sect they were baptised, what practice should be observed concerning them?

Response. Those who confess that they do not know who baptised them are not ignorant of whether they were baptised but into which faith. Hence since they have received baptism in some form or other, they should not be baptised; but let them be joined to catholic communion through the laying on of hands, with the invocation of the power of the Holy Spirit,[47] which they could not receive from heretics.

Question 19. Concerning those who were indeed baptised while young, (but) were captured by pagans and lived with them as pagans, and came to Roman territory while they were still young: if they seek communion, what practice should be observed?

Response. If they were accustomed solely to eating burned offerings at pagan feasts, they can be cleansed by fasting and the laying on of hands, so that they can participate in the sacraments of Christ, while abstaining from offerings to idols from now on. But if they worshipped idols, or were corrupted by murders or illicit sex, it is not fitting for them to be admitted to communion unless they perform public penance.[48]

Letter 170 to Gennadius, Bishop of Constantinople

Introduction

This is Leo's only known letter to Gennadius, patriarch of Constantinople (458–71), the successor of the 'monophysite' candidate Anatolius. It was composed on 18 June 460, after the usurper Timothy Aelurus had been expelled from the patriarchate of Alexandria by Emperor Leo. From the time of Proterius's murder by a mob of anti-Chalcedonian monks in Alexandria, Leo had exerted strong pressure on the emperor to find a suitable replacement (see introduction to *Letter* 124). This pressure eventually resulted in the appointment of a new bishop, the pro-Chalcedonian Timothy Salofaciolus, by August 460.

After usurping Proterius's position even before his death, Timothy Aelurus had broken off communion with Rome, Constantinople and Antioch, denouncing all the pro-Chalcedonian bishops of Alexandria (Wace and Piercy 1994: 988). From Leo's letters to Basil of Antioch, Juvenal of Jerusalem, Euxitheus, vicar of Thessaloniki, Peter of Corinth and Luke of Dyrrhacium, it appears that Timothy went on to ask the emperor to rescind the canons of Chalcedon and to summon a new council (*epp.* 149, 150). Pope Leo opposed this proposal in an obsequious letter of 458, praising the new emperor for upholding the faith of his predecessor, and seeking from him the deposition and exile of 'the plunderer and cruel assassin' Timothy (*ep.* 162). In 460 Emperor Leo finally expelled Timothy from Alexandria. Even after he had been exiled to Gangra, however, Timothy sought out his supporters in Constantinople. At this point Leo wrote *Letter* 170 to Gennadius, warning the relatively new patriarch not to allow Timothy Aelurus to remain in Constantinople, or to speak with other people, especially the patriarch himself, or to return to his former see of Alexandria. Leo's final three letters in August 460 concern the same issue: he praises the restoration of harmony to the Alexandrian church by the consecration of Timothy Salofaciolus, while warning the Alexandrian bishops not to maintain any contact with Aelurus (*epp.* 171–3).

Timothy Aelurus's exile in Gangra lasted sixteen years, until the usurpation of the imperial throne by Basiliscus in 475. The same Basiliscus had led the unsuccessful Byzantine military campaign against the Vandals in North Africa in 468. As emperor, Basiliscus reversed the religious policy of Emperor Leo I's successor Zeno and declared his support for the Eutychian party, recalling Timothy to Alexandria. Timothy Salofaciolus was driven into exile. Pope Leo did not live to see this day, for he had died in November 461. Timothy Aelurus again travelled to Constantinople to lobby for a new council which would overturn the decisions of Chalcedon (Wace and Piercy 1994: 908). He was unsuccessful, however, and the reign of his patron Basiliscus was cut short when Zeno returned from exile and overthrew him in August 476. Four years after being ejected, Timothy Salofaciolus was restored permanently to the see of Alexandria. With Byzantine imperial attention focused on other things, the deposition of the last Roman emperor, Romulus Augustulus, in early September 476 passed almost without notice, and when Odovacer sent the newly reinstalled eastern emperor the imperial regalia, Zeno had little choice but to endorse the new leader with the title of ruler (*dux*) of Italy.

Translated from CSEL 35: 119–20; not previously translated into English.

Text

Bishop Leo to Gennadius, bishop of Constantinople.

From the letters of Your Affection and from conversation with our brothers and fellow bishops Domitian and Geminian,[49] I have understood that Timothy[50] was allowed to come to Constantinople by the actions of some adversaries of the faith, after he was expelled from the church of Alexandria. (This was allowed), as far as I could understand, so that he might be converted to catholic teaching, even against his will, when he is pressed by the opinions of all the Lord's priests: and, although it seems he was ejected for just this reason after the error of (his) heretical perversion was condemned, so that he might agree with apostolic teaching in order to return to Alexandria. However, even if he is proven catholic, this remains a firm charge against him: that while the bishop of such a great see was still alive, he usurped his position and appeared to be the instigator of an act of unspeakable cruelty that was committed.[51]

And for that reason Your Affection ought to strive with care, for which he is renowned, and take pains that no one associates with such a wicked man privately or publicly, and offer him no opportunity to meet with anyone under the guise of reproof, lest he seize the full freedom of returning. Our most Christian leader has already passed judgement on him in his edicts.[52] Therefore, dearest brother, you would do well to strive with every effort and ever-watchful circumspection for ecclesiastical unity, so that his supporters are deprived of hope and a catholic bishop is consecrated from his own Alexandrian clergy according to the ancient custom of the orthodox Egyptians.[53] That parricide will not be deserted[54] by his defenders elsewhere, unless the church of Alexandria, which should be restored to the honour of its fathers and its own liberty, has obtained a most approved leader for the healing of all these evil actions.

Dated 18 June in the consulship of Magnus and Apollonius,[55] through the agency of Filoxenus.

NOTES

INTRODUCTION

1 Cf. two recent Italian studies treating Leo's christology and soteriology (Casula 2000; Casula 2002), and two English monographs on similar themes (Armitage 2005; Green 2008). Recent articles on these subjects include those of Studer (1986); Barclift (1997); Dunn (2001a and 2001b). Leo's achievements in the field of canon law have deservedly commanded recent attention (Jasper 2001; Pietrini 2002). General studies in English of Leo's pontificate are, however, fairly limited (Jalland 1941; Grillmeier 1987; Studer 1993).

CHAPTER 1

1 Prosper, *Epitoma chronicon* 1341, Mommsen 1892: 478. Prosper twice uses the designation 'deacon' to describe Leo in this passage.
2 *British Museum* 36589, ff. 134–5v, dates to the eleventh or twelfth century. The Greek menological and synaxary notices for Leo, whose feast in the Greek calendar is 18 February, do not depend on this *Life* and have been attributed to another *Life*, as yet undiscovered, perhaps held in the monastery of Iviron (van De Vorst 1910: 400–1).
3 Cf. *ep.* 113.4, where Leo asks Julian of Cos to make a Latin translation of the *Acts of Chalcedon*.
4 *Pratum spirituale* 147, PG 87: 3012.
5 Zosimus, *Historia nova* 5.41.4–42.2, Paschoud 2003: 61–3.
6 Leo's successor, Pope Hilary (461–8), later used a similar phrase in the dedicatory inscription of the Baptistery of St John Lateran (*ILCV* 1, 978: 183), further confirmation that the bishop of Rome was by now acting in place of the emperor in the sphere of church dedication.
7 *Liber Pontificalis*'s account of the involvement of Valentinian 'then residing at Ravenna' (*LP* 1: 227) cannot be accepted, since Valentinian was born only in the following year, i.e. 419!
8 Heather (2007: 137–8) points out that, while the Nicene sources dismissed Geiseric as an Arian, he was in fact a 'Homoean', that is, an opponent of the Homousian doctrine that had been proclaimed orthodox at the Ecumenical Council of Nicaea I (325).
9 *Letter of Paschasinus, bishop of Lilybaeum, to Leo, ep.* 3.1, PL 54: 606A; Prosper, *Epitoma chronicon* 1342, Mommsen 1892: 478.

10 According to calculations based on findings of pig bones in southern Italy, there were *c.* 120,000 recipients of the pork dole in Rome in 419, a number which had increased to *c.* 140,000 in 452, implying a total population of between 300,000 and 500,000 (Barnish 1987: 160).

11 Fragmentary sources for this story are the histories of John of Antioch (*frag.* 199 [2], Gordon 1960: 104–5) and Priscus (*frag.* 15, Gordon 1960: 105–6).

12 *Liber Pontificalis* places Leo's diplomatic mission to Attila *after* 'the Vandal disaster', i.e. the invasion of Rome by Geiseric in May 455 (*LP* 1: 239, Davis 2000: 39).

13 John Malalas, *Chronographia*, Dindorf 1831: 359.1–4, and *Chronicon paschale*, Dindorf 1832: 588. Both authors acknowledge Priscus of Thrace as their source.

14 Placidia is closely associated with the pope in the dedicatory inscription beneath the triumphal arch at St Paul's: *Placidiae pia mens operis decus omne paterni gaudet pontificis studio splendere Leonis* (*ILCV* 1, 1761b: 342). The following imperfect translation is based on the partially restored text: 'The pious soul of Placidia rejoices for all the glory of paternal labour to shine with the zeal of Pope Leo.'

15 *LP* 1: 239, Davis 2000: 39–40. Duchesne and Davis identify the dedication as an interpolation.

16 Sixtus III was said to have established a monastery 'at the Catacombs', the first mention in *Liber Pontificalis* of a monastery founded near a suburban basilica, the basilica of St Sebastian (*LP* 1: 234 n.13).

17 'She dedicated herself to the monastery at the church of the blessed apostle Peter for the service of the almighty God … ' (Gregory the Great, *Dialogi* 4.14, Moricca 1960: 247). This sixth-century monastery may also be identifiable with a monastery in the vicinity of St Peter's that was dedicated to St Stephen in the eighth century (Cooper 2007: 170–1).

18 An inscription in the apse ascribes it to the work of Flavius Constantius Felix and his wife Padusia. Flavius held the consulship in 428, and was assassinated by Aetius in 430, placing the apse-vault's construction in the pontificate of Celestine (422–32) (*LP* 1: 241 n.8).

19 Fl. Avitus Marinianus's and his wife Anastasia's contributions to the restoration of St Peter's, as well as those of Rufius Viventius Gallus, perhaps his son (*PLRE* II: 492), are recorded in inscriptions associating them with the pope (*ILCV* 94, 1758 and 1759).

20 On the Roman cult of St Stephen see *Homily* 85, below.

21 The testimony of *Liber Pontificalis* (*LP* 1: 238) is supported by an inscription recording the dedication (*ILCV* 1, 1765: 343): 'When the virgin Demetrias Amnia, leaving the world, closed her final day, though she was not about to die, she consecrated to you, Pope Leo, the last of her vows, that she would build the hall for a sacred house … '. See further discussion in Neil 2006: 245.

22 *LP* 1: 239. There were some twenty-five endowed churches in Rome at this time (Davis 2000: xli).

23 Pope Cornelius had allegedly plotted with a noble widow, Lucina, to move the remains of the apostles Peter and Paul from the catacombs to more suitable accommodation. The pair secretly relocated the body of St Paul to Lucina's estate on the Ostian Way, near the site of his beheading. Peter's body was also moved nearer to where he had been crucified, and

placed among the bodies of the holy bishops at the temple of Apollo on Mt Aureus (*LP* 1: 150).

24 Gillett 2001: 165. Cf. the letters of Valentinian to Theodosius (*ep.* 55, PL 54: 857–60), and of Galla Placidia to Theodosius (*ep.* 56, PL 54: 859–62) on the reverence of the imperial family for the cult of St Peter. Valentinian refers to Leo as 'the most blessed bishop of the city of Rome, on whom antiquity conferred the headship of the priesthood above all others ... ' (*ep.* 55, PL 54: 859A).

25 CIL 6, 1756a and b, Bormann and Henzen 1876: 389. On Sextus Claudius Petronius Probus, consul in 371, several times praetorian prefect, and father of the two consuls of 395, see Dunn 2007a: 110.

26 Cf. Silva-Tarouca (1932b) who judged many of these letters suspect or spurious, mostly on the basis of slim stylistic evidence (*epp.* 27, 36, 39, 43, 47–9, 74, 111–13, 118, 120, 141, 154, 157–8, 160–1). Künstle (1905: 117–26) disputes the authenticity of *Letter* 15, basing his argument on the similarity between these sixteen chapters and the seventeen anathemas of the Synod of Braga (563). Künstle's argument that the letter was produced in Braga and first attributed to Leo in 563 has not been taken up in recent scholarship.

27 Cf. *ep.* 119.4, PL 54: 1044–5; cf. note [i], where the Ballerini conclude on the basis of this text that Leo was already an archdeacon under Pope Celestine. In regard to this letter the editors entertain two possibilities: Cyril addressed this letter to Leo, or Cyril actually addressed his letter to Celestine and Leo found it in the papal archive.

28 Leo's exegesis of the Beatitudes in *Homily* 95 is highly allegorical, but this homiletic text was not written to expound doctrine, but rather to facilitate spiritual growth.

29 ACO 2.4: 119–31, FOTC 34: 275–88. A similar collection of patristic testimonies adduced by Eutyches for the opposing argument was attached to the *Tome* (ACO 2.2.1: 35–42). Eutyches's 'witnesses' included excerpts from letters of Popes Julius, Felix I and Celestine!

CHAPTER 2

1 Preface to *ep.* 15 below. Cf. Excursus V: *Manichaean Astrology*, CFML 1: 93–7.

2 Cf. Zec. 8: 19.

3 Cf. Stökl Ben Ezra 2003: 263 who maintains that the solemn fast during Lent was not introduced until after the time of Leo.

4 A modified version of the translation in Stökl Ben Ezra 2003: 273–4.

5 E.g. *Admonitio in sequentes sermones de collectis*, PL 54: 155–8, and, following the Ballerinis' lead, NPNF 12: 118 n.669 (*serm.* 9).

6 The reference to the beginning of the collections 'next Wednesday' posed a problem for the Ballerini brothers, whose edition is reprised in PL 54. According to their reckoning, this had to refer to Wednesday 6 July in 443. They were rightly perplexed as to how this sermon could then refer to the outcome of an investigation into the Manichees which was yet to take place. For this reason they wanted to emend the text from 'next Wednesday' to 'next Thursday' so that it would refer to Thursday 6 July in 444, but were unwilling to do so against all the manuscript witnesses (Preface, PL 54: 157–8, and 162 [note h]). Their difficulty is easily resolved if this homily

was delivered, as Chavasse maintains, in November of 443, that is, after the Manichean investigation, rather than in July, as the Ballerini supposed.

7 See Hoyce (1941) for evidence for private penance in the West in the second and third centuries. Hoyce argues that public penance was reserved for the three mortal sins of murder, apostasy and adultery, and that a bishop could absolve ordinary sins after confession, with no abstinence from communion required.

8 The assumption that Leo was archdeacon, i.e. head of the seven suburbicarian bishops in Rome, is often made in scholarship on the basis of his apparent clerical pre-eminence before his ordination, illustrated by his appointment to the embassy to Gaul in 440.

9 Pope Siricius in his letter to Himerius of *c.* 385 (PL 13: 1137).

CHAPTER 3

1 Cf. also the translation of *Homily* 73 on the Ascension, below.
2 See the introduction to *ep.* 28, below, for further discussion of these two terms and their usage.
3 *ep.* 101.1, PG 37: 181C–184A. In this letter to the priest Cledonius, Gregory of Nazianzus sought to refute the Apollinarian notion that Christ had a divine mind rather than a human one.
4 E.g. *sermones* 22.1–4, 28.3, 49.3 and *ep.* 31.2.
5 See Maier 1996: 441 n.1.
6 *Codex Theodosianus* 16.5.62, SC 497: 328.
7 *Valentiniani Novella* 18, CFML 1: 51.
8 Also *serm.* 9.4, CCSL 138: 37; *serm.* 34.5, CCSL 138: 186–7; *serm.* 42.5, CCSL 138a: 246–8. See Maier 1996: 448–50, 455–7; Lieu 1992: 204–6.
9 Leo may be the acolyte of the same name who had delivered a letter from Sixtus, not yet pope, to Bishop Aurelius on the subject of Pelagianism, as mentioned by Augustine in *ep.* 191.1 (PL 33: 867).
10 *Epitoma chronicon* 1336, Mommsen 1892: 477.
11 *On the predestination of the saints* and *On the gift of perseverance*.
12 PL 54: 594–5 and PL 54: 597–8. The latter is translated below.
13 Modified version of the translation of NPNF 12.
14 E.g. *sermones* 32.4; 33.1 and 5; 35.1 and 4; 36.2; 38.1.
15 Green 2008: 78–80.
16 Cf. Chapter 10, n.9 below.
17 Socrates of Constantinople, *Historia ecclesiastica* 7.32, Hansen and Maraval 2007: 114.
18 Wace and Piercy 1994: 753–8, s.v. 'Nestorius and Nestorianism'. See also McGuckin 1994: 151–74 on associative difference in Christ.
19 John Cassian, *De incarnatione Christi* 1.3, Petschenig 2004: 239–40; *De inc.* 5.1–2, Petschenig 2004: 301–4; *De inc.* 5.4, Petschenig 2004: 306. See further Green 2008: 32–4.

CHAPTER 4

1 Ullmann 1960: 25–51; Ullmann 2003: 20–1.
2 Cf. *ep.* 133, in which Proterius of Alexandria offers proofs that the Roman date of Easter is wrong, and argues for the eastern date.

3 I have translated the original Greek text. The Ballerini questioned whether the Latin version of the text was original or a translation made from the Greek (PL 54: 899 n.[b]).

4 Wace and Piercy 1994: 866–7, s.v. 'Proterius of Alexandria'.

CHAPTER 5

1 *ep.* 10.4, PL 54: 632A; FOTC 34: 42.

2 *ep.* 10.2, PL 54: 630B; FOTC 34: 40.

3 *Nov. Val.* 17 = *ep.* 11, PL 54: 636–40.

4 *Decretales papae Vigilii* 7, Hinschius 1963: 712.

5 Jasper 2001: 81–7 furnishes more detail on these three important collections.

6 He was not, as *Liber Pontificalis* recounts, buried on 11 April.

7 Popes buried there after Leo include Simplicius (468–83), Gelasius (492–6), Anastasius II (496–8), and Symmachus (498–514).

8 The text of the epitaph has been preserved only in De Rossi (1888: 98). See *LP* 1: 379 n.35. The text was taken over in SC 200 (Dolle 1973: 302, 304), and is partially translated here.

CHAPTER 7

1 Casula dates *Homily* 87 to Sunday 4 October 442 (Casula 2002: 297).

2 As Leo put it in a later homily on the September fast, using military imagery to great effect: 'The soldier of the church, even if he can fight special battles with boldness, still will fight safer and better if he stands in rank openly against the enemy, when he does not enter the fray on his own strength, but engages in the universal war under the rule of the unconquered King, in the company of a host of brothers' (*serm.* 89.2, CCSL 138a: 552.31–5).

3 Cf. also Leo, *sermones* 6.3, 9.2, 10.4, 16.2, 49.6, 78.4 *et al.*

4 The doctrine of traducianism, the idea that parents transmitted both body and soul in the act of conception, and that original sin was thus passed down materially through the male seed, in the act of procreation, was opposed to the doctrine of creationism, whereby God creates a new soul for each newborn: on both these ideas in Augustine, see Rist 1994: 317–20, 326.

5 Spiritual longings (*spiritalia desideria*) are opposed to longings of the flesh (*corporales concupiscentiae* and *cupiditates*).

6 Matt. 17: 21; Mark 9: 29. Verse 21 is missing in some versions of Matt. 17, and the phrase 'and fasting' is missing from some versions of Mark 9: 29.

7 I assume Leo means prayers of intercession, and 'the other' is the one for whom such prayers are offered.

8 This concession to human frailty opened the door to the abuses of the Middle Ages with the selling of indulgences in lieu of penance.

9 The language of the harvest (e.g. 'the yearly cycle', the elements of fire, floods and hail which threaten crops, reaping in greater abundance, etc.) is appropriate to the season in which this homily was delivered.

10 Here Leo picks up the metaphor of the seed and its produce, introduced in Chapter 1, and presents it in a more positive light.

11 The charging of interest on loans was forbidden for Christians, cf. Leo, *ep.* 4 (PL 54: 610–14). On 'holy interest' see 'Fasting and almsgiving' in Chapter 2.

12 *De officiis* 1.41.205–7 and 2.28.140–1, and *Hymnus* 73. See Conybeare 2002: 179–80.

13 We exclude the supplementary homily 13 on the feast of the Spanish martyr Vincent (PL 54: 501–4), whose attribution to Leo in a single manuscript has been judged spurious by several editors (PL 54: 501).

14 The cult of St Stephen had been brought to Rome, along with his relics, early in the fifth century, and its enthusiastic following is evidenced by the shrine built by Demetrias on her estate and dedicated to Stephen in the 450s. On Demetrias Anicia see Chapter 1, Leo's life and times.

15 10 August. The cult of St Lawrence was popular in both East and West.

16 Cf. Matt. 22: 37–40.

17 Cf. Rom. 5: 6–7.

18 Lit. 'none of his own' (sc. followers).

19 The 'gentile powers' were the western emperor Gallienus (253–68) and his father Valerian (253–60), who ruled in the East. Eusebius relates that while Valerian was initially positive towards Christians, he was persuaded by the equestrian Macrianus to initiate persecution of them in Egypt (*Historia ecclesiastica* 7.10.5–6, Winkelmann 1999: 652). Eusebius attributed to Gallienus the reversal of his father's religious policy after Valerian's death, and the restoration of freedom of worship and ecclesiastical property (*Historia ecclesiastica* 7.13, Winkelmann 1999: 666).

20 As archdeacon, Lawrence had been in charge of the church sacristy, where the sacred vessels and robes were kept. He was also responsible for the management of church funds, especially those reserved for the poor.

21 Sc. the prefect or other agent of imperial edicts.

22 Lat. *sacrarium*, where the sacred vessels and holy books were kept.

23 The inalienability of church property was the subject of Leo's admonition to the bishops of Sicily (*ep.* 17, PL 54: 703–6).

24 Cf. *Hom.* 87.4 above, on the increase of holy treasure.

25 The evocation of 'the plunderer' would bring to mind for Leo's audience its own experience of siege and despoliation at the hands of Alaric and, if this homily was delivered in or after May 455, also Geiseric.

26 The legend of Lawrence's martyrdom is recounted by Prudentius in the poem *Peristephanon* 2, written before 405 (Conybeare 2002: 178). In Prudentius's comical account, Lawrence suffers this excruciating torment with a light heart, and jokes with his torturers: 'Turn me over now, this side is done.' In Prudentius's representation Lawrence is the epitome of defiance of secular authority.

27 Ps. 67: 36 in the Septuagint.

28 The relics of Stephen the Protomartyr were allegedly discovered in Jerusalem in 415 and brought to Rome shortly afterwards. The church of St Stephen *in Rotondo*, still surviving, was built on the Caelian Hill by Pope Simplicius (468–83). The relics of Stephen were transferred to St Lawrence Outside the Walls in 578.

29 Cf. Philo, *De migratione Abrahami* 194: The mind that has embraced right religion no longer believes 'that the motions and agitations of the stars were the cause to men of disaster, or, on the contrary, of good fortune' (Cohn and Wendland 1962: 2, 306, Yonge 1993: 272). The heavenly bodies – the planets and fixed stars, together called the 'rulers' – exercise power not as autonomous agents but as subordinates of the one Father of

all and are thus not deserving of worship (Philo, *De specialibus legibus* 1.13–16, Cohn and Wendland 1962: 5, 3–4). See Runia 1993: 177–8.

30 Delivered on 25 December 451. Cf. *Hom.* 22.6, delivered on Christmas Day 441, where Leo also warned the congregation against the practice of sun worship.

31 Leo's emphasis on the proper understanding of the Incarnation is inspired by events at the Council of Chalcedon earlier in the same year (Green 2008: 232). At this stage Leo would have been basking in the glory of his achievements, since news of the negative reaction in some quarters took some time to reach him.

32 The equal danger of denying our nature in Christ or Christ's equality with the Father is a theme common to the *Tome, ep.* 28.5 (Green 2008: 232 n.188).

33 Again, the idea that the Son of God assumed our characteristics without losing his own (cf. *serm.* 27.2) is found in the *Tome, ep.* 28.3 (Green 2008: 232 n.190).

34 The teaching of two natures being taken up into one person in Christ is often repeated in the *Tome*.

35 This is another of Leo's carefully balanced double phrases: *Ad humana ascensio ... hominis ad divina provectio* (CCSL 138: 134). See Barclift 1997: 231 on the interchangeable use of *homo* and *humanus* for 'human nature' in the first decade of Leo's pontificate; cf. 27.1 the Son renewed humanity (*homines*) in his human nature (*in homine*).

36 In Latin there is a word play in the use of rhyming nominal participles: 'higher places' (*eminentioribus*) and 'very foolish people' (*insipientioribus*).

37 The unusual orientation of St Peter's basilica towards the west necessitated that those who wished to bow towards the rising sun turn around to face east before entering the church.

38 The 'wicked' (*impii*) are both pagan adherents to cosmic religion and Manichees who worshipped the sun and the moon.

39 Job is 'without complaint' in the sense of not having any accusation against him.

40 The phrase 'to shine upon the earth' seems to have crept into v. 14 from the following verse.

41 Cf. *Hom.* 63.4 (CCSL 138a: 384) for a similar citation of Col. 3: 10, from Holy Week 452.

42 Cf. Gen. 1: 18. The ascription of the substantive adjective 'Good' for God is reminiscent of Platonism, where *To Agathon* (the Good) is one title and predicate of divinity.

43 *Hom.* 22.6, reworked in 449, ends with an emphasis on the difference between the uncreated orders and those created *ex nihilo* (CCSL 138: 99–100) as Gregory of Nyssa had done in the previous century. 'The sun, the moon and the stars are convenient for use, and beautiful to look at, but in such a way as to refer thanks for them to their creator, and so that God, who made these things, should be worshipped and not the creation which serves him' (CCSL 138: 100).

44 Irenaeus, *Adversus haereses* 3.21.10, Sagnard 1952: 370–2.

45 This is a version of the ransom theory, even though Armitage (2005: 69 n.12), commenting on Leo's *Hom.* 22, claims that Leo knows nothing of Gregory of Nyssa's theory that a ransom was paid to the devil to free humankind from sin.

46 Holy Saturday, 4 April 454.

47 Leo perhaps felt the need to justify returning to the well-worn theme of Christ's humanity and divinity, which had occupied most of his sermons since 449, especially those delivered on the feasts of Easter, the Nativity and the Ascension.

48 Cf. Luke 19: 23; Matt. 25: 27. Cf. the concept of holy usury discussed in 'Fasting and almsgiving' in Chapter 2.

49 Cavalcanti and Montanari (2001: 458) suggest that the reading was from the Gospel of John, either John 3: 13 ff. or John 12: 23 ff.

50 Lat. *ratio*, suggesting a rational plan.

51 Just as the advent of Christ was postponed until a certain point in history to fulfil God's salvation plan (cf. *serm.* 73).

52 Cf. Ex. 31: 18; Deut. 9: 10.

53 On the doctrine of Christ's double consubstantiality see Armitage 2005: 7–18, 205–9.

54 The belief in two persons in Christ was the Christological error of which Nestorius was accused; the confusion of Christ's essence in one nature was the error of Eutyches. On these heresies see Chapter 3.

55 Cf. n.51 above on 'the plan of postponements'. Christ's suffering was not necessary of itself, but it was part of God's salvation plan.

56 The devil apparently did not realise that Christ was the immortal son of God and thought he could overcome Christ by killing him, and this was his downfall. By making the sinless Christ suffer and die, he lost his right to control human beings, who, captive to sin, were subject to the devil and to death. Leo calls this right the 'iron law' (*ius ferreum*).

57 Cf. Irenaeus's doctrine of the recapitulation of Adam in Christ, the 'second Adam', discussed briefly in the introduction to this text.

58 The figures of the Old Testament (*serm.* 69.2) have been made redundant by Christ's new covenant.

CHAPTER 8

1 Lieu 1992: 204–6. See also 'Inquiry against the Manichees' in Chapter 3.

2 Pelagianists: *Letter* 1.1, discussed in relation to *Letter* 2 below; Priscillia-nists: *ep.* 15 below.

3 Lieu 1992: 205.

4 Prosper, *Epitoma Chronicon* 1350 [s. a. 443], Mommsen 1892: 479.

5 12 December 443.

6 Cf. *serm.* 95.7: ' … and in the mirror of the human heart the image of God may shine forth, reproduced through the traces of imitation.'

7 Note the use of harvest imagery in this paragraph: the harvest (*percep-tionem*), 'every year's turn' (*singulorum annorum reuolutione*), the earth's bounty (*terrae fecunditatem*). The December fast was a time to remember and give thanks for the bounty of the harvest in the previous autumn, which sustained people through the winter.

8 Cf. Prov. 11: 25: *The soul who blesses will prosper, whoever satisfies others will be satisfied.*

9 Note the alliteration of the parallel verbs *discessit* ('departed') and *descivit* ('deviated').

10 The male and female Manichean Elect undertook three oaths or 'seals': 1) the seal of the mouth, which proscribed blasphemy, and eating meat or

drinking wine; 2) the seal of the hands, which meant not performing any task which might harm the particles of light which were said to be held captive in matter; these activities included tilling the soil, harvesting any plant or killing any animal, and bathing; 3) the seal of the breast (or 'seal of the thoughts' in eastern Manichean texts), which forbade sexual inter-course, which leads to procreation and the further enslavement of the Light in matter (Lieu 1992: 26–7). The lower rank of Hearers, to which group Augustine belonged throughout his eight-year adherence to the sect, had to serve the material needs of the Elect.

11 Fasting on Saturday, the Jewish Sabbath, was discouraged in the West, except before Easter, and completely outlawed in the East (Stökl Ben Ezra 2003: 266), as was fasting on Sundays. The Manichees fasted on Sundays and Mondays as well.

12 Leo's encapsulation of Manichean teachings on Christ's physical body, death and resurrection, as a form of docetism (e.g. *serm.* 34.4–5), is an oversimplification: some Manichean texts seem to assign a degree of cor-poreality to Christ (CFML 1: 99–102).

13 1 June 444.

14 That is, God's plan for the salvation of humankind.

15 A reference to the road to Emmaus story in Luke 24: 13–35.

16 Lat. *praevaricatione*, a legal term for the mismanagement of a case where the prosecution colludes with the defence. The use of the term here implies that Adam and Eve colluded with the devil in their fall.

17 As the Niceno-Constantinopolitan creed asserts.

18 Cf. Eph. 1: 20–1.

19 Wis. 2: 24. The envy of the devil also appears in *serm.* 9.1 (CCSL 138: 32); *serm.* 40.2 (CCSL 138a: 224); *serm.* 49.3 (CCSL 138a: 287); and *serm.* 77.2 (CCSL 138a: 488).

20 Our main source for these events is the *Chronicle* of Bishop Hydatius, the bishop mentioned at the end of the letter (*ep.* 15.17) (Burgess 1993).

21 Innocent, *ep.* 3, PL 20: 485–93. In contrast, Spanish bishops turned to the bishop of Carthage for advice on Nestorianism, e.g. the letter of Vitalis and Constantius to Bishop Capreolus of Carthage, written at the time of the Council of Ephesus (PL 53: 847–9) (Moorhead 2001: 60).

22 Hydatius (*Chronicon* 135, MGH 11: 24) identified the deacon as Pervincus.

23 Cf. the letter of Turibius of Astorga to the bishops Hydatius and Cepo-nius, of unknown date, edited and translated in CFML 1: 78–85. Hyda-tius also reports that Turibius had contact with Manichees in 445, in the same year as Leo the Great set up an inquiry into the presence of Man-ichees in the provinces (*Chronicon* 130, 133, MGH 11: 24) (CFML 1: 5). This wider inquiry would have been two years after Leo's investigation into Manichees in Rome.

24 See CFML 1: 94–7, *Excursus* IV on Manichean astrology. Cf. *serm.* 42.5 on Manichean fasting on Sundays ('the day of the Lord') and Mondays. Leo calls this the 'stupid abstinence' which they devote to the sun and moon. Leo condoned fasting on Mondays, Wednesdays and Fridays, but not on the Sabbath, i.e. Saturdays (*serm.* 42.6), or Sundays.

25 That is, the signs of the Zodiac.

26 Priscillianism was proscribed by Honorius I, Arcadius and Theodosius II in Rome in 407, whereby any property where a Priscillianist meeting had

been held with the landowner's knowledge was forfeit to the state (*Codex Theodosianus* 16.5.40) (Chadwick 1976: 188). An edict of the following year (*Codex Theodosianus* 16.5.43) permitted Catholics to seize Priscillianist churches and property.

27 Reading *destrictio* for the Latin *districtio* 'state of distraction', a frequent point of confusion in the manuscripts; cf. similarly the translation of CFML 1: 55 as 'severity'.

28 Leo refers to the trial of Priscillian and several of his followers by Emperor Maximus in Triers in *c.* 386.

29 The invasion of Spain by the Visigoth, Vandal, Suevi and Alan peoples from 409 onwards caused widespread chaos and destruction but it also allowed heretics to flourish unopposed.

30 That is, Mani.

31 Sabellius, the third-century author, taught a form of modalism in relation to the Trinity, whereby the single person of the Godhead had three modes of existence, which it could adopt like masks that could be put on and off. The Patripassians were called after their belief that God the Father (*Pater*) suffered in the suffering (*passio*) of the Son because the Father and the Son were one and the same person.

32 This was the confession of faith approved by the Nicene Council in 325, which proclaimed Christ 'of one being with the Father' (Lat. *consubstantialis*, Greek *homoousios*).

33 The Chalcedonian Definition of Faith contained a similar definition of the union of natures in Christ using the four famous adverbs: 'without confusion, without change, without division, without separation'.

34 Arius, priest of Alexandria (313–36), was condemned at the first and second Ecumenical Councils of Nicaea (325) and Constantinople (381) for teaching that there must have been a time when Christ did not exist, since God brought him into existence. Thus, Christ the Son was a created being and subordinate to God the Father. The position upheld at Nicaea was that Christ was coeternal and consubstantial with the Father. Arianism was the form of Christianity adopted by the Vandals and Goths and thus had a long life in the West. It also enjoyed imperial support in the East under Constantine's second son, Constantius II (337–61). Even Felix II, bishop of Rome (355–65), supported it early on during his reign, although the *LP* recounts only that Felix condemned Constantius as a heretic and was subsequently beheaded (*LP* 1: 211). Given that Constantius died four years before Felix he could not have been instrumental in the pope's death (cf. *LP* 1: 207–8, which gives a contradictory account, according to which Felix was deposed but died in peace). Athanasius, present at the Council of Nicaea (325) as a deacon, and later patriarch of Alexandria (328–73), was instrumental in the condemnation of Arianism in the East in the fourth century.

35 Paul of Samosata, the 'monarchian' bishop of Antioch, was condemned at a number of synods from 264 and was finally condemned at the Synod of Antioch in 268 for heresy and immorality.

36 Gennadius, *De viribus inlustribus* 14 (Herding 1924: 77) notes that the Photinians were condemned by Audentius the Spanish bishop, who showed that the Son was coeternal with the Father. Audentius also wrote against the Manichees, Sabellians and Arians.

37 The practice of fasting on feast days was also common to followers of Mani and Marcion of Sinope. Marcion, the second-century Gnostic dualist, rejected most of the books that came to be included in the canon of Christian scriptures. The Marcionite heresy arose in Rome in 144 and continued in the West until the mid fifth century, in spite of being condemned by Tertullian in his tract *Against Marcion* (*c.* 208). Marcion seems to have joined forces in Rome with Cerdo (see note below).

38 Cerdo, a Syrian Gnostic, came to Rome during the pontificate of the Greek pope Hyginus (*c.* 138–42). According to Irenaeus, who treats the heresies of Cerdo and Marcion together, Cerdo taught that the God proclaimed by the law and the prophets was not the father of Jesus Christ. The God of the Old Testament was righteous, while the God of the New Testament was benevolent. Marcion of Pontus developed Cerdo's doctrine (*Adversus haereses* 1.27.1–2, Rousseau and Doutreleau 1979: 348–50). Leo here describes them both as docetists.

39 Augustine assimilates the Priscillianists with the Manichees and other 'plagues' who do not believe that Christ had real flesh but that he was spirit alone (*serm.* 238.2, PL 38: 1125).

40 Cf. *serm.* 27.4 above on sun worship.

41 This distinction is found in Augustine, e.g. 'For whatever seems to be predicated there (sc. in God) in terms of qualities, should be understood in terms of substance (*substantia*) or essence (*essentia*)' (*De trinitate* 15.5.8, Mountain 1968: 470). See Casula 2002: 277 n.24; CFML 1: 61 n.89.

42 Cf. Casula's translation: ' … because being is a constitutive characteristic of that which is everlasting' (Casula 2002: 277).

43 This is an example of the gender-exclusive language of the original Latin, with the use of the masculine pronoun *ille* for God.

44 Cf. *Homilies* 26.2, 30.7, 63.2, and *ep.* 28.2 (above), discussed by Armitage 2005: 25–34: 'children of the promise' refers to God's promise to Abraham that all his offspring would be blessed. Christ, the descendant of David, was the fulfilment of that promise, through whom all Christians are blessed. This doctrine counters the Manichean spiritual caste system, with its segregation of Hearers from the more spiritually advanced Elect.

45 Other texts read: 'to that condition', so as to avoid the 'equivocal wording' of the text (CFML 1: 65 n. 99). See *Excursus X* on Manichean anthropology (CFML 1: 106–7). According to the Coptic Manichean text, *Chapters* (*Kephalaia*), Adam and Eve were created by the evil Rulers or Archons after Christ, the 'Third Messenger', revealed his image to them (*Kephalaia* LV and LVI) (CFML 1: 100, 107).

46 Leo comments that Origen was rightly condemned for this doctrine (*ep.* 35.3 to Julian of Cos, PL 54: 807C). The Origenist doctrine of diversity nominates free will, resulting in defection from the good, as the cause of differences in moral calibre among human beings and heavenly beings, and their accordingly diverse fates (*Peri Archon* 2.9.5–8, Crouzel and Simonetti 1978: 360–72). Refuting the Gnostic doctrines of Marcion, Valentinus and Basilides, Origen taught that the devil was one such soul that fell from heaven through satiety with contemplation of the Good. Many souls joined in the devil's fall. Human beings fell into dense, cool bodies; angels into finer, warmer bodies. The degree of corporeal density and warmth correlates with the measure of sin of the individual soul.

47 Lit. 'from the body of its unity'.

48 It is not quite true that this was the constant Christian position, as the doctrine of traducianism was occasionally entertained by Augustine (cf. Chapter 7 n. 4 above). Cf. Leo, *ep.* 35.3, ACO 2.4: 7–8, a refutation of the Eutychian notions that Christ's soul existed before his body and that the flesh assumed by Christ did not originate in Mary's womb.

49 Cf. *serm.* 27.3 above.

50 Augustine of Hippo was also consulted by Spanish bishops on the proper attitude to the writings of Dictinius, a reformed Priscillianist: Augustine, *Contra mendacium* 2.2, Zycha 1900: 471–2.

51 That is, the three persons of the Father, Son and Holy Spirit.

52 Tarragona is a town on the north-eastern coast of Spain; Lusitania was a territory on the western side of the Iberian Peninsula; Carthage is not the city by the same name in North Africa but New Carthage (*Carthago Nova*), founded by the Carthaginians on the south-eastern coast of Spain; on Galicia see the introduction to this letter.

53 Cf. Schipper and van Oort's translation: 'that the official instrument which contains our decision is delivered', which 'official instrument' they take to mean the present letter (CFML 1: 77 n.77).

54 On Bishop Hydatius of Chaves, a town in Galicia, see the introduction to this letter.

55 Schipper and van Oort (CFML 1: 5) note that there is no evidence that the requested assembly of the Iberian bishops or a provincial synod ever took place.

56 In 447.

57 Except of course in relation to the single person of Christ, e.g. 'joining in one person' (*ep.* 28.3).

58 It should be noted, however, that neither Nestorius nor Nestorianism are specifically mentioned in this letter.

59 *Sermones* 21, 22, 23, 24, 51, 54, and 71 (Chavasse 1973: cliii).

60 Followed by Barclift (1997: 221–2) and Pietrini (2002: 5). There has also been debate over whether Prosper or Leo was the author of the tract *On the calling of all nations*: Green (2008: 197–8) summarises the evidence, which points to Prosper as the more likely author.

61 See 'Leo's soteriology and christology' in Chapter 3.

62 Casula 2000: 77; Green 2008: 201.

63 The letter or 'tome' was composed on 13 June 449.

64 *Letter* 22 of Flavian to Leo, written after the council that was convened in Constantinople in November 448 ('some time since', as Flavian put it in *ep.* 22.4), took some six months to arrive in Rome. Leo wrote *Letter* 23 to Flavian, complaining about not being informed of the Eutychian controversy, before belatedly receiving *Letter* 22 in May 449. On the chronology of the letters between Leo and Flavian cf. *ep.* 38, FOTC 34: 118 n.2.

65 I.e. the Council of Constantinople in November 448, where Eutyches was excommunicated, deprived of the priesthood, and expelled from the monastery where he was archimandrite. The *Acts* are found in ACO 2.2.1: 3–19.

66 That is, the confession of the creed by catechumens before baptism. See Leo's *Homily* 98, 'On the symbol of the faith for the chosen' (Dolle 1973: 294–300).

67 Cf. the first lines of the Apostolic creed: 'I believe in God the Father almighty, maker of heaven and earth, and in Jesus Christ his only Son, our Lord, who was conceived by the Holy Spirit, born of the virgin Mary ... '.

68 A phrase from the Niceno-Constantinopolitan creed from the Council of Constantinople I in 381: *We believe in one Lord, Jesus Christ ... God from God, Light from Light, true God from true God, begotten not made, of one being with the Father. ...*

69 I have translated the alternative reading *totum*, rather than *totam*, which would mean: 'the birth expended itself completely ... '

70 I have attempted to maintain the assonance of the two infinitives with the verbs 'stain' (*contaminare*) and 'detain' (*detinere*).

71 'Passible' in the sense of being capable of suffering.

72 Cf. *serm.* 21.2.

73 Or 'of God's protection': the Latin noun *muneribus* can mean both; cf. the noun *dote* in the next clause also meaning 'gift'.

74 *Pietas* can mean the devotion of a parent to a child, or of a child to a parent. It can also mean something close to 'pity' in Christian texts, as in God's 'pity' for human beings.

75 Or 'he that could not be contained wished to be contained'. The Latin verb *comprehendo* will bear both meanings. Cf. *serm.* 37.1, CCSL 138: 200, of the infant Jesus: 'He is contained in the lap of the mother who is contained by no limit.'

76 Cf. *serm.* 54.2. This was the passage to which the monks of Palestine took particular exception, characterising it as 'Nestorian'.

77 This passage, from 'His birth in the flesh ... ' was inspired by *serm.* 19 of Gaudentius of Brescia, PL 20: 983A–C.

78 The previous section, from 'To hunger, to thirst, to grow weary ... ' is closely modelled on Gaudentius of Brescia's *serm.* 19, PL 20: 984A–B.

79 Compare the more elegant formulation of this passage in *ep.* 124.4 below, cf. *serm.* 64.4.

80 A similar reference is found in both the Apostolic creed and the Niceno-Constantinopolitan creed.

81 Cf. Augustine, *Contra sermonem Arianorum* 8, PL 42: 688, with the opening of this paragraph.

82 I.e. Christ, the cornerstone (cf. 1 Pet. 2: 6–7). Peter's name (*Petrus*) was derived from the Greek word for 'rock' (*petra*) (cf. Matt. 16: 18: '*You are Peter and on this rock I will build my church*').

83 Cf. *serm.* 4.2 below, and *serm.* 51.1.

84 Cf. *serm.* 73.3 above.

85 Cf. the translation of NPNF 12: 'and that we might know the Word not to be different from the Flesh'. There is no manuscript support for such a translation in the ACO version.

86 See the record of the trial, ACO 2.2.1: 17–18, sections 145 and 154, in which Eutyches cites Cyril, Athanasius and other holy fathers as holding the same opinion.

87 Cf. ACO 2.2.1: 16–17, sections 134–40, and 147.

88 Lat. *pietatis*. See n. 74 above on *pietas*.

89 A scribal note appears at this point: 'And in another hand: I, Tiburtius the notarius, copied this by order of my venerable lord Pope Leo.'

90 Julius of Puteoli; Renatus of the Roman titular church of St Clement; and Hilary, the deacon who would be Leo's successor as bishop of Rome.

91 In 449.

92 *Homilies* 64 and 65 are really one long homily split into two and delivered three days apart, on Easter Sunday and the following Wednesday, so as not to fatigue the audience (*serm.* 64.4, CCSL 138a: 394).

93 Cf. introduction to *ep.* 28 above.

94 Green 2008: 230–47 gives a detailed analysis of the theological content of *Letter* 124.

95 ' ... so that the ears of the faithful may have proof that we preach nothing other than what we have received from our precedessors' (*ep.* 129.2, ACO 2.4: 85; FOTC 34: 216).

96 Evagrius, *Historia ecclesiastica* 2.8 (Hübner 2007: 238–40). Wace and Piercy (1994: 866–7) follow Evagrius's account; cf. Horn (2006: 95–6), who cites Liberatus of Carthage's *Breviarium* 15 as an alternative source on Proterius's death. According to Liberatus, Proterius died on Holy Thursday, 28 March 457, twelve days after Timothy Aelurus had been chosen as patriarch.

97 Many of the ideas here are presented again in *ep.* 165, almost *verbatim*, except for the substitution of *natura* in that letter where *substantia* is used here: see the introduction above.

98 In *Letter* 130 of March 454, Leo asked Marcian to promulgate an official Greek version of the *Tome* to replace the falsified version that Alexandrian monks were citing as confirmation that Leo accepted the heresy of Nestorius (cf. *epp.* 124, 131 and 152).

99 In *Letter* 113.3 to Julian of Cos (dated 11 March 453), Leo seems to be unsure of the motives of the monks of Palestine and asks for more information (ACO 2.4: 66.15–23). In the final section of *Letter* 113 Leo requests a complete Latin version of the *Acts* of the Council of Chalcedon.

100 See, e.g., *Letter* 31 to Pulcheria, sister of Theodosius II (13 June 449); *Letter* 32 to Faustus and Martin and other eastern abbots (13 June 449); *Letter* 69 to Emperor Theodosius (16 July 450) and *Letter* 59 to the clergy and people of Constantinople (17 March 450).

101 Cf. the reading of *Letter* 165: 'according to the reality of both natures' (FOTC 34: 264).

102 Pope Damasus condemned Apollinarism at several Councils of Rome held between 374 and 382. In the seventh anathema of one of these councils he and the assembled bishops of Rome condemned the teachings of Apollinaris as follows: 'We pronounce anathema against those who say that the Word of God was changed into human flesh in place of the rational soul. For the Son himself was made the Word of God in the flesh not to replace the rational and intellective soul, but rather he assumed and saved our soul, that is the rational and intellective soul' (*Professio catholicae fidei quam Papa Damasus destinavit ad Paulinum Antiocenum episcopum*, Hinschius 1963: 517). Apollinaris was also condemned at the Second Ecumenical Council convened in Constantinople in 381.

103 Cf. the Niceno-Constantinopolitan creed.

104 Whereas Marcion is paired with the Manichees here, in *Letter* 165 Valentinus and Mani are singled out as the two prime examples of Docetism (ACO 2.4: 114 line 11).

105 Cf. *Letter* 59.3 (Pope Leo to the clergy and people of Constantinople, ACO 2.4: 34–7), where Leo describes those who believe in a phantom body in Christ, or who say that all bodily actions and passions belong to the Godhead rather than the flesh, as belonging to the Arians.

106 In *Letter* 165 Leo inserts a long quotation from the Niceno-Constantinopolitan creed. This insertion was made to answer the claims of the Eutychians that they conformed with the definition of Nicaea, whereas the Chalcedonians did not. In the *Tome*, Leo had focused more on the Apostles' creed in its early form, which is known as the Old Roman creed.

107 Note the imagery of the military triumph being employed here. This complete paragraph is drawn from *serm.* 64.3 (CCSL 138a: 391–2).

108 *Letter* 165 adds the Chalcedonian adverbs: 'without separation and without division'.

109 In *Letter* 165 Leo makes an allusion at this point to Peter's confession of Jesus: 'You are the Christ, the Son of the living God' (Matt. 16: 16).

110 This whole paragraph up to this point is taken from *serm.* 64.4 (CCSL 138a: 392–3) and inspired by Gaudentius of Brescia's *serm.* 19 (cf. *ep.* 28.3 above).

111 Cf. *Letter* 28.5 above.

112 This section is borrowed from *serm.* 65.4 (CCSL 138a: 398), almost *verbatim*.

113 Cf. n.74 above on the translation of *pietas* as 'pity'.

114 This note in the manuscripts indicates that the duplication of material in *Letter* 165 to the Emperor Leo ends here.

115 The monks are addressed in the singular here, a switch from the plural form of address used earlier.

116 Leo here refers to the riots that had spread from Jerusalem throughout Palestine, culminating in the murder of Severian of Scythopolis. Juvenal, bishop of Jerusalem, sought safety in exile.

117 The claw was an ancient instrument of torture in the shape of a bird's talon, and was often paired with the rack in the accounts of early Christian martyrdoms.

CHAPTER 9

1 Leo makes a pun based on the similarity between the Latin words for 'city' (*urbs*) and 'world' (*orbis*), as Jerome had done before him when he bemoaned the fact that 'in one city the whole world had perished' (*Prologus, Comm. in Hiezechielem*, Glorie 1964: 3 line 14) (Moorhead 2001: 41 and n.7).

2 Both these nouns are in the feminine gender: 'female teacher', 'female disciple'. Recension A reads: 'you who were the mother of error have been made the daughter of truth'.

3 Recension C adds: 'by whose zeal the foundations of your walls were first placed, of whom he [who gave you his name ...]'.

4 Romulus, who murdered his twin brother Remus, was traditionally known as the founder of Rome.

5 In place of 'than those men (founded), of whom the one who gave you his name defiled you with fratricide. They are the ones who advanced you to this point of glory', Rec. A reads: 'than those twins, who were in conflict to the point of parricide, (founded) ... '.

6 The pun on *urbs* and *orbis* is repeated (see n.1 above).

7 The passage 'But so that the effect of his ineffable grace ... ignoring the author of its progress' in Rec. B is an expansion of the same section in Rec. A, which reads: 'But this city, dearly beloved, ignorant of the creator of its dignity ... '.

8 The date of the feast of Saints Peter and Paul (29 June and the following week) may have been chosen to compete with the *Ludi Apollinares* on 6–13 July.

9 In the city of Rome, the stronghold or citadel (*arx*) was the *Capitolium* dedicated to the god Jupiter. Later, in ch. 5, Leo refers to 'Roman strongholds' in the plural to indicate other Roman cities that Peter had conquered by establishing churches there.

10 The rest of this section is not found in Rec. A.

11 Rec. A omits 'Peter'.

12 Rec. C omits 'as a source of fear' and adds 'you should give way to terror while you sought their salvation'.

13 Rec. C reads 'emotion'.

14 Rec. A reads 'you should serve the food of heavenly nourishment'.

15 Cf. Gal. 2: 7, where Paul speaks of his gospel as that of the foreskin (i.e. the uncircumcised Gentiles), while Peter's is the apostolate of circumcision.

16 Rec. A reads 'Already you had imbued many peoples with the laws sanctioned by the Gospel ... '.

17 Rec. A reads 'by divine dispensation'.

18 Nero instituted a local persecution after the fire in Rome in 64 CE, which he blamed on Christians.

19 Cf. Tertullian's famous dictum: 'The blood of martyrs is the seed of the church'.

20 Rec. A reads 'ranks'.

21 Rec. A omits 'single'.

22 Cf. Eph. 1: 22–3; Col. 1: 18.

23 Rec. A adds a final paragraph: 'But as we ourselves have experienced, and our forefathers proved, we believe and confess that, among all the trials of this life, we are always helped by the prayers of our special patrons to obtain the mercy of God: so that, as far down as our own sins press us, we are so far raised up by the merits of the apostles.'

24 Alaric's third siege of Rome, 25–27 August 410.

25 In 399 John Chrysostom delivered a similar condemnation of horse races in the Hippodrome in Constantinople, in his sermon *Against the Games and Theatres, New Homily* 7 (PG 56: 263–70; Mayer and Allen 2000: 119–25). Evidence of their continued appeal for Christians is found in John's homily *On 'My Father's Working Still', New Homily* 10 (PG 63: 511–16, Mayer and Allen 2000: 144–7).

26 Circus games were held on 28 August, the festival of the Moon and the Sun, according to the *Chronography of 354*, and likely still included in the calendar in the early 440s.

27 Cf. *serm.* 27 on astrological fatalism, the belief that human destinies were governed by the movements of the heavenly bodies.

28 Contrary to Leo's assertion that Siricius (384–99) made the original grant of such powers to Anysius of Thessalonica, some scholars believe that it was Pope Damasus (366–84) who first made Acholius his vicar, citing

Letter 2 of Damasus to Acholius (ST 23: 18–19). Dunn (2007b: 133) disagrees, interpreting this letter as merely the request of one bishop to another.

29 See 'The reception of Leo's letters into canon law' in Chapter 5.

30 Reading the PL emendation of *alterni* to *fraterni* (PL 54: 617 n.[a]).

31 The word for priest (*sacerdos*) is used throughout this letter to indicate 'bishop'; cf. n.36 below.

32 Cf. Hunt's translation 'there appears to be a more important motive (*affectio*) for us' (FOTC 34: 27).

33 On 'watchtowers' (*speculis*) in Leo's rhetoric of episcopal vigilance in this text see Maier (1996: 454).

34 Pope Siricius (384–99) was predecessor of Anastasius (399–401/2) and Innocent I (401/2–17).

35 Cf. ST 23: 19, *ep.* 3: Pope Siricius to Anysius of Thessalonica. Anysius's successor Rufus (412–35) held the vicariate before Anastasius was granted it in 444.

36 Although the word used is *sacerdotium* and this same prohibition applied to deacons and priests, the context indicates that bishops are meant, as Hunt observes (FOTC 34: 29 n. 4).

37 That is, before being baptised.

38 The same restriction applies to deacons and priests in *ep.* 12 to the bishops of Caesarea Mauritania (PL 54: 645–56), probably issued on 10 August in 446 (the date is questioned by Hunt in FOTC 34: 48 n.1).

39 Cf. the letters of Innocent on this subject, *ep.* 3 to the Synod of Toledo (*c.* 404 CE), and *ep.* 17 to the bishops of Macedonia and Dacia (414 CE).

40 This emendation of a lacuna in the text is suggested by Silva-Tarouca (ST 23: 55 line 58).

41 Here the hierarchy of the churches in Illyricum is spelled out: provincial bishops answer to the metropolitan of each province, and the metropolitans answer to the papal vicar Anastasius.

42 The same verse is quoted in *Letter* 12 to the bishops of Caesarea Mauritania, where Leo spells out what this verse means: 'What does "*lay hands hastily*" mean except to give the episcopal honour to the untried, to those who have not reached the age of maturity [25 for deacons; 30 for priests], before the time of examination, before their obedience has been tried, before they have experienced discipline?' (PL 54: 647B, FOTC 34: 49–50).

43 A translation of the emendation suggested by Silva-Tarouca (ST 23: 56 line 89).

44 I.e. *ep.* 5 to the bishops of Illyricum (= *ep.* 24, ST 23: 57–9), issued on the same day.

45 Again, I have followed Silva-Tarouca's emendation of the lacuna (ST 23: 57 line 102).

46 See *Liber Diurnus Romanorum Pontificum* 6 (Sickel 1889: 6.16–19) on the ordination of priests and deacons.

47 In 444.

48 On the dispute with Hilary of Arles, see Chapter 5; on the inquiry against the Manicheans, see Chapter 3.

49 In Gal. 3: 16–17, Paul interprets Gen. 12: 7 (*Then the Lord appeared to Abram and said: 'To your offspring [Heb. seed] I will give this land'*) as referring to Christ. God's promise to Abraham, and the concept of

Abraham's seed, are important Leonine themes (Armitage 2005: 25–45). Armitage describes Leo's claim that 'Peter properly reigns over all those whom Christ rules' (*serm.* 4.2) as 'universalist' 'in the biblical sense of the word ... which is to say, the inclusion of the Gentiles in the restored Israel' (2005: 44).

50 Other sources, including Irenaeus and Tertullian, offer alternative genealogies which make Clement the third bishop of Rome rather than the fourth, as in the *Liber Pontificalis* (Neil 2003: 25–30).

51 Cf. Leo's complaint in *serm.* 84.1 about the lack of attendance two years before at the liturgical celebration of Rome's delivery from Alaric.

52 Lat. *pontifex*, a term used in pre-Christian Rome for 'one of the college of priests having supreme control in matters of public religion in Rome' (Clare 1982: 1403). The title of *pontifex maximus*, given to the head of the college, was assumed even by Christian emperors up until the time of Gratian (see introduction to *Homily* 84 above). Leo's adoption of the title *pontifex* for himself suggests that the bishop had assumed the civic function of offering sacrifices for the safety and prosperity of the city and the empire by this time. Cf. *serm.* 64.3 (CCSL 138a: 391) for the crucified Christ, the 'true high priest', offering up the sacrifice of his own body on the altar of the cross.

53 Lit. 'whatever it did not refuse to others'.

54 From this point the text is borrowed from *serm.* 83, a sermon on St Peter and St Paul from 443, except for three minor additions.

55 Cf. *serm.* 83.1, CCSL 138a: 519: 'For that confession has obtained this, dearly beloved, (the confession) inspired by God the Father in his apostolic breast, transcended every wavering human opinion, and became as solid as a rock, which cannot be shaken by any blow.' Cf. the same passage in *serm.* 3, CCSL 138: 13.

56 Cf. Is. 22: 22: '*I will place on his* (sc. Eliakim son of Hilkiah's) *shoulder the key of the house of David; he shall open, and no one shall shut; he shall shut, and no one shall open.*'

57 The subject of the verb *intretis* is plural: 'lest you (sc. Peter and your brothers) enter into temptation'.

58 Peter's penance after denying Christ, and the Lord's forgiveness, gave hope to all Christians. As Uhalde puts it, 'Peter taught Christians that penance worked as an antidote to human fallibility and mendacity alike' (Uhalde 2007: 119).

59 The pronoun 'us' refers to Leo and to all Christians everywhere, as the next sentence shows.

60 The coda, inc. *Therefore* ... , is original to this homily.

CHAPTER 10

1 Casula 2002: 264; Pietrini 2002: 85.

2 From the various titles of *Letter* 1 offered by the manuscripts (PL 54: 589–90 n.24) it is clear that the identity of its addressee was unknown even at the earliest stages of the transmission process. One can say with relative certainty, however, that the addressee of *Letter* 1 should be identified with the metropolitan of the province of Venice, to whom Leo says he sent letters of instruction on the proper treatment of Pelagian clergy (*ep.* 2.1).

3 'If any bishop, objecting to the small size of his diocese, seeks to administer one with greater reputation and transfers himself to a larger congregation for any reason at all, he will indeed be expelled from the see which is not his and will likewise lose his own' (*ep.* 14.8, PL 54: 674A, FOTC 34: 64).

4 *Ep.* 18 to Januarius of Aquileia is dated 30 December 447. Its contents are very similar to those of *ep.* 2.

5 The Ballerini suggest that the anonymous bishop of Aquileia to whom Leo addressed *ep.* 1 was the predecessor of Januarius (444–7) (PL 54: 593–4).

6 See 'Pelagianism' and 'Nestorianism' in Chapter 3.

7 E.g. *ep.* 1, *ep.* 15, *ep.* 18, *ep.*170; less frequent in homilies, e.g. *serm.* 16.

8 Cf. *serm.* 16 above on Manicheism, and *ep.* 15 on Priscillianism.

9 Cf. two letters of Pope Gelasius (492–6) to Bishop Honorius (JK 625 and 626) condemning the revival of Pelagianism in Dalmatia (*epp.* 5 and 6, PL 59: 30–3). Gelasius also wrote to the bishops of Picenum in 493 condemning three Pelagian doctrines (JK 621) (PL 59: 34–41).

10 Lit. 'the letter of your Brotherhood', an honorific title reserved for fellow priests and bishops.

11 I.e. *ep.* 1 to the bishop of Aquileia, on which see the introduction to this text.

12 There were crucial differences between the teachings of Pelagius and his disciple Caelestius, who developed his own following. Caelestius exaggerated the Pelagian separation between grace and free will, and denied original sin, arguing that Adam would have died even without the Fall, as he had been created mortal. According to Caelestius, infants who died without baptism attained eternal life, since they were in a sinless state (Casula 2002: 105–6).

13 Similar canons prohibiting priests and bishops from transferring between dioceses are the Apostolic Canons 13–14 (Mansi I.31), Nicaea I, canons 15–16 (Mansi II.681–2), Arles 2, canon 21 (Mansi II.473), and Carthage 4, canon 27 (Mansi III.953).

14 Cf. the similar concern expressed in *ep.* 2 above.

15 Forum Julii, a town in south-eastern Gaul, not to be confused with the Roman town of the same name in northern Italy, now known as Cividale del Friuli.

16 This is an indirect allusion to the practice of closing the main doors of the church on catechumens and penitents before the liturgy of the Eucharist to keep them from participating in or observing the rite of communion.

17 Reading *ac necessarium* for *ab necessarium*.

18 Accepting the manuscript variant *confessio* (rather than *conversio* 'conversion') provided in PL 54: 1013 n. (a).

19 These two scriptural quotations are made from the Septuagint version of Isaiah.

20 The mortal sin of apostasy, like those of adultery and murder, warranted greater penalties: the fulfilment of public penance is required by the canons.

21 In 452 CE.

22 Cf. *epp.* 83, 89, 90, 94, 104, 111, 115, 121, 126, 128, 130, 134, 136, and 142. The majority of these concern the convocation of the Council of Chalcedon and the problems that ensued.

23 Wace and Piercy 1994: 866, s.v. 'Proterius, patriarch of Alexandria'.

24 Gennadius, *De viris inlustribus* 87 (Herding 1924: 108); Bede, *De temporum ratione* 43 (CCSL 123b: 417). Bede cites an unnamed source, possibly Victor of Capua (James 1993: 563 n.38).

25 Patriarch of Alexandria (385–412).
26 In *Laterculum paschale* Theophilus calculated Easter for 100 years from
375. Latin Easter calendars were calculated in eighty-four-year cycles and
contained a different date for 455, 17 April: Leo had already raised this
discrepancy in 451, in *ep.* 88.4 to Paschasinus of Lilybaeum (PL 54: 929).
27 I have translated the editorial addition of Schwartz, ACO 2.4: 90 l.7.
28 This might be read as a gentle reminder to Marcian that the success of his
rule depended on the devotions of the Christian priesthood.
29 Proterius, *ep.* 133, PL 54: 1084–94.
30 Lit. 'times'.
31 The adjective *sacerdotali* here means 'episcopal' rather than 'priestly'. See
ep. 6 above on the use of *sacerdos* to mean 'bishop' rather than 'priest'.
32 In 454. Silva-Tarouca has reconstructed the text at the end of *ep.* 136, issued
on the same day as *ep.* 137, so that it reads 'after the consulship of the
most illustrious Opilio' (ST 20: 146 = *ep.* 57), and similarly for *epp.* 126,
127 and 138, issued in the same year, since Leo at that time did not know
the names of the two eastern consuls chosen for that year, as Hunt notes
(FOTC 34: 211 n.3). The correct identification of the consulship of Aetius
and Studius at the end of *ep.* 137 may well have been added after the event.
33 Note the frequent references to the Gospel of John, chapters 10, 15, and 16.
34 Translating the reading *consecratio* offered in PL 54: 1204 (h) and accepted
by Hinschius 1963: 616.
35 PL 54: 1203B here inserts *publicam* following Sirmond's emendation, so
that the text reads: 'public penance'.
36 A misquote of 1 Sam. 2: 25: '*If someone sins against a man God will med-
iate for him, but if someone sins against the Lord who can intercede for
him?*' Augustine, *Answer to the Letters of Petilian the Donatist*, Book 2, ch.
106, misquotes the verse twice in the same way: '*If the people shall sin, the
priest shall pray for them: but if the priest shall sin, who will pray for him?*'
(NPNF 4: 240, 241).
37 The creation of Adam and Eve in Gen. 1: 27 gives man and woman an
equality which is absent from the account of Gen. 2: 21–5, where Eve is
created out of Adam's flesh. However, Gen. 2: 24 offers a more obvious
reference to the institution of marriage.
38 I.e. *libera*, a manumitted slave. The distinctions of social class made here
are entirely typical of Leo's time, however obnoxious they may appear to
the modern reader.
39 Gen. 21: 10, cf. Gal. 4: 30. Hagar's son Ishmael is recognised as a true heir
of Abraham in the Islamic faith.
40 Lit. 'in this body'.
41 See Uhalde 2007: 29–32 on the bishop's court (*audientia episcopalis*),
which took over much of the business of secular law courts towards the
end of the fourth century.
42 2 Tim. 2: 3–4 refers to serving God as a soldier of Christ.
43 Cf. Deut. 23: 21; Ps. 50: 14.
44 I.e. Romania, a name encompassing both the eastern and western parts of
the empire in the fifth century.
45 Reading *dabatur* as does Hinschius 1963: 617, for *dacatur* (PL 54: 1209 A1).
46 Refugees from the Vandal invasions had poured into Rome from North
Africa after the collapse of Carthage in 439, and from the neighbouring

province of Mauritania, which was under Vandal control from 429 to 534. The Donatist sect was strong in North Africa, as were the Manichees. The Vandals themselves were Arians. Thus it is possible that Christians could have been unwittingly (or willingly) baptised into any of these sects, all of which Leo regards as heretical.

47 Cf. *ep.* 159.7 to Nicetas, bishop of Aquileia, which instructs that people baptised by heretics should be received back into the church by the laying on of hands with the invocation of the Holy Spirit 'since they have received the bare form of baptism without the power of sanctification' (PL 54: 1139, FOTC 34: 251). *Ep.* 159 was written within a year of the composition of *ep.* 167. Compare *ep.* 166.2 to Neo, bishop of Ravenna, on the laying on of hands for those who have returned from captivity but were baptised by heretics (PL 54: 1194–5).

48 In *ep.* 159.5, Leo ruled that those who were polluted during captivity by eating foods used for sacrifices should be cleansed by penance: 'Whether terror forced them or hunger urged them to do this, there should be no hesitation in absolving them, since this type of food was taken out of fear or need, not out of reverence for their pagan religion' (PL 54: 1138, FOTC 34: 250).

49 The Roman bishops Donatian and Geminian mentioned here are known from only one other source, Leo's letter of September 458 to Emperor Leo I, as the emissaries he promised to send to Constantinople (*ep.* 164, FOTC 34: 257). Almost two years later, they had finally returned to Rome and reported on the state of affairs in the imperial capital.

50 Timothy probably merited his sobriquet *Aelurus*, meaning 'The Cat' or 'The Weasel', for his cunning and political nous. See *ODB* 1991: 2086–7, s. v. 'Timotheos Ailouros'. Several of his letters survive, along with fragments of a polemical work *Against the Definition of the Council of Chalcedon* in an Armenian and a Syriac version (Ebied and Wickham 1970).

51 A reference to the murder of Proterius, patriarch of Alexandria, in 457.

52 Emperor Leo I (457–74) expelled Timothy from Alexandria in 460.

53 By August 460, Timothy Salofaciolus had been installed as patriarch of Alexandria.

54 Lit. 'is not deserted' (*deseritur*).

55 In 460.

BIBLIOGRAPHY

TEXTS OF LEO THE GREAT

P. and H. Ballerini produced an early edition of the works of Leo in 1753–7, which was based on the 1675 edition of Pasquier Quesnel. The Ballerini edition was taken over in Patrologia Latina:

Migne, J.-P. (1881–8) *Sancti Leonis magni Romani pontificis opera omnia post Paschasii Quesnelli recensionem.* 3 vols. Paris: Garnier (PL, 54–6).

SERMONS

Chavasse, A. (1973) *Sancti Leonis magni Romani pontificis tractatus septem et nonaginta.* Turnhout: Brepols (CCSL, 138 and 138a).

Naldini, M. (ed.) (1997) *Sermoni. Leone Magno, 1. Introduzione: I sermoni di Leone Magno fra storia e teologia.* Fiesole: Nardini (Biblioteca patristica, 30).

Montanari, E. and Naldini, M. (eds and trans.) (1998) *Sermoni. Leone Magno, 2. Sermoni del Ciclo Natalizio.* Fiesole: Nardini (Biblioteca patristica, 31).

Montanari, E. and Puccini, S. (eds and trans.) (1999) *Sermoni. Leone Magno, 3. Sermoni quaresimali e sulle collette.* Fiesole: Nardini (Biblioteca patristica, 33).

Cavalcanti, E. and Montanari, E. (eds and trans.) (2001) *Sermoni. Leone Magno, 4. I Sermoni sul Mistero Pasquale.* Bologna: Devoniane (Biblioteca patristica, 38).

LETTERS

Schwartz, E. (1932a) *Acta conciliorum oecumenicorum 2: Concilium universale Chalcedonense* vol. 2: *Versiones particulares,* part 1: *Collectio Novariensis de re Eutychis.* Berlin: de Gruyter (= ACO 2.2.1).

——(1932b) *Acta conciliorum oecumenicorum 2: Concilium universale Chalcedonense* vol. 4: *Leonis papae I epistularum collectiones.* Berlin: de Gruyter. (= ACO 2.4).

Silva-Tarouca, C. (1932) *S. Leonis magni Tomus ad Flavianum episcopum Constantinopolitanum (epistula XXVIII) additis testimoniis patrum et eiusdem S. Leonis magni Epistula ad Leonem I imperatorem (epistula CLXV)*. Rome: Pontificia Universitas Gregoriana (ST, 9).

——(1934) *S. Leonis magni epistulae contra Eutychis haeresim*, part 1: *Epistulae quae Chalcedonensi concilio praemittuntur (aa. 449–451)*. Rome: Pontificia Universitas Gregoriana (ST, 15).

——(1935) *S. Leonis magni epistulae contra Eutychis haeresim*, part 2: *Epistulae post Chalcedonense concilium missae (aa. 452–458)*. Rome: Pontificia Universitas Gregoriana (ST, 20).

——(1937) *Epistularum romanorum pontificum ad vicarios per Illyricum aliosque episcopos. Collectio Thessalonicensis*. Rome: Pontificia Universitas Gregoriana (ST, 23).

Several letters were not included in the editions of Schwartz and Silva-Tarouca. Other editions containing one or more letters include:

Campos, J. (1962) 'La epístola antipriscilianista de S. León Magno.' *Helmantica* 13: 269–308.

Günther, O. (1895) *Epistulae imperatorum pontificum aliorum inde ab a. CCCLXVII usque ad a. DLIII datae Avellana quae dicitur collectio*, vol. 1. Vienna: Tempsky (CSEL, 35).

Schipper, H. G. and van Oort, J. (eds and trans.) (2000) *St Leo the Great. Sermons and Letters against the Manichaeans, selected fragments*. Turnhout: Brepols (CFML, 1).

Vollmann, B. (1965) *Studien zum Priszillianismus. Die Forschung, die Quellen, der fünfzehnte Brief Papst Leos des Grossen*. St Ottilien: EOS-Verlag (Kirchengeschichtliche Quellen und Studien, 7).

TRANSLATIONS OF LEO'S WORKS

Dolle, R. (ed. and trans.) (1961–2003) *Sermons de Léon le Grand*. 4 vols. Paris: CERF (SC, 22bis, 49bis, 74bis, 200).

Feltoe, C. (trans.) (1894) *The Letters and Sermons of Leo the Great*, in P. Schaff and H. Wace (eds) (1955), *Leo the Great, Gregory the Great*, repr. Grand Rapids, MI: Eerdmans (NPNF, ser. 2, 12).

Freeland, J. P. and Conway, A. J. (trans.) (1995) *St Leo the Great, Sermons*. Washington, DC: The Catholic University of America Press (FOTC, 93).

Hunt, E. (trans.) (1957) *St Leo the Great, Letters*. Washington, DC: The Catholic University of America Press (FOTC, 34).

OTHER TEXTS AND TRANSLATIONS

References to works edited in Patrologia Graeca and Patrologia Latina are not listed individually.

Bormann, E. and Henzen, G. (1876) *Corpus inscriptionum latinarum consilio et auctoritate Academiae Litterarum Regiae Borussicae editum*, vol. 6: *Inscriptiones urbis romae latinae*. Berlin: George Reimer.

Burgess, R. W. (1993) *The Chronicle of Hydatius and the Consularia Constantinopolitana: two contemporary accounts of the final years of the Roman Empire.* Oxford: Clarendon Press (Oxford classical monographs).

Cohn, L. and Wendland, P. (1962) *Philonis Alexandrini opera quae supersunt.* 7 vols. Berlin: de Gruyter.

Courtonne, Y. (2002) *Saint Basile, Correspondance.* 3 vols, 2nd edn. Paris: Les belles lettres.

Croke, B. (1995) *The Chronicle of Marcellinus: a translation and commentary.* Sydney: Australian Association for Byzantine Studies (Byzantina australiensia, 7).

Crouzel, H. and Simonetti, M. (1978) *Origène. Traité des Principes*, vol. 1: *Livres 1 et 2.* Paris: Cerf (SC, 252).

Davidson, I. (2001) *Ambrose, De officiis.* 2 vols. Oxford: Clarendon (Oxford early Christian studies).

Davis, R. (2000) *The Book of Pontiffs (Liber Pontificalis): The ancient biographies of the first ninety Roman bishops to AD 715*, 2nd edn. Liverpool: Liverpool University Press (Translated texts for historians, 6).

Dekkers, E. and Fraipont, I. (1956) *Aurelii Augustini opera pars 10, Enarrationes in Psalmos 3, CI–CL.* Turnhout: Brepols (CCSL, 40).

De Rossi, I. B. (1888) *Inscriptiones christianae urbis Romae septimo saeculo antiquiores*, vol. 2, part 1. Vatican City: Pont. inst. archeologiae Christianae.

Diehl, E. (1961) *Inscriptiones latinae christianae veteres.* 3 vols, 2nd edn. Berlin: Weidmann.

Dindorf, L. (1831) *Joannis Malalae Chronographia.* Bonn: Weber (Corpus scriptorum historiae Byzantinae).

——(1832), *Chronicon paschale.* 2 vols. Bonn: Weber (Corpus scriptorum historiae Byzantinae).

Duchesne, L. and Vogel, C. (1955–72) *Le Liber Pontificalis.* 3 vols. Paris: E. de Boccard.

Giunta, F. (1991) *Jordanis De origine actibusque Getarum.* Rome: Istituto storico italiano per il medio evo (Fonti per la storia d'Italia, 117).

Glorie, F. (1964) *S. Hieronymi presbyteri Opera Pars 1.4, Opera exegetica. Commentariorum in Hiezechielem libri XIV.* Turnhout: Brepols (CCSL, 75).

Gordon, C. D. (1960) *The Age of Attila. Fifth-century Byzantium and the Barbarians.* Ann Arbor: University of Michigan Press.

Hansen, G. C. and Maraval, P. (2007) *Socrates, Histoire ecclésiastique Livre VII.* Paris: CERF (SC, 506).

Herding, W. (1924) *Hieronymi de viris inlustribus liber. Accedit Gennadii catalogus virorum inlustrium.* Leipzig: Teubner.

Hinschius, P. (1963) *Decretales pseudo-Isidorianae et Capitula Angilramni.* Leipzig: B. Tachnitz (1863); repr. Aalen: Scientia Verlag.

Hubner, A. (2007) *Evagrius Scholasticus, Historia ecclesiastica. Kirchengeschichte.* 2 vols. Turnhout: Brepols (Fontes christiani, 57).

Jaffé, P. and Kaltenbrunner, F. (1956) *Regesta pontificum Romanorum I (a S Petro ad a. MCXLIII).* Leipzig: Veit (1885, 2nd edn); repr. Graz: Akademische Druck.

Jones, C. W. (1943) *Bedae opera de temporibus*. Cambridge, MA: Mediaeval Academy of America.

Labourt, J. (1949–63) *Saint Jérôme, Lettres*. 8 vols. Paris: Les belles lettres.

Lambot, C. (1961) *Sancti Aurelii Augustini sermones de vetere testamento, Sermones I–L*. Turnhout: Brepols (CCSL, 41).

Laourdas, B. and Westerink, L. G. (1983–8) *Photii Patriarchae Constantinopolitani epistulae et amphilochia*. 6 vols. Leipzig: Teubner (Bibliotheca scriptorum Graecorum et Romanorum Teubneriana).

Mayer, W. and Allen, P. (2000) *John Chrysostom*. London–New York: Routledge (The Early Church Fathers),

Mommsen, T. (1863) *Corpus inscriptionum latinarum consilio et auctoritate Academiae Litterarum Regiae Borussicae editum*, vol. 1: *Inscriptiones latinae antiquissimae ad C. Caesaris mortem*. Berlin: George Reimer.

——(1892) *Chronicorum minorum saec. IV–VII*, vol. 1. Berlin: de Gruyter (MGH auctorum antiquissimorum, tomus 9).

——(1893), *Chronica minora saec. IV–VII*, vol. 2. Berlin: de Gruyter (MGH auctorum antiquissimorum, tomus 11, 1).

Mommsen, T. and Rougé, J. (2005) *Code théodosien livre XVI*, 2nd edn. Paris: CERF (SC, 497).

Moricca, U. (1960) *Gregorii Magni dialogi libri IV.* Rome: Senato (1924); repr. Turin: Bottega d'Erasmo (Fonti per la storia d'Italia, 57).

Mountain, W. J. (1968) *De trinitate. Aurelius Augustinus*. 2 vols. Turnhout: Brepols (CCSL, 50–50A).

Nau, F. (1910) *Le livre de Héraclide de Damas*. Paris: Letouzey et Ané.

Paschoud, F. (2003) *Zosime. Histoire nouvelle*, 3/1: *Livre V*, 2nd edn. Paris: Les belles lettres (Collection des Universités de France).

Perels, E. (1978) *Nicolai I. papae epistolae*. Berlin: de Gruyter, 1902–25, repr. Munich: de Gruyter, 257–690 (MGH epistolae, 6).

Petschenig, M. (2004) *Iohannis Cassiani opera*. 2 vols. Vienna: Verlag der Österreichischen Akademie der Wissenschaften (CSEL, 17).

Richardson, E. C. (1890) *The Life of Constantine by Eusebius*, repr. in P. Schaff and H. Wace (eds) (1955) *Eusebius of Caesarea. The Life of the Blessed Emperor Constantine*. Edinburgh: T&T Clark, repr. Grand Rapids, MI: Eerdmans (NPNF, ser. 2, 1).

Roberts, A. and Rambaut, W. (1885) *Irenaeus of Lyons. Against the Heresies*. Buffalo, NY: Christian Literature Publishing (Ante-Nicene Fathers, 1).

Rolfe, J. C. (1986) *Ammianus Marcellinus*. 3 vols, 2nd edn. London: Heinemann/Cambridge, MA: Harvard University Press (Loeb classical library, 331).

Rousseau, A. and Doutreleau, L. (1979) *Irénée de Lyon. Contre les hérésies Livre I*. Paris: Cerf (SC, 264).

Sagnard, F. (1952) *Irénée de Lyon. Contre les hérésies Livre III*. Paris: Cerf (SC, 34).

Schepps, G. (1889) *Priscilliani quae supersunt, accedit Orosii Commonitorium de errore Priscillianistarum et Origenistarum*. Vienna: Tempsky (CSEL, 18).

Schwartz, E. (1925) *Acta conciliorum oecumenicorum* 1: *Concilium universale ephesenum*, pars 1: *Collectio Palatina sive qui fertur Marius Mercator.* Berlin: de Gruyter (=ACO 1.1).

——(1963) *Acta conciliorum oecumenicorum* 1: *Concilium universale ephesenum*, pars 2: *Collectio Veronensis*, 2nd edn. Berlin: de Gruyter.

Sickel, T. (1889) *Liber diurnus Romanorum pontificum.* Vienna: C. Gerold.

van De Vorst, C. (1910) 'La vie grecque de s. Léon.' *Analecta Bollandiana* 29: 400–408.

van den Hout et al. (1969) *De heresibus sancti Aurelii Augustini, Aurelii Augustini Opera*, part 13/2. Turnhout: Brepols (CCSL, 46).

van Heck, A. (1992) *Gregory of Nyssa, De beneficentia.* Brill: Leiden (Gregorii Nysseni opera, 9).

Winkelmann, F. (1999) *Werke. Eusebius*, vol. 2: *Die Kirchengeschichte. Eusebius*, 2nd edn. Berlin: Akademie-Verlag (Die griechischen christlichen schriftsteller der ersten jahrhunderte NF, 6).

Yonge, C. D. (1993) *The Works of Philo, Complete and Unabridged.* Peabody, MA: Hendrickson.

Zycha, J. (1891) *Sancti Aureli Augustini Contra Fortunatum.* Prague–Vienna: Tempsky (CSEL, 25, sect. 6/1).

——(1900) *Sancti Aureli Augustini Contra Mendacium.* Prague–Vienna: Tempsky (CSEL, 41).

REFERRED SECONDARY LITERATURE

Armitage, J. M. (1997) 'The Economy of Mercy: The Liturgical Preaching of Saint Leo the Great', PhD diss. Durham: University of Durham.

——(2005) *A Twofold Solidarity: Leo the Great's Theology of Redemption.* Strathfield: St Pauls (Early Christian Studies, 9).

Barclift, P. (1997) 'The Shifting Tones of Pope Leo the Great's Christological Vocabulary.' *Church History* 66/2: 221–39.

Bark, W. (1943) 'The Doctrinal Interests of Marius Mercator.' *Church History* 12/3: 210–16.

Barnish, S. (1987) 'Pigs, Plebeians and *potentes*.' *Papers of the British School at Rome* 55: 157–85.

Bolkestein, H. (1958) *Economic Life in Greece's Golden Age*, rev. Eng. edn., trans. E. J. Jonkers. Leiden: Brill.

Brown, P. (2002) *Poverty and Leadership in the Later Roman Empire.* Hanover–London: The University of New England Press (Menaham Stern Jerusalem Lectures).

Cappuyns, M. (1927) 'L'auteur du *De vocatione omnium gentium*.' *Revue Bénédictine* 39: 198–226.

Casula, L. (2000) *La cristologia di san Leone Magno. Il fondamento dottrinale e soteriologico.* Milan: Glossa (Dissertatio series Romana, 27).

——(2002) *Leone Magno: Il conflitto tra ortodossia ed eresia nel quinto secolo.* Rome: Tiellemedia Editore.

Chadwick, H. (1976) *Priscillian of Avila: the Occult and the Charismatic in the Early Church*. Oxford: Clarendon Press.

Clare, P. G. (ed.) (1982) *Oxford Latin Dictionary*. Oxford: Clarendon Press.

Conybeare, C. (2002) 'The Ambiguous Laughter of St Laurence.' *Journal of Early Christian Studies* 10/2: 175–202.

Cooper, K. (2007) 'Poverty, Obligation, and Inheritance: Roman Heiresses and the Varieties of Senatorial Christianity in Fifth-century Rome', in K. Cooper and J. Hillner (eds) *Religion, Dynasty, and Patronage in Early Christian Rome, 300–900*. Cambridge: Cambridge University Press, 165–89.

Croke, B. (1981) 'Anatolius and Nomus: Envoys to Attila.' *Byzantinoslavica* 42/2: 159–70.

di Capua, F. (1934) *De clausulis a s. Leone Magno adhibitis*, in K. Silva-Tarouca, *S. Leonis Magni epistulae contra Eutychis haeresim*, Pars prima: *Epistulae quae Chalcedonensi concilio praemittuntur (aa. 449–451)*. Rome: Pontificia Universitas Gregoriana (ST, 15), xxiii–xxxii.

Dunn, G. D. (2001a) 'Divine Impassibility and Christology in the Christmas Homilies of Leo the Great.' *Theological Studies* 62: 71–85.

——(2001b) 'Suffering Humanity and Divine Impassibility: The Christology of the Lenten Homilies of Leo the Great.' *Augustinianum* 41: 257–71.

——(2007a) 'The Validity of Marriage in Cases of Captivity: the Letter of Innocent I to Probus.' *Ephemerides theologicae Lovaniensis* 83: 107–21.

——(2007b) 'Innocent I and Anysius of Thessalonica.' *Byzantion* 77: 124–48.

——(2009) 'The Care of the Poor in Rome and Alaric's Sieges', in G. D. Dunn, D. Luckensmeyer and L. Cross (eds) *Prayer and Spirituality in the Early Church*, vol. 5: *Poverty and Riches*. Strathfield: St Pauls.

Ebied, R. Y. and Wickham, L. R. (1970) 'A Collection of Unpublished Syriac Letters of Timothy Aelurus.' *Journal of Theological Studies* 21: 321–69.

Finn, R. (2006) *Almsgiving in the Later Roman Empire: Christian Promotion and Practice*. Oxford–New York: Oxford University Press (Oxford classical monographs).

Gaidioz, J. (1949) 'Saint Prosper d'Aquitaine et le Tome à Flavien.' *Revue des sciences religieuses* 23: 270–301.

Gillett, A. (2001) 'Rome, Ravenna and the Last Western Emperors.' *Papers of the British School at Rome* 69: 131–67.

——(2003) *Envoys and Political Communication in the Late Antique West, 411–533*. Cambridge–New York: Cambridge University Press (Cambridge studies in medieval life and thought, 4th ser., 55).

Granata, A. (1960) 'Noti sulle fonti di S. Leone Magno.' *Rivista di storia della Chiesa in Italia* 14: 263–82.

Green, B. (2008) *The Soteriology of Leo the Great*. Oxford: Oxford University Press (Oxford theological monographs).

Grillmeier, A. (1987) *Christ in Christian Tradition*, vol. 2: *From the Council of Chalcedon (451) to Gregory the Great (590–604)*. Pt.1, *Reception and Contradiction: the Development of the Discussion about Chalcedon from 451 to the Beginning of the Reign of Justinian*, Eng. trans. London: Mowbray.

Halliwell, W. J. (1939) 'The Style of Pope St Leo the Great', PhD diss. Washington, DC: The Catholic University of America Press (Patristic Studies, 59).

Heather, P. (2007) 'Christianity and the Vandals in the Reign of Geiseric', in J. Drinkwater and B. Salway (eds) *Wolf Liebeschuetz Reflected: Essays Presented by Colleagues, Friends and Pupils.* London: Institute of Classical Studies, 137–46.

Horn, C. B. (2006) *Asceticism and Christological Controversy in Fifth-century Palestine. The Career of Peter the Iberian.* Oxford: Oxford University Press (Oxford early Christian studies).

Hoyce, G. H. (1941) 'Private Penance in the Early Church.' *Journal of Theological Studies* 42/1: 18–42.

Humphries, M. (2000) 'Italy, A.D. 425–605', in A. Cameron, B. Ward-Perkins and M. Whitby (eds) *Late Antiquity: Empire and Successors A.D. 425–600.* Cambridge: Cambridge University Press (The Cambridge Ancient History, 14), 525–51.

Jalland, T. (1941) *The Life and Times of St Leo the Great.* London: SPCK.

James, N. W. (1984) 'Pope Leo the Great, the City of Rome and the Western Churches', PhD diss. Oxford: University of Oxford.

——(1993) 'Leo the Great and Prosper of Aquitaine: a Fifth-century Pope and His Advisor.' *Journal of Theological Studies* ns 44/2: 554–84.

Jasper, D. (2001) 'The Beginning of the Decretal Tradition: Papal Letters from the Origin of the Genre through the Pontificate of Stephen V', in D. Jasper and H. Fuhrmann, *Papal Letters in the Early Middle Ages.* Washington, DC: Catholic University of America Press (History of medieval canon law), 1–133.

Jones, A. H. M., Martindale, J. R. and Morris, J. (eds) (1980) *The Prosopography of the Later Roman Empire* II: AD 395–527. Cambridge: Cambridge University Press.

Kazhdan, A. P. et al. (1991) *Oxford Dictionary of Byzantium.* 3 vols. New York–Oxford: Oxford University Press.

Klingshirn, W. (1985) 'Charity and Power: Caesarius of Arles and the Ransoming of Captives in sub-Roman Gaul.' *Journal of Roman Studies* 75: 183–203.

Künstle, K. (1905) *Antipriscilliana: dogmengeschichtliche Untersuchungen und Texte aus dem Streite gegen Priscillians Irrlehre.* Freiburg im Breisgau–St Louis, MO: Herder.

Lepelley, C. (1998) 'Le patronat episcopal aux IVe et Ve siècles: continuités et ruptures avec le patronat classique', in E. Rebillard and C. Sotinel (eds) *L'Évêque dans la cité du IVe au Ve siècle. Image et autorité.* Rome: Ecole française du Rome, 17–33.

Lieu, S. N. C. (1992) *Manichaeism in the Later Roman Empire and Medieval China*, 2nd edn. Tübingen: J. C. B. Mohr (Wissenschaftliche Untersuchungen zum Neuen Testament, 63).

McGuckin, J. (1994) *Cyril of Alexandria: the Christological Controversy, its History, Theology, and Texts.* Leiden: Brill (Supplements to Vigiliae christianae, 23).

McShane, P. (1979) *La romanitas et le pape Léon le Grand: l'apport culturel des institutions impériales à la formation des structures ecclésiastiques.* Tournai: Desclée–Montreal: Bellarmin.

Maier, H. O. (1995) 'Religious Dissent, Heresy and Households in Late Antiquity.' *Vigiliae christianae* 49/1: 49–63.

——(1996) '"Manichee!": Leo the Great and the Orthodox Panopticon.' *Journal of Early Christian Studies* 4/4: 441–60.

Markus, R. (1990) *The End of Ancient Christianity.* Cambridge: Cambridge University Press.

Mathisen, R. W. (1996a) 'Valentinian III.' *De imperatoribus Romanis: an online encyclopedia of Roman emperors.* Available HTTP: <www.romanemperors.org/valenIII.htm> (consulted 30.7.08).

——(1996b) 'Justa Grata Honoria.' *De imperatoribus Romanis: an online encyclopedia of Roman emperors.* Available HTTP: <www.roman-emperors. org/justa.htm> (consulted 30.7.08).

Matthews, J. (1990) *Western Aristocracies and Imperial Court AD 364–425.* Oxford: Clarendon Press (1975); repr. Oxford: Clarendon Press.

Moorhead, J. (2001) *The Roman Empire Divided, 400–700.* Harlow: Longman.

Mueller, M. M. (1943) 'The Vocabulary of Pope St. Leo the Great', PhD diss. Washington, DC: The Catholic University of America Press (Patristic studies, 67).

Neil, B. (2003) 'Rufinus' translation of the *Epistola Clementis ad Iacobum.' Augustinianum* 43/1: 25–39.

——(2006) '*On True Humility*: an Anonymous Letter on Poverty and the Female Ascetic', in P. Allen, W. Mayer and L. Cross (eds) *Prayer and Spirituality in the Early Church*, vol. 4: *The Spiritual Life.* Strathfield: St Pauls, 233–46.

——(2007) 'Blessed is Poverty: Leo the Great on Almsgiving.' *Sacris Erudiri* 46: 143–56.

——(forthcoming) 'Imperial Benefactions to the Fifth-century Roman Church', in G. Nathan and L. Garland (eds) *Legitimising the Emperor.* Canberra: Australian Association for Byzantine Studies (Byzantina australiensia).

Pásztori-Kupán, I. (2006) *Theodoret of Cyrus.* London–New York: Routledge (The Early Church Fathers).

Pietri, C. (1976) *Roma Christiana: recherches sur l'église de Rome, son organization, sa politique, son idéologie de Miltiade à Sixte (331–440).* 2 vols. Rome: École française de Rome.

Pietri, L. (2002) 'Évergetisme chrétien et fondations privées dans l'Italie de l'antiquité tardive', in R. Lizzi Testa and J.-M. Carrié (eds) *Humana sapit: études d'antiquité tardive offertes à Lellia Cracco Ruggini.* Turnhout: Brepols, 253–63.

Pietrini, S. (2002) *Religio e ius romanum nell'epistolario di Leone Magno.* Milan: A. Guiffré (Materiali per una palingenesi delle costituzioni tardoimperiali, 6).

Ramsey, B. (1982) 'Almsgiving in the Latin Church: the late fourth and fifth centuries'. *Theological Studies* 43: 226–59.

Rist, J. (1994) *Augustine: Ancient thought baptized.* Cambridge: Cambridge University Press.

Runia, D. (1993) *Philo in Early Christian Literature: A survey.* Assen: Van Gorcum.

Salzman, M. (forthcoming) 'Leo the Great: Religious responses to crisis in fifth-century Rome', in C. Rapp (ed.) *City, Empire and Christianity: Changing contexts, power and identity in Late Antiquity* (under contract).

Sieger, J.D. (1987) 'Visual Metaphor as Theology: Leo the Great's Sermons on the Incarnation and the Arch Mosaics at S. Maria Maggiore.' *Gesta* 26/2: 83–91.

Silva-Tarouca, K. (1932) *Nuovi studi sulle antiche lettere dei Papi,* 1. Rome: Pontificia Universitas Gregoriana (Gregorianum, 12).

Stökl Ben Ezra, D. (2003) 'Whose Fast is it? The Ember Day of September and Yom Kippur', in A. Becker and A. Yoshiko Reed (eds) *The Ways that Never Parted: Jews and Christians in Late Antiquity and the Early Middle Ages.* Tübingen: Mohr Siebeck (Texts and studies in ancient Judaism, 95), 259–82.

Studer, B. (1986) 'Les pontifes romains de Sirice à Léon le Grand', in J. Quasten (ed.), *Initiation aux Pères de l'Église IV: Du concile de Nicée (325) au concile de Chalcédoine (451): Les Pères latins.* Paris: CERF, 735–77.

——(1993) *Trinity and the Incarnation: the Faith of the Early Church,* ed. Andrew Louth, Eng. trans.. Collegeville, MN: Liturgical Press.

Uhalde, K. (2007) *Expectations of Justice in the Age of Augustine.* Philadelphia: University of Pennsylvania Press.

——(forthcoming) 'Leo I on Power and Failure.' *Catholic Historical Review.*

Ullmann, W. (1960) 'Leo the First and the Theme of Papal Primacy.' *Journal of Theological Studies* ns 11: 25–51.

——(2003) *A Short History of the Papacy in the Middle Ages,* 2nd edn. London: Routledge.

Wace, H. and Piercy, W. C. (eds) (1994) *Dictionary of Christian Biography and Literature to the End of the Sixth Century AD, with an Account of the Principal Sects and Heresies.* London: Murray (1911); repr. Peabody, MA: Hendrickson. Available HTTP: <www.ccel.org/ccel/wace/biodict.dcb.html> (consulted 18.8.08).

Wallraff, M. (2001) *Christus versus sol: Sonnenverehrung und Christentum in der Spätantike.* Münster: Aschendorff (Jahrbuch für Antike und Christentum, 32).

Wickham, C. (2005) *Framing the Early Middle Ages: Europe and the Mediterranean, 400–800.* Oxford: Oxford University Press.

INDEX

Acacian Schism (484–519) 122
Acts of the Council of Chalcedon 94,
    95
adoptionism, Nestorian 37
Aelurus, Timothy 106, 146, 147–48
Aetius, General 3, 8, 10, 133
Africa 40
African bishops 40
Alaric 8–9; *Homily* on anniversary
    of sack of Rome by 41, 55, 118–
    20; sieges of Rome 4–5, 41, 118
Albinus 3
Alexandrian monks: uprising of
    138–39
almsgiving 18–21, 23, 25, 55–56, 57,
    59
Altar of Victory: dispute over (384
    CE) 5
Altinum 131
Ambrose of Milan 5, 7, 58, 16, 17,
    19, 21, 22, 29, 63, 95
Ammianus Marcellinus 6
Anastasius, Bishop of Thessalonica:
    Leo's letter to 120–25
Anastasius, Emperor 33, 36
Anastasius, Pope 31
Anatolius 94, 137
Anicia, Demetrias 33
Antelmi, Canon Joseph 15
Antiochene formula 104–5
apocryphal scriptures 91
Apollinaris 38, 107

Apollo 25
Aquileia 131
Arcadius 5
Arians/Arianism 29, 35, 85
Armitage, J.M. 27, 68
Ascension: *Homily* on 78–81
astrology: condemnation of by Leo
    21, 62, 65; and Priscillianism 83,
    89, 90
Athanasius 17
Atticus: appeal of 47–48, 121–22
Attila the Hun 7, 8–10, 43, 73, 121,
    133
Augustine 16, 17, 19, 31, 32, 33, 34,
    63, 74, 95, 118, 119; *City of God* 29
Augustulus, Romulus 11
Avellana Collection 49
Avitus, Emperor 11

Balkans 121
baptism 24–25, 139, 145–46
Bark, W. 37
Basil of Caesarea 20
Basiliscus 147
Bede, Venerable 137
bishops: as civic leaders 4–6;
    negotiation of ransom of captives 9
Bolkestein, H. 20
Boniface, Pope 6
*Book of Authorities of the Church of
    Arles* 49
Byzantines 122

179

Caelestius 33, 36, 132, 133
calendar: importance of Christian 1, 22–26; *see also* Easter; fasts/fasting
Callistus 23
Canon 28: 39, 43
Cappadocians 19
Carthage: conquest of by Vandals 7
Carthage, Synod of 33
Cassian, John 18, 34, 37
Catalaunian Plains, Battle of the 133
Celestine, Pope 6, 36, 37
Celidonius of Besançon, Bishop of 45
Cerdo 83, 86
Chalcedon, Council of (451) 1, 29, 39, 43, 48, 62, 95; Leo's rejection of *Canon 28* 39, 43–44; non-attendance of by Leo 43; unrest in aftermath 104, 105
Chavasse 118, 119
Chrysostom, John 17, 21, 35, 119
church building 11–13
church property: sale of 47
Cicero 16
Clement I, Pope 39, 127
clerical ordination 139, 142
Collection of Novara 48
Collects 25
Constantine I (the Great) 11, 13, 29, 62, 119
Constantinople 5, 121; conflict between Rome and 39, 42–44
Constantinople, Council of: (381) 35, 36, 42; (448) 27; (533) 4, 49
consubstantiality 85, 101, 107; two-fold 27–28, 31
Cornelius, Pope 13
Cyprian of Carthage 40
Cyril of Alexandria 17, 35, 36, 37, 94, 137
Cyrillians 94

Damasus, Pope 5, 58
December Fast 18, 23; *Homily* on 73–78, 83
decretals 46–49, 131, 133
deification, doctrine of 79
devil 21, 25, 28–29, 70–71, 77–78, 82, 87, 88, 114, 130

Dictinius 91
Dioscorus of Alexandria 3, 38, 94, 105, 106
disciples 79, 80–81
divine accounting, theme of 19
Dorus, bishop of Benevento 47

Easter 24–25, 67; dating of 24, 40, 45, 137, 138
Ephesus, Council of: (431) 34, 36–37, 132; (449) *see* 'Robber Council'
essence 28, 64, 69, 85, 87, 93, 107–11
Eudoxia, Empress Licinia 10, 12
Eulalius 6
Eusebius of Caesarea 127
Eutyches 3, 37–38, 41, 42, 94, 96–97, 102, 103, 107
Eutychianism 14, 27, 30, 37–38, 48, 94, 96, 137
Euxitheus 122

False Decretals 47, 48
fasts/fasting 18, 23–24, 55; December Fast 18, 23, 73–78, 83; and Manichees 32; September Fast 18, 23, 24, 55–58
Feast of the Nativity: *Homily* on 22, 61–67
Feast of St Lawrence: *Homily* on 58–61
Feast of St Peter and St Paul 40; *Homilies* on 59, 113–18
feasts 1; pagan 22–23
Felix III, Pope 11, 23
Flavian, Bishop of Constantinople 30, 37–38; Leo's letter to *see* *Tome to Flavian*
Franks 8

Gaidioz, J. 15
Galla Placidia 8, 10, 12, 13
Gallicanism 46
Gaudentius of Brescia 17
Gaul 3, 8, 40; bishops of 45, 46, 125
Geiseric, King 7, 10, 11, 68, 73, 118
Gelasius, Pope 8, 23, 32, 35, 44; *General Decretal* 49
Gennadius, Bishop of Constantinople: Leo's letter to 146–48

Gennadius of Marseilles 15, 95, 137
Goths 8, 29
Gratian, Emperor 5
Green, B. 15, 27, 96
Gregory the Great: *Dialogues* 12
Gregory of Nazianzus 17, 19, 20
Gregory of Nyssa 19, 68
Grimani Collection 49

Hadrian I, Pope 122
Hellenistic religion 62, 63
heresy: condemnation of by Leo 27, 29–30, 68, 71
Hilary of Arles 14, 40, 45–46, 125
Hilary of Poitiers 16, 17, 95
Hilary, Pope 41–42, 46, 49, 58, 59
Holy Saturday: *Homily* on 59, 67–72
holy usury 19–20
Homilies 18–20; (4) (anniversary of Leo's ordination) 125–30; (8) 25; (9) 25; (16) (December Fast) 73–78, 83; (19) 34–35; (27) (Feast of the Nativity) 22, 61–67; (69) (Holy Saturday) 59, 67–72; (73) (Ascension) 78–81; (82B) (Feast of the Apostles) 113–18; (84) (anniversary of Alaric's sack of Rome) 41, 55, 118–20; (85) (Feast of St Lawrence) 58–61; (87) (September Fast) 24, 55–58; (89) 23–24; influence of Prosper on 15; literary style of 15
Honoria, Justa Grata 8, 10
Honorius, Emperor 4–5, 6, 13, 82
Hormisdas, Pope 33, 74
Huns 7, 8–9, 10, 59, 121, 133 *see also* Attila the Hun
hypostasis 36

Ibas of Edessa 49
Illyricum (Balkans) 120–21, 122, 123
Innocent I, Pope 5, 26, 33, 83, 118, 134, 139
Irenaeus of Lyons 28, 68

James, N.W. 15
Jerome 4, 16, 49, 114
Jerusalem 59, 61
Jesus Christ 28–29; controversy over natures of 4, 28–29, 30, 38, 62, 63–65, 79, 94–95, 104, 107–11, 98–103; humanity of 16, 28–29, 35, 36, 37, 69, 94, 103, 105, 109–10; resurrection of 28, 71, 79–81, 86, 88, 90, 93, 101, 102, 138
Jews 68, 70
John of Antioch 10
Jordanes 8–9
Julian, Bishop of Eclanum 33, 34, 132
Justinian, Emperor 140
Juvenal, Bishop of Jerusalem 14, 105
Juvenal of Cos 105

Lawrence, St 58–59; cult of 41, 58; *Homily* on Feast of 58–61
Lent 23
Leo, Emperor 38, 104, 146; Leo's letter to *see Second Tome to Emperor Leo*
Leo I, Pope: acclaimed pope 3; accumulation of power due to weakness of Valentinian III 10; achievements 1; as administrator of the wider church 45–50, 131–48; and almsgiving 18–21, 23, 25, 55–56, 57, 59; attributes 50; background 3; burial 49; championing of cult of St Peter 13; and Christian calendar 22–23; christology and theology 27–29, 35, 62, 63–64, 73–112; church building campaign 11–13; and church Collects 25; concern with liturgical uniformity 24; condemnation of astrology and pagan religious practices 21–22, 62, 65; condemnation of heresy 27, 29–30, 68, 71; condemnation of Manicheism and investigation into 25, 27, 31–33, 73–74, 76–78, 83, 86, 91–92, 125, 132; condemnation of Nestorianism 27, 37, 41, 95–96, 104, 107; condemnation of Pelagianism 33–35, 37, 74, 131–32, 133; condemnation of Priscillianism 27, 30–31, 74, 82–83; conflict with Constantinople 43–44; death 49;

dispute with Hilary of Arles 14, 40, 45–46, 125; epithet 'the Great' 50, 95; and Eutychian controversy 27, 30, 37–38, 48, 96–97, 102–3, 107; extension of influence 1; and fasting 18, 23–24, 55–58; as heir of St Peter 39, 114, 126, 127, 129–30; and humanity of Christ 16, 28–29, 35, 36, 37, 69, 94, 103, 105, 109–10; literary style 15–17; and martyr saints 41, 59, 60, 113, 119; on natures of Christ 62, 94–95, 104, 107–11; negotiation of truce with Attila 8–9; opposition to clergy being tried in open courts 137, 138; ordination of (440) 41; ordinations performed by 23; as pastoral caregiver 18–26, 55–72, 134; on primacy of the bishop of Rome 39, 40–42, 43–44, 114, 119; reburial at St Peter's basilica 49; and salvation 27–29, 34–35, 67–68, 69, 126; sees Rome as Christian community 25, 29; sermons 13–14, 16–17; sources of and influences on literary output 17; on sun worship 63, 65–66, 41; and unity of church 125, 126, 127–28; and Vandal attack on Rome 10–11; writings on life of 3–4
Leo (priest) 139, 140
Letter of Pope Clement I to James the brother of the Lord 39, 127
Letters 13, 14–15; (1) 34, 131; (2) (to Septimus, Bishop of Altinum) 34, 48, 131–33; (4) 19, 46; (6) (to Anastasius, Bishop of Thessalonica) 120–25; (7) 48; (14) 47–48, 131; (15) (to Turibius, Bishop of Astorga) 82–94; (16) 46–47; (17) 47; (18) 132; (19) 47; (28) *see Tome to Flavian*; (108) (to Theodore, Bishop of Fréjus) 133–36; (124) (to the Monks of Palestine) 16, 38, 96, 104–12; (136) 137; (137) (to Emperor Marcian) 136–38; (159) 139; (165) (to Emperor Leo) *see Second Tome to Emperor Leo*; (167) (to Rusticus, Bishop of Narbonne)

26, 133, 134, 138–46; (170) (to Gennadius, Bishop of Constantinople) 146–48; literary style of 16–17; reception of into canon law 46–49
Liber Pontificalis 3, 5, 9, 13, 14, 23, 41, 59, 127
Life of St Leo 3–4
liturgical time, concept of 79, 80
Livy: *History of Rome* 114
Ludi Apollinares 25, 113, 118
Lupercalia, festival of 23

Macedonia/Macedonians 47
magic: Leo's condemnation of 21–22
Maier, H.O. 83
Majorian, General 11
Malchus 10
Manichees/Manicheism 14; and astrology 22; beliefs 73; condemnation of by Leo and investigation into 25, 27, 31–33, 73–74, 76–77, 83, 86, 91–92, 125, 132; likened to Priscillianism by Leo 30, 31, 82–83, 87
Marcian, Emperor 8, 38, 42, 43, 44, 106; Leo's letter to 136–38
Marcion 83, 86
Marinianus 12
marriage 139–40, 142–43, 144–45
martyr-saints 41, 59, 60, 113, 119
Maximus, Bishop of Antioch 105
Maximus the Confessor 4
Maximus, Emperor Magnus 30
Maximus, Petronius 10, 11, 12
Melania the Younger 19, 33
Mercator, Isidore 48
Mercator, Marius 36
Milan 7
Milevis synod (416) 33
monasteries 12
Mongus, Peter 106
monophysitism/monophysites 42, 94, 104
Moschus, John: *The Spiritual Meadow* 4

Narbonne 139
Nativity, Feast of the: *Homily* on 22, 61–67

neo-Platonism 63
Nero, Emperor 117
Nestorianism/Nestorius 33, 35–37, 49, 78, 94, 105; accusing of Leo by monks of Palestine 30, 37, 48, 104; background to controversy over 35–36; condemnation of by Leo 27, 37, 41, 95–96, 104, 107; support of Pelagius 36; and *Tome to Flavian* 37
Nicea, Council of (325) 137
Nicene Creed 27
Nicetas of Remesiana 17
Nicholas I, Pope 50, 122
North Africa: Vandal invasions 7, 73
Novatianists 35

Odovacer 11
Orange: second Synod of (529) 35
ordinations 23
Orosius of Braga 31

pagan feasts 22–23
pagan religious practices: Leo's condemnation of 21–22, 25
Palestine: Leo's letter to monks of 16, 38, 96, 104–12
Pannonia 121
Paschasinus, Bishop of Lilybaeum 24
passion of Christ 67, 68–71, 102, 112, 130, 138
Patripassians 85
Paul of Samosata 83
Paul, St 113, 116, 117
Pelagian clergy 132, 133
Pelagianism/Pelagians 27, 33–35, 74; Leo's condemnation of 33–35, 37, 74, 131–32, 133
Pelagius 33, 36, 132
penance 26, 134, 139, 140, 142, 143–44
penitence 135–36
Pentecost 23, 25
Peter and Paul, Feast of 40; *Homilies* on 59, 113–18
Peter, St 13, 41, 113, 116, 128–30; Leo as heir of 39, 114, 126, 127, 129–30
Philo of Alexandria 62–63

Photius, Patriarch of Constantinople 50
Plato: *On the confusion of languages* 22
Priscillian, Bishop of Avila 30, 82
Priscillianism/Priscillianists 22; and astrology 83, 89, 90; beliefs of 82; Leo's condemnation of 27, 30–31, 74, 82–83; Leo's letter to Turibius condemning 82–94; similarities with Manicheism 30, 31, 82–83, 87; trial and execution of 82; Turibius's dossier condemning 82
Priscus of Thrace 9–10
Probus, Sextus Petronius 13
Projectus 45–46
Prosper of Aquitaine 9, 11, 15, 74, 95, 96, 137; *On the Calling of all the Nations* 15
Proterius of Alexandria 43, 105–6, 137, 139, 146
Prudentius 29
Pseudo-Isidorean Decretals 48
Pulcheria 42, 43

Quartodecimans 35
Quesnellian Collection 48

Ravenna 5, 6, 118
Ravennius, bishop of Arles 46
Regensburg Collection 48
resurrection of Christ 28, 71, 79–81, 86, 88, 90, 93, 101, 102, 138
'Robber Council' (Ephesus) (449) 27, 38, 42, 94, 95
Rome: Alaric's sieges of 4–5, 41, 118; barbarian invasions 1, 8–11; bishops of as civic leaders 4–6; conflict between Constantinople and 39, 42–43; contributions made by prominent citizens 12; cutting off of food supplies from North Africa due to Vandal invasions 7–8; and dispute over Altar of Victory (384 CE) 5; divisions within urban population 6; economic and demographic crisis 7,11; pagan 113–14; and Romulus and Remus myth 114, 115; sparing of citizens during

sack of 41, 118, 119; Vandal invasion of 10–11, 12–13, 59, 139
Romulus and Remus myth 114, 115
Rufinus of Aquileia 39
Rusticus, Bishop of Narbonne: Leo's letter to 26, 133, 134, 138–46

Sabellius 85
Sabinian 139, 140
St Lawrence Outside the Walls 58
St Paul's Outside the Walls 12
St Peter's basilica 12, 13, 63
Salofaciolus, Timothy 146, 147
salvation 27–29, 34–35, 67–68, 69, 126
Salzman, Michele 118, 119
Sardinia 7
Saturnalia, feast of 22, 62
Schipper, H.G. 31
Second Tome to Emperor Leo 16, 17, 38, 96, 104, 106
semi-Pelagianism 34, 35
September Fast 18, 23; *Homily* on the 24, 55–58
Septimus, Bishop of Altinum: Leo's letter to 34, 48, 131–33
Serapeum 21
Sergius I, Pope 49
Severian, bishop of Scythopolis 105
'shadow' emperors 10
Sicily 7, 40, 73; bishops of 45, 46–47
Simplicius 26
Siricius, Pope 26
Sixtus III, Pope 3, 5–6, 11, 33, 58–59
slaves 46
Socrates 36
Sophronius of Jerusalem 4
Spain 40
Stephen, bishop of Rome 40
Stephen, St 59, 61
Stilicho 121
Studer, Basil 27
substance: Leo's concept of 27–28
Suevi 82
sun worship 62, 63, 65–66
Sunday 22
Symmachus, Pope 5, 9, 32–33, 47

taxes: *siliquaticum* 12
Tertullian 27, 115
Theodore, Bishop of Fréjus: Leo's letter to 133–36
Theodore of Mopsuestia 36, 49
Theodoret of Cyrrhus 49, 74, 105
Theodoric 11
Theodosius I, Emperor 5, 10, 21, 120–21
Theodosius II, Emperor 6, 8, 10, 14, 28, 32, 38, 42, 43
Theodosius (son of Galla Placidia) 13
Theophilus of Alexandria 17, 35
Thessalonica 120–21
Thessalonica Collection 41–42, 49
Three Chapters controversy 48–49
Toledo, Council of (400) 5, 82, 83
Tome to Flavian 4, 15, 27, 28, 38, 49, 50, 94–103, 105; attempt at discrediting by 'monophysite' monks 104; impact of 2; influences on writing of 17, 95; and Nestorius 37; questioning of Leo's authorship 95–96; and relationship between two natures of Christ 4, 38, 94–95, 98–103; translation into Greek 104, 105
Trinitarian doctrine 27–28
Turibius, Bishop of Astorga: *Letter* to 82–94
'two powers' theory 44, 137–38
twofold consubstantiality 27–28, 31

Uhalde K. 126
Ullman, W. 39
usury 19, 46

Valentinian III, Emperor 6, 8, 10, 11–12, 14, 21, 32, 46, 125; *Novella 18* 74
van Oort, J. 31
Vandals 8, 29, 32, 82; invasion of North Africa 7, 73; invasion of Rome (455) 10–11, 12, 59, 139
Victor of Tunnuna 10
Vienne, bishops of 46, 47

Vigilius, Pope 48
Visigoths 139

Wickham, C. 7
Word of God 107, 108, 109, 110,
  111, 112, 115–16, 128

Yom Kippur, Jewish festival of 23,
  55

Zeno, Emperor 147
Zosimus (historian) 4
Zosimus, Pope 33